# Intellectual Property and TRIPS Compliance in China

NEW HORIZONS IN INTELLECTUAL PROPERTY

**Series Editors**: Christine Greenhalgh, Robert Pitkethly and Michael Spence, *Senior Research Associates, Oxford Intellectual Property Research Centre, St Peter's College, Oxford, UK*

In an increasingly virtual world, where information is more freely accessible, protection of intellectual property rights is facing a new set of challenges and raising new issues. This exciting new series is designed to provide a unique interdisciplinary forum for high quality works of scholarship on all aspects of intellectual property, drawing from the fields of economics, management and law.

The focus of the series is on the development of original thinking in intellectual property, with topics ranging from copyright to patents, from trademarks to confidentiality and from trade-related intellectual property agreements to competition policy and antitrust. Innovative theoretical and empirical work will be encouraged from both established authors and the new generation of scholars.

Titles in the series include:

The International Political Economy of Intellectual Property Rights
*Meir Perez Pugatch*

Software Patents
Economic Impacts and Policy Implications
*Edited by Knut Blind, Jakob Edler and Michael Friedewald*

The Management of Intellectual Property
*Edited by Derek Bosworth and Elizabeth Webster*

The Intellectual Property Debate
*Edited by Meir Perez Pugatch*

Intellectual Property and TRIPS Compliance in China
Chinese and European Perspectives
*Edited by Paul Torremans, Hailing Shan and Johan Erauw*

# Intellectual Property and TRIPS Compliance in China

## Chinese and European Perspectives


*Edited by*
Paul Torremans
*School of Law, University of Nottingham, UK and Faculty of Law, University of Ghent, Belgium*

Hailing Shan
*School of International Law, East China University of Politics and Law, Shanghai, People's Republic of China*

Johan Erauw
*Faculty of Law, University of Ghent, Belgium*

The University of Nottingham
East China University of Politics and Law
UNIVERSITEIT GENT



NEW HORIZONS IN INTELLECTUAL PROPERTY

**Edward Elgar**
Cheltenham, UK • Northampton, MA, USA

Published by
Edward Elgar Publishing Limited
Glensanda House
Montpellier Parade
Cheltenham
Glos GL50 1UA
UK

Edward Elgar Publishing, Inc.
William Pratt House
9 Dewey Court
Northampton
Massachusetts 01060
USA

A catalogue record for this book
is available from the British Library

**Library of Congress Cataloguing in Publication Data**

Intellectual property and TRIPS compliance in China : Chinese and European perspectives / edited by Paul Torremans, Hailing Shan, Johan Erauw.
p. cm. — (New horizons in intellectual property)
Includes bibliographical references and index.
1. Intellectual property—China. 2. Foreign trade regulation—China. 3. Intellectual property (International law) 4. Intellectual property (International law)—Compliance costs. I. Torremans, Paul. II. Shan, Hailing, 1959– III. Erauw, Johan.
KNQ1155.I59 2007
346.5104′6—dc22

2006102434

ISBN 978 1 84542 875 4

Typeset by Cambrian Typesetters, Camberley, Surrey
Printed and bound in Great Britain by MPG Books Ltd, Bodmin, Cornwall

# Contents

# Contributors

**John Adams**, Professor, Schools of Law, University of Sheffield (Emeritus), UK and University of Notre Dame, France

**Johan Erauw**, Professor, Faculty of Law, University of Ghent

**Daniel J. Gervais**, Acting Dean, Vice-Dean (Research) and Osler Professor of Intellectual Property Law, Faculty of Law (Common Law), University of Ottawa, Canada

**Hon. Dr H.C. Cao Jianming**, Vice-President of the Supreme People's Court of the People's Republic of China, Grand Justice of the first rank

**Jingzhou Tao**, DLA Piper Rudnick Gray Cary UK LLP

**Zhu Lanye**, Professor, East China University of Politics and Law

**Fientje Moerman**, Deputy Minister–President and Flemish Minister for Economics, Business, Science, Innovation and Foreign Trade, Flemish Regional Government, Flanders, Belgium

**Hailing Shan**, Professor, School of International Law, East China University of Politics and Law

**Guo Shoukang**, Professor, Supervisor of PhD candidates, Law School of Renmin University of China, Chair of UNESCO Seminars on Copyright and Neighbouring Right

**Sigrid Sterckx**, Professor, Department of Philosophy and Moral Science, University of Ghent, Belgium

**Kristie Thomas**, Teaching Fellow, University of Nottingham in Ningbo

**Paul Torremans**, Professor, School of Law, University of Nottingham, UK and Faculty of Law, University of Ghent, Belgium

**Zou Weining**, Partner, Jun He Law Office (Beijing)

**Zuo Xiaodong**, Director and Legal Counsel, Legal Department, China Grand Enterprises Group

**Hon. Jiang Zhipei**, Justice of the Supreme People's Court of China, Director of the Third Civil Chamber, PhD in Law

# Foreword: the recent development and current status of judicial protection of intellectual property in China

**Hon. Dr H.C. Cao Jianming***

## INTRODUCTION

In recent years, Chinese courts at all levels have strengthened all aspects of their work regarding the judicial protection of intellectual property rights. These include increasing the degree of judicial protection for intellectual property rights, efficient fulfilment of judicial functions, acceptance and trial of cases in accordance with the law, strictly punishing crimes against intellectual property rights through a combination of all mechanisms of trial and enforcement measures, maintaining the order of the market economy with great resolve and creating a legal environment suitable for innovation. Significant progress has been made.

## GENERAL REVIEW OF JUDICIAL PROTECTION OF INTELLECTUAL PROPERTY RIGHTS IN CHINA

The Chinese intellectual property regime has been established and has constantly been improved over the last 20 years, which coincides in time with the development of a market economy and the emergence and increase of intellectual property cases in Chinese courts. Alongside the rapid growth of the Chinese economy, especially after China's accession to the WTO and the adoption of innovation as a national strategy, the importance and urgency of protecting intellectual property rights has gained historical attention. The focus of the construction of the intellectual property legal framework has shifted from legislation to implementation. After years of efforts, China has primarily established a relevant and complete legal framework protecting

* Vice-President of the Supreme People's Court of the People's Republic of China, Grand Justice of the first rank.

intellectual property rights, which complies with the requirements of the WTO and is capable of meeting the needs of the nation's development. Judicial protection of intellectual property rights is an important component of such a framework for the protection of intellectual property rights. Corresponding to Chinese procedural laws which divide into civil, administrative and criminal procedural law, judicial protection of intellectual property rights in China divides into three categories: civil, administrative and criminal judicial protection with civil judicial protection as the basis. By carrying out their judicial duties in accordance with the law, Chinese courts have been effectively promoting works with respect to judicial protection of intellectual property rights, as a result of which the strength and the degree of protection has increased continuously.

### Acceptance and Trial of all Types of Cases Involving Intellectual Property Rights in Accordance with the Law

Chinese courts have been resolving various disputes involving intellectual property rights and protecting the lawful rights and interests of the proprietor through trial in accordance with the law of civil disputes between equal parties over intellectual property rights. In recent years, and especially in those after China's accession to the WTO, the following characteristics of civil cases involving intellectual property rights have manifested themselves.

First, there has been a wide range of different types of cases which have involved not only all types of rights covered by TRIPs, such as patents (inventions, utility models, industrial designs), new varieties of plants, trademarks, copyright, computer software, layout designs (topographies) of integrated circuits, trade secrets, geographical indications and so on, but also new types of intellectual property such as cyber copyright, practical arts and folk literature and folk arts.

Second, the number of cases has increased dramatically. According to the statistics, in 2005, Chinese courts nationwide accepted 16 483 first instance, appeal and retrial cases concerning intellectual property, including anti-unfair competition cases, an increase of 20.66 per cent over the previous year. They disposed of 16 453 cases, which represents an increase of 29.6 per cent over the previous year.

Third, the uneven geographical allocation of cases has become apparent. Cases involving intellectual property are concentrated in economically developed areas such as Guangdong, Beijing, Jiangsu, Zhejiang, Shandong and Shanghai. Civil intellectual property cases accepted in these six provinces/municipalities have accounted for 65.38 per cent of the overall accepted intellectual property cases nationwide, and this percentage has been stable in recent years.

Fourth, the percentage of cases involving a foreign factor or that are associated with parties from Hong Kong, Macao and Taiwan has increased as a whole. There were 449 such cases in 2005, which accounts for 3.35 per cent of the intellectual property cases concluded at first instance. This represents an increase of 23.01 per cent over the previous year.

Chinese courts have been facilitating the administrative protection of intellectual property rights through the trial of administrative cases involving intellectual property, and the supervision and support of administrative measures. These administrative cases involve administrative proceedings brought against decisions of the intellectual property authority on authorization, administrative penalties and other issues. It is particularly noteworthy that lawsuits with the Patent Review Committee under the State Intellectual Property Office or the Trademark Examination Committee under the State Administration of Industry and Commerce as defendant have increased rapidly following the recent amendments to the Patent Law and Trademark Law that stipulate that such judicial judgment shall be the final decision with respect to the authorization and withholding of a patent or a trademark. That increase has levelled off only recently. In 2005, 575 administrative intellectual property cases of first instance were accepted by Chinese local courts, an increase of 9.32 per cent over the previous year, and 576 such cases have been disposed of, which represents an increase of 4.92 per cent over the previous year.

Chinese courts have been handing down criminal penalties against intellectual property infringement in breach of the criminal code and above the threshold, through trials of criminal cases involving intellectual property. In 2005, Chinese local courts accepted 3567 criminal cases of first instance involving intellectual property, an increase of 28.36 per cent over the previous year. This demonstrates that the arsenal to deal with crimes against intellectual property has been strengthened and the implementation of criminal judicial interpretations involving intellectual property has achieved obvious effects. One important reason for such a rapid increase of cases is that the Interpretation on Several Issues regarding the Implementation of Law in Trial of Criminal Cases involving Intellectual Property Infringement, enacted at the end of 2004, has lowered the threshold for an infringement to be deemed a crime, combined with the execution of the special action plan of the State Council for the protection of intellectual property.

The above-mentioned facts show that China's WTO accession has an important impact on the trial of intellectual property cases in China. Judicial protection of intellectual property has gained more trust and attention of the society with the mechanism of such protection running smoothly, and with the strength and the level of protection increasing.

## The Jurisdiction of Civil Cases involving Intellectual Property has been relatively Centralised

According to the Civil Procedure Law and the relevant Judicial Interpretations enacted by the Supreme Court, civil cases involving intellectual property cases are, in principle, within the jurisdiction of courts at intermediate level or above, except for a few primary courts that are authorized by the Supreme People's Court to handle certain intellectual property cases. The underlying consideration of such an arrangement is that, since intellectual property cases are a new type of case for Chinese courts, relative concentration and centralization of jurisdiction will enable experience to be accumulated and research to be conducted. According to statistics, around 90 per cent of intellectual property cases in China have been tried at first instance by courts at intermediate level or above. Until the end of 2005, the number of Intermediate Courts with jurisdiction as the court of first instance over cases involving patents, new plant varieties and layout designs of integrated circuits has increased to 51, 37 and 43, respectively. Also, 15 primary courts that are reasonably located have been authorized to try certain intellectual property cases.

## The Organization of Intellectual Property Trials has been Improved Continuously

In order to meet the demand of the development of the market economy, in order to emphasize the special and professional nature of trials of intellectual property cases and to comply with international legal rules, specialized intellectual property divisions were established within Beijing High Court and Intermediate Courts as early as 1993 and in the Supreme Court since 1996. Since then, especially after the institutional reform of the Chinese court system in 2000, specialized intellectual property divisions have flourished in Chinese courts. Almost all High Courts and Intermediate Courts located in a provincial capital or in other large cities have established special divisions dedicated to the handling of intellectual property cases. Even those courts without a special intellectual property division have a dedicated collegial panel in charge of the trial of intellectual property cases. Until now, more than 170 intellectual property divisions and more than 140 dedicated intellectual property collegial panels have been set up in Chinese courts, in which more than 1600 judges have been allocated to the trial of intellectual property cases. This has provided important guarantees for the task of dealing effectively with intellectual property cases.

# MAIN MEASURES OF JUDICIAL PROTECTION FOR INTELLECTUAL PROPERTY RIGHTS IN CHINA

## Equal Protection of the Legitimate Interests of both Chinese and Foreign Parties through Strict Enforcement of Domestic Laws and Implementation of International Treaties

Chinese courts have always adhered to the judicial doctrine of equal protection in trials; that is, all legitimate interests enjoyed in accordance with the law or rights granted by the law shall be protected equally, without regard to the nationality, occupation, geographic origin or financial status of the party concerned. Chinese courts have been trying to create an environment of equal judicial protection through granting foreign parties 'national treatment' in accordance with treaty obligations and by protecting their lawful interests in accordance with the law.

## Granting the Right Holder and the Aggrieved Party a Full Remedy by Imposing Tough Judgment Civil Penalties and Liabilities upon the Infringer and the Party in Breach of Agreement

Chinese courts have been adhering to the doctrine of full compensation in trials of intellectual property cases: all losses caused by infringing activities, together with expenses occurred for the investigation, prevention of further infringement and appointing legal counsel, shall be included in the total sum of compensation for which the infringer will be ordered to take liability. In recent years, the amount of compensation awarded in the judgments has increased. In cases where the actual loss is hard to estimate, statutory compensation applies. In some cases a ceiling of half a million Yuan has been set for such statutory compensation, which has again strengthened the compensation for intellectual property infringement. For example, in *American Autodesk* v. *Beijing LongFa Construction and Decoration Company*, a case regarding the infringement of software copyright, the defendant, after having administrative penalties imposed upon him, was ordered by Beijing High Court to pay 1.49 million Yuan in compensation and 30 000 Yuan in legal expenses to the plaintiff in the law suit for civil compensation. This ruling has been widely praised by academics and the software industry alike.

## In an Appropriate Manner, Ending Infringement and Effectively Preventing Further Losses to the Right Holder by Applying Provisional Measures Available in Civil Proceedings

The overall judicial doctrine of Chinese courts regarding pre-trial injunctions is that both an active and a cautious attitude shall be taken. An active attitude means that the courts shall be active in accepting cases, rapid in their investigation, and that measures shall be taken in a timely manner. Caution means that the application for an injunction shall be examined carefully in order to prevent any detriment of the party's interest due to an improper application of such measures. As long as the application has been deemed to comply with the relevant judicial interpretations after examination, the court shall order the party against which the application has been submitted to stop the infringement. According to the statistics, in the period from the amending of three major intellectual property laws until October 2005, 90 per cent of all applications for a pre-trial injunction were supported by Chinese courts and over 95 per cent of applications for the preservation of evidence and assets were supported. This percentage is high even compared to that of developed countries and other major jurisdictions. In most cases, the parties have reached an agreement or have gone for mediation after provisional measures such as injunctions and Mareva orders were adopted by the court, which in turn facilitates the timely solution of many disputes without the need for formal litigation. This is similar to the approach and effect of handling such cases in many countries.

## Strengthening the Judicial Protection of Well-known Trademarks by Identifying them in Accordance with the Law

From July 2001 to October 2005, Chinese courts identified 72 well-known trademarks in accordance with the law based upon principles of individuality, passiveness and necessity. From January to October 2005, 42 well-known trademarks were identified, of which nine belong to foreign right holders. This has demonstrated that all registered trademarks, no matter whether they belong to Chinese or to foreign right holders, will be equally identified and protected by Chinese courts in accordance with the law in order to protect the legitimate interests of both domestic and foreign proprietors. For example, in July 2001, in the *Procter & Gamble Company* v. *Shanghai Chen Xuan Intelligence Technology Developing Ltd* case regarding an unfair competition claim arising from the defendant's registration of a domain name, the Shanghai High Court ruled that the registered trademark 'Safeguard' (the combination of its words and graphics) should be identified as a well-known trademark and protected accordingly. This was the first case where a Chinese court judicially identified and protected a well-known trademark.

## Emphasizing the Mediation Approach and Resolving Civil Disputes in a Timely Manner

In the trial of civil disputes involving intellectual property, Chinese courts have earnestly followed the guideline to 'mediate where possible, adjudicate when necessary, combine mediation and adjudication, defuse the issue when the case is closed'. Chinese courts have put the emphasis on the establishment of the legal approach of mediation and used the mediation during trial and the settlement between the parties as important means to conclude cases. Through this approach, the independent value of mediation in resolving intellectual property disputes has been realized to a large extent, conflicts have been defused in time and social coherence has been promoted. In recent years, the rate of civil disputes involving intellectual property resolved through mediation or closed owing to the withdrawal of the charges has been maintained at around 50 per cent.

**Establishing a Supervision Mechanism for High-profile Cases Involving Crimes against Intellectual Property and Strengthening the Force of Criminal Punishment**

In May 2005, the Supreme Court issued the Notice on Actively Participating in the Consolidation and Regulation of the Order of Market Economy by Fulfilling Fully the Function of Adjudication. This notice requires that courts at various levels shall devote their major efforts to punishing strictly, decisively and in a timely fashion, in accordance with the law, crimes against intellectual property. If suspects of economic crimes are discovered in civil proceedings, any relevant information or material shall be transferred in time to the police or prosecutor for further investigation. Recently, the Supreme Court has issued the Notice on Strengthening the Work of Adjudicating Criminal Offences Violating Intellectual Property Rights. This notice requires once again that courts at various levels shall work closely with other relevant authorities and establish a supervision mechanism for high-profile intellectual property criminal cases, which will enable such cases to be registered, followed and supervised and crimes against intellectual property to be punished properly and rooted out decisively.

**Strengthening the Work Concerning Judicial Interpretations and Improving the Litigation Regime for Intellectual Property Cases**

Clarifying, in accordance with the law, detailed judicial principle and setting the standards for the judicial protection of intellectual property rights has been a major characteristic of Chinese judicial protection of intellectual property rights and an important task for the Supreme Court. In recent years, in order to meet the needs of economic and social development, the Supreme Court has adopted, in a timely manner, several judicial interpretations with respect to intellectual property rights that have effectively facilitated the completion of the Chinese intellectual property legal framework and that have achieved positive results. After the Interpretation on Several Issues regarding the Application of Law in Handling Criminal Cases involving Infringement of Intellectual Property, Interpretation on Several Issues regarding the Application of Law in the Trial of Disputes over Technology Contracts, which was adopted in 2004, and the Reply on Relevant Issues regarding the Handling of Phonograms and Videos in Criminal Cases involving Infringement of Copyright, which was adopted in 2005, four more judicial interpretations regarding unfair competition, infringement of new plant varieties, conflict over intellectual property rights and copyright of music television have been drafted, based upon in-depth research and opinions acquired from various sources. In order to ensure the quality of the judicial interpretation, these four drafts have been published through the Internet to consult the general public. Domestic and foreign parties, by various means, have raised a lot of sincere and constructive opinions and suggestions relating to their amendment. At present, the Supreme Court is carefully studying these opinions and suggestions and, on that basis, it will amend and improve the drafts in order to submit them in due course to the Judicial Committee of the Supreme Court for discussion.

## Strengthening the Professional Training of Judges and Improving the Overall Quality of Adjudication

Chinese courts have paid particular attention to the establishment of a team of professional judges who specialize in intellectual property cases, selecting distinctive talents to join the adjudication team. They have been emphasizing the need for professional training and they have been introducing new training methods. After years of adjudicating practice and professional training, a generation of intellectual property judges with concrete theoretical knowledge and practical experience has been created. The Supreme Court holds every year (or every two years) intellectual property adjudication training courses in the National Academy of Judges. Similar courses and symposiums have been run by local High Courts, which enables the training of intellectual property judges to be conducted on a nationwide basis. In addition, Chinese courts have been continuously expanding their international exchanges and cooperation in the field of intellectual property and they have actively been learning from foreign experience and from foreign approaches regarding the judicial protection of intellectual property. In March 2006, for example, the Supreme Court and the EU held the successful 'Sino–EU Conference & Forum on Criminal Protection of Intellectual Property' in Xiamen, China, which achieved positive results. In the future, we will further strengthen our cooperation with the EU and others and try to improve the overall quality of adjudication through research visits, professional conferences, training courses and so on.

### Actively Adopting all Feasible Measures to Increase the Transparency of Judicial Protection of Intellectual Property Rights

According to the law, Chinese courts have to observe the doctrine of an open trial: that is, the court proceedings of all cases shall be accessible to parties; the judgment of all cases shall be published; and the trial proceedings of all cases shall be open to the general public audience unless otherwise required or permitted by law. The courts provide a library service for the general public with respect to legal documents. Recently, the Supreme Court has issued the Notice on the Preparation for Making Intellectual Property Judgments Available Online, which requires that High Courts shall, as far as possible, make intellectual property judgments which entered into force within their respective jurisdiction gradually available online. In fact, courts located in some relatively developed areas such as Beijing have already made their civil intellectual property judgments available online. Recently, the 'Chinese Intellectual Property Rights Judgments Website' (http://ipr.chinacourt.org) hosted by the Intellectual Property Rights Division of the Supreme Court has been opened, an effective step towards demonstrating judicial transparency. It so far contains all valid judgments, decisions and mediation documents of intellectual property cases concluded in 2005.

## THE PROSPECTS FOR THE JUDICIAL PROTECTION OF INTELLECTUAL PROPERTY RIGHTS IN CHINA

In general, owing to the advance of science and technology and the emerging of a knowledge-based economy, the protection of intellectual property will increasingly become the focus of market competition and the attention of society. With the globalization of the economy and the internationalization of the intellectual property regime, the protection of intellectual property will increasingly become the key issue of international conflicts and trade relationships. At present, the protection of intellectual property rights in China has entered a new phase of development, with serious challenges as well as huge opportunities and bright prospects of development. In particular, China has adopted, as her important strategic mission, the policy of promoting an innovation-oriented nation. Intellectual property, as a stimulant for creative innovation, is closely linked to the establishment of an innovative nation. Protection of intellectual property is not only necessary for China to fulfil international obligations and to create a healthy investment environment, but it is even more necessary for China's own development and the establishment of an innovative nation.

## CONCLUSION

Although the Chinese economy has developed rapidly, China will remain a developing country for a long time. Piracy, counterfeiting and other infringements of intellectual property rights are still a serious problem in certain areas. As an important aspect of intellectual property enforcement, the status, function and task of judicial protection of intellectual property rights will become even more important, apparent and difficult with respect to domestic development and international competition. How to realize the fundamental and leading role of judicial protection in the overall protection system is a major topic for all of us. China has successfully established its regime for the protection of intellectual property rights. Although with shortcomings, this regime is working actively and creatively. China's determination to secure the protection of intellectual property rights has never changed. Her attitude towards strict punishment of criminal offences against and infringement of intellectual property rights is clear. China's stand on protecting intellectual property rights in accordance with the law is firm. At the same time, the protection of intellectual property rights is not only the task of administrative authorities and judiciaries. It also requires active participation and cooperation of the owners of intellectual property and the awareness of the general public. We hope that all right holders, including foreign enterprises and individuals, will actively protect their legitimate rights and interests and seek judicial remedies through legal procedures where necessary.

Chinese courts will fulfil even further and with even more determination their function regarding the judicial protection of intellectual property rights. They will equally protect the legitimate interests of both domestic and foreign right holders, increase the degree of protection and try to create a good environment of judicial protection for intellectual property rights, where owners protect their rights actively, courts adjudicate appropriately and fairly, and enforce their rulings effectively, and where infringement is punished without doubt or hesitation.

# Preface

## Paul Torremans,[*] Hailing Shan[**] and Johan Erauw[***]

As its title indicates, this book sets out to deal with intellectual property rights and their protection in China. It does so in the light of China's entry into the World Trade Organization (WTO), which meant that the TRIPs Agreement was extended to China. The book offers both Chinese and European perspectives on the issues surrounding the development of intellectual property norms and their enforcement.

The academics that conceived the project that eventually resulted in this book have been working together for quite some time now. The links between East China University of Politics and Law in Shanghai and the University of Ghent go back a couple of decades. What started with a series of visits by members of staff of both faculties to Shanghai and Ghent, respectively, was gradually broadened into staff training and teaching exchanges. Gradually the idea of a joint research programme in the area of intellectual property was conceived. This project further took shape when the University of Nottingham joined, because one of the members of its Law School started teaching and researching at the Faculty of Law in Ghent too.

The project started to focus on the rapid changes that were taking place in China's intellectual property rights legislation and practice. The issue of TRIPs compliance took centre stage in the context of China's accession to the WTO and gradually the issues surrounding the enforcement of intellectual property rights in China took centre stage jointly with those surrounding the further development of Chinese intellectual property legislation.

It was felt that a first milestone in the project that was now at cruising speed would be the presentation of the outcome of this first phase in the research at an international conference. The result became known as the 'Shanghai

* Professor, School of Law, University of Nottingham, UK and Faculty of Law, University of Ghent, Belgium.

** Professor, School of International Law, East China University of Politics and Law.

*** Professor, Faculty of Law, University of Ghent.

Conference on Intellectual Property Rights and WTO compliance: Chinese and European Perspectives', and took place at the magnificent campus of East China University of Politics and Law in Shanghai on 24 November 2004. On that occasion the academic team was joined by senior judges of the Supreme People's Court, the then Director of Directorate General Trade at the European Commission and by a Minister of the Flemish Regional Government, who was in China as part of a Belgian trade mission. This reinforced the political and judicial angle on the topic, which blended in very nicely with the academic emphasis of the research project.

This book should be seen as the second milestone of our research project. Various speakers at the conference have developed their topics further in the light of the debates at the conference and several contributions have been written specifically for this book. All contributions also take account of the developments that have taken place since the date of the conference in this rapidly changing area of law. Especially in a dynamic and rapidly developing Chinese economy, the protection and enforcement of intellectual property rights is not only an essential element and tool, but also a constantly moving target that develops new aspects in symbiosis with the economic development. We hope that this book will allow the readers to develop an insight in these issues and that it may contribute to the continuing debate on these topics, not only inside China, but also at a global level amongst right holders and users in all of China's trading partners. A better mutual understanding and in-depth and comparative knowledge of all the factors and issues involved is essential if the intellectual property system and its enforcement, in China and around the world, is to be able to live up to the challenges of a rapidly changing global economy.

It is our aim to continue our research cooperation and to expand it to other legal issues. There is a running programme of staff exchanges and we plan to organize more international conferences. That research will no doubt result in further publications and this book may become the first in a series of publications on Chinese and European law.

It is appropriate at this stage to record our thanks to the various people and institutions without the continuing support of whom this project would not have been possible. East China University of Politics and Law hosted the conference in its grand conference hall. We are very grateful to the President of East China University of Politics and Law, Professor He Qinhua, for making this facility available to us and for encouraging the project, and the excellent practical organization of the conference in Shanghai by Professor Liu Xiaohong and her team. The Hon. Cao Jianming, Grand Justice and Executive Vice President of the Supreme People's Court, generously offered his guidance to bring the project to fruition.

Thanks are also due to the then Rector of the University of Ghent, Professor André De Leenheer, for his support for the project and his presence in

Shanghai. The Faculty of Law and the Department of Private International Law of the University of Ghent have been nurturing the link with East China University of Politics and Law for many years, which enabled us to develop this project.

We received generous financial support from the provincial authorities in East Flanders in Belgium. They did not only sponsor us from Ghent, but the province's then acting Governor, Mr Marc De Buck, also joined us for the conference. We are especially grateful for their continuing commitment to support our joint research activities.

The University of Nottingham, its School of Law and its China Policy Institute also offered financial and practical support. In Shanghai, they were represented by Richard Pascoe, the Director of the China Policy Institute, and they were instrumental in the translation and the editing of the various contributions that make up this book. Special thanks are in this respect due to our young Nottingham colleague Ping Wang for his efforts in translating the contributions that were originally written in Chinese.

The Shanghai Bar Association and the Belgian–Chinese Economic and Commercial Council also supported the conference we held in Shanghai. Our project is and remains, however, in the first place an academic endeavour. It would never have seen the light of day without the tireless efforts of Professor Johan Erauw of the Department of Private International Law of the Faculty of Law at the University of Ghent.

At East China University of Politics and Law the scientific part of the project was headed by Professor Hailing Shan, whilst, from a joint University of Nottingham–University of Ghent perspective, Professor Paul Torremans coordinated efforts.

We hope that readers will enjoy the outcome of our research project and that they will find the various contributions to this book informative, useful and challenging at the same time.

Paul Torremans, Hailing Shan and Johan Erauw
August 2006

# Table of cases

# Table of legislation

## CHINA

### National Laws

**Regulations**

**Local Regulations**



**Implementation Measures**



**Judicial Interpretations (Supreme People's Court)**

**Other Instruments**

## UK



## USA



## EU LEGISLATION

# Table of treaties and conventions

# Introduction: setting the scene

**Paul Torremans***

Intellectual property rights were a prominent element in the Uruguay Round of trade negotiations that resulted in the WTO agreement. In terms of intellectual property the TRIPs Agreement, as part of that WTO agreement, set the scene for the developments over the past decade, during which the Chinese economy saw rapid development and with it the growth in importance of intellectual property rights.

Right holders that enter the Chinese economy saw rapid development and with it the growth in importance of intellectual property rights.

Right holders that enter the Chinese markets seek protection for their rights. Chinese manufacturing facilities are more and more often used to produce branded, patented or copyright protected goods, that are then exported and marketed globally. More and more Chinese companies and individuals also seek protection for their own intellectual property by using the international intellectual property system.

Chinese intellectual property laws have therefore developed rapidly over the past decade. There was an obvious need for a more structured and modern intellectual property system in the context of the adoption of the market economy and, in order to join the WTO, China also needed to comply with the standards set in the TRIPs Agreement.

Substantive rights and modern intellectual property laws are, however, only a first step. Once the necessary legislation is in place, and once industry starts using it, enforcement becomes the next big issue. The theory then has to be put into practice. On this point too there have been fascinating developments in China during the last couple of years.

This book offers a variety of perspectives from academics, judges, politicians and practitioners on these developments in the area of intellectual property law in China. These developments are looked at both from a Chinese and from a European point of view.

The foreword was written by the Hon. Dr H.C. Cao Jianming, Vice-President of the Supreme People's Court of the People's Republic of China

* Professor, School of Law, University of Nottingham, UK and Faculty of Law, University of Ghent, Belgium.

and Grand Justice of the first rank. From his unique position at the top of the Supreme People's Court he looks at these recent developments in Chinese intellectual property law. He looks at substantive law, but mainly at enforcement issues, in an essay entitled 'The Recent Development and Current Status of Judicial Protection of Intellectual Property in China'. He summarized his findings as follows:

> Although the Chinese economy has developed rapidly, China will remain a developing country for a long time. Piracy, counterfeiting and other infringements of intellectual property rights are still a serious problem in certain areas. As an important aspect of intellectual property enforcement, the status, function and task of judicial protection of intellectual property rights will become even more important, apparent and difficult with respect to domestic development and intellectual competition. How to realize the fundamental and leading role of judicial protection in the overall protection system is a major topic for all of us. China has successfully established its regime for the protection of intellectual property rights. Although with shortcomings, this regime is working actively and creatively. China's determination to secure the protection of intellectual property rights has never changed. Her attitude towards strict punishment of criminal offences against and infringement of intellectual property rights is clear. China's stand on protecting intellectual property rights in accordance with the law is firm. At the same time, the protection of intellectual property rights is not only the task of administrative authorities and judiciaries. It also requires active participation and cooperation of the owners of intellectual property and the awareness of the general public. We hope that all right holders, including foreign enterprises and individuals, will actively protect their legitimate rights and interest and seek judicial remedies through legal procedures where necessary.
>
> Chinese courts will fulfil even further and with even more determination their function regarding the judicial protection of intellectual property rights. They will equally protect the legitimate interests of both domestic and foreign right holders, increase the degree of protection and try to create a good environment of judicial protection for intellectual property rights, where owners protect their rights actively, courts adjudicate appropriately and fairly, and enforce their rulings effectively, and where infringement is punished without doubt or hesitation.

Part I of the book thus looks both from a Chinese and from a European perspective at issues surrounding the question whether the substantive intellectual property laws are TRIPs compliant.

The Chinese perspective is offered in an essay that was written by Professor Guo Shoukang of the School of Law at Renmin University and by Zuo Xiaodong, who is Director and Legal Counsel at the China Ground Enterprises Group. Professor Guo Shoukang is the *éminence grise* of Chinese intellectual property and he is therefore ideally placed to paint the picture of the substantive law developments before asking the final question, whether the result is TRIPs compliant. The essay then goes on to consider future developments of the system and the need for it to serve also the specific demands of the developing

Chinese economy and society. The authors in the end come to the following conclusion:

> To sum up, China's intellectual property law offers protection basically consistent with the requirement of TRIPs. It shall be made clear that the existence of infringement of intellectual property rights does not necessarily mean that the intellectual property law or its enforcement has a problem. Attention shall be paid to whether effective remedies have been provided in respect of activities infringing intellectual property rights. China's intellectual property protection regime is being improved; its enforcement is being strengthened. In the process of implementing international treaties, China has demonstrated the credibility of a responsible super nation.
>
> Besides meeting the requirement of TRIPs, China's intellectual property laws also need to be adjusted to the requirement of the development of society and to technological advance. In such a process, certain regulation of China's intellectual property law have exceeded the requirement of TRIPs. For example, in order to meet the need of developing information technology, the right of dissemination through information networks is provided in the 2001 Copyright Law. And the 'Interpretation of the Supreme People's Court on Several Issues concerning the Application of Law in the Trial of Cases in Relation to Copyright Disputes over Computer Network'[1] was adopted by the Supreme People's Court. The Regulation on the Protection of the Right to Dissemination through Information Network is being drafted at the moment and is presumably going to be promulgated soon.[2] This will pave the way for China to join the WIPO Copyright Treaty (WCT) and the WIPO Performances and Phonograms Treaty (WPPT). At the moment, a new wave of amendments of China's intellectual property laws is being prepared in order to meet the need of social, economic, technological and cultural development and the challenge of emerging new issues. Alongside the development and advance of the society, economy and technology, the protection of intellectual property in China will be continuously improved and strengthened.

I next offer a European perspective that focuses more heavily on the shortcomings and problems that have been identified in the TRIPs framework over a decade of experience. Through a thorough analysis of the TRIPs provisions concerning substantive patent, trade mark and copyright law, an overall assessment of the fairness and effectiveness of TRIPs is made. This is then coupled with an analysis of the objectives and principles of the agreement and its place in the overall WTO agreement. From this analysis emerges a suggestion that Article 7 TRIPs and its role should be reviewed and enhanced in order to restore the balance.

---

1 Adopted 22 November 2000, amended 2 January 2004.

2 It is also translated as *Regulations on the Protection of the Right of Communication through Information Network*. However, it is the view of the translator that the Chinese term '传播' is better represented by the word 'dissemination' than 'communication'. The draft can be found in http://www.chinaiprlaw.com/english/laws/laws22.htm. (Note by the translator.)

Part II of the book then shifts the TRIPs compliance emphasis to the issues surrounding enforcement of rights. In order to situate these issues correctly Professor Daniel Gervais of the University of Ottawa sets the ball rolling, looking at the TRIPs Agreement and the changing landscape of international intellectual property. This leads him to the following conclusions:

> Without adequate IP protection, economic development will not occur at an optimal level, though it is unclear whether IP rules have any positive effect on the development of the truly poorer nations. In addition, we now know that, while IP is an essential ingredient, it does not, by itself, make an economic plan. Many more elements are required. I argue that, for both practical reasons and on the basis of available empirical data, TRIPS should be seen, and accepted, as a given. Further, it may be defended as an appropriate reference point for developing nations in the context of TRIPS Plus bilateral trade discussions. Indeed, post-TRIPS developments have been going in two (arguably diverging) directions. On the one hand, TRIPS-related development within WTO, as well as recent developments in WIPO, have tried to be more responsive to the perceived needs of developing countries and the interests of users in securing access to protected content and material on terms they consider reasonable. This even includes broad exceptions to obligations to obtain permissions and licences. On the other hand, IP developments in bilateral and regional trade agreements mirror the so-called 'maximalist' approach. This latter trend to regulate IP rights through bilateral regimes may not immediately threaten the balanced approach of WTO and WIPO, but these bilateral initiatives likely will have a significant impact in the long run. TRIPS contains a number of rules that WTO members must implement, but it also affords a fair margin of 'policy flexibility'. Thus, implementing TRIPS may and should be viewed as part of a broader knowledge strategy resting on priority setting, education and institutional capacity-building, regulatory adaptation, FDI 'marketing', and patent mining. Finally, if TRIPS were defended as the 'correct' international norm, it would have the effect of buttressing the position that TRIPS Plus is inadequate at this juncture for many, and perhaps most, developing countries.

Afterwards the emphasis shifts towards enforcement in the strictest sense. Piracy and counterfeiting are still a significant threat for right holders, with which the Chinese enforcement system grapples on a day-to-day basis. One of the unique aspects of that Chinese enforcement system is its administrative component. That administrative enforcement system and its role in the fight against piracy is examined in Chapter 4, by Kristie Thomas of the University of Nottingham in Ningbo. Her analysis leads her to conclude as follows:

> It is clear that, despite significant changes in the intellectual property enforcement system in China as a result of WTO accession, enforcement of IP rights through administrative means still dominates. Not only is administrative enforcement chosen by rights holders for its cost-effectiveness, availability and quick resolution, it is also the preferred choice of the state. This official preference for public enforcement mechanisms has been attributed to social and cultural factors such as Confucianism and socialism, leading to a lack of emphasis on individual rights, as well as the role of the legal system in the Chinese economy generally as a tool for policy implementation.

However, despite the key role of administrative enforcement within the IP framework, there are still various criticisms levelled at the administrative agencies. The most significant criticism is that local protectionism dominates the enforcement of IP at the local level, leading to delays in enforcement and the imposition of insignificant fines. A further observation of the administrative enforcement system is the numerous agencies that compete for dominance within the IP enforcement framework. These bureaucratic rivalries make the implementation of any comprehensive IP strategy virtually impossible, a task already complicated by the perceived gap in authority between central and local governments.

It is undeniable that China's WTO entry and subsequent attempts to comply with the TRIPS Agreement have had a significant effect on the protection of IP in China. The effect of TRIPS has been felt most strongly in the legislative arena, but it has also had a significant effect on the enforcement system. The main change to the administrative enforcement system has been the introduction of judicial review of final administrative decisions, which was previously unavailable. Other changes include the removal of barriers to national treatment within the administrative enforcement system, increases in the maximum fines available for IP infringements, the availability of preliminary injunctions and the lowering of thresholds for criminal liability. It is believed that these changes will have a considerable long-term effect on the IP enforcement system in China, but it is perhaps too soon to see their full impact.

It is clear that administrative enforcement remains an IP holder's main choice for enforcement, but it is also undeniable that the system is beginning to change. With judges gaining more experience of IP disputes and beginning to issue preliminary injunctions more regularly, the civil system will begin to appeal more to rights holders. However, it is unlikely that administrative enforcement will ever be abandoned; it is more likely that it will continue to play an important role in IP enforcement in China, as a fast and cost-effective method to curb infringements as part of a wider strategy of IP protection.

In the foreword we were offered a view from the bench on the issues surrounding enforcement. But the administrative, as well as the judicial (civil and criminal), enforcement system need to be put into practice by the right holders and their lawyers. They look at it from a different perspective and that perspective is offered in Chapter 5, by Jingzhou Tao, of DLA Piper Rudnick Gray Cary UK LLP. His conclusion is a rather critical one. In his words:

> The shortcomings in intellectual property rights enforcement in China and the sluggish pace of improvement have invited much criticism from other WTO members, in particular the US, EU members and Japan. In recent years, the US trade delegation has repeatedly visited China and negotiated with the Chinese government with regard to intellectual property rights enticement issues. Faced with great international pressure and the risk of trade wars triggered by the dissatisfaction of the other WTO member countries, the Chinese government's habitual reaction is to launch periodic anti-counterfeiting and anti-piracy campaigns and to issue various specific rules to show to the world that it continues to make progress in its intellectual property rights legislation. Nevertheless, such actions have thus far produced little effect. It may take decades for the Chinese government to thoroughly curb rampant intellectual property rights infringement in China.

Having dealt with the enforcement of mainstream intellectual property rights in the traditional markets, we return to the bench for an analysis of the protection which the Chinese legal system offers copyright and trademark owners in cyberspace. The Hon. Dr Jiang Zhipei, Justice of the Supreme People's Court of China and Director of the Third Civil Chamber, demonstrates that China has successfully faced up to these advanced and complex issues that surround the use, infringement and enforcement of copyright and trade mark rights on the Internet. He is therefore able to draw the following broad conclusion:

> It has been more than four years since China's WTO accession. China's reform and opening up has reached the new era of building a harmonious socialist society. The reform of the Chinese judicial system has also progressed further in order to provide effective legal protection, in order to fulfil the goal of building a harmonious society. The much-noticed 'professionalisation of Chinese judges' has also made continuous and in-depth progress. The judicial protection of intellectual property in China will surely become fairer and more effective. This will not only facilitate the protection of intellectual property in China but also contribute to the international protection of intellectual property.

Part III of the book then moves away from the TRIPs Agreement in a narrow sense. Until now we have also primarily looked at mainstream intellectual property rights such as patents, trade marks and copyright and this focus too changes in Part III. Here we look at confidentiality, non-competition clauses, transfer of technology agreements and traditional knowledge.

Professor John Adams, of Notre Dame University and emeritus professor at the University of Sheffield, starts the discussion on confidentiality and non-competition in Chapter 7 by offering a European perspective. His analysis highlights the tension between the need to allow employees freedom to practise their trade, wherever they choose to go, and the need for employers to protect their legitimate interests. He concludes by reminding ourselves what an employer's legitimate interests are. Once one accepts that only these interests can be taken into account in the balancing act, a solution becomes a bit more obvious. The emphasis falls here on the protection of the employer's genuine trade secrets; that is, the information has the character that the law recognizes as having the character of a trade secret.

In Chapter 8, this is followed up from a Chinese perspective by Professor Hailing Shan of the School of International Law of East China University of Politics and Law. She focuses on the protection of know-how in Chinese enterprises and in employment relationships:

> Protection of trade secrets in China has been through a process of improving from no protection to protection, from a piecemeal approach to consolidated protection, from protection that was narrow in scope to wide protection, from domestic law protection to protection under bilateral agreements, international treaties and global conventions. However, like the protection of other intellectual properties, China still

> has a huge task in establishing a coherent regime of trade secrets protections. This task is particularly difficult because, for historical reasons, the enactment of Chinese laws, including those regarding trade secrets, has been subject to external pressures and a lack of basic infrastructure, which has influenced, to a certain extent, the fairness and effective implementation of the legislation. Therefore, the improvement of the Chinese legal framework on the protection of trade secrets shall be based upon experiences of other jurisdictions, taking into consideration, as the starting point, the reality of the country and the need for further development. It shall aim at establishing a trade secrets protection regime with special characteristics and in accordance with international standards, in order to facilitate the advance in technology and investment and to protect the public interest.

Leaving confidentiality behind, we turn to the protection of traditional knowledge in Chapter 9. Professor Zhu Lanye of East China University of Politics and Law asks in this respect the question whether this is really an efficient way to protect poor countries' intellectual property. She looks at this from an international as well as from a Chinese perspective before concluding:

> Compared with the huge amount of traditional knowledge existing today, all work done cannot meet the requirement of protection, not to say adequate and effective protection. As mentioned in the first part of this essay, before the answers to many questions will be found, this topic will be a long-term important task of WIPO. The existing intellectual property system is obviously not suitable to be used directly on traditional knowledge protection. The developing countries should cooperate and find out a better means to protect traditional knowledge.

Transfer of technology is the final issue which we address in Part III of the book. In Chapter 10, Zou Weining, who is a partner in the Jun He Law Office in Beijing, looks at the new Chinese rules concerning contract for the importation of technology. It is clear that this new system for technology importation contracts represents a vast improvement over the old system and that it reflects China's WTO commitments. Parallel importation, however, remains, as in many other countries, a difficult issue.

Part IV of the book looks at the development agenda and the role of intellectual property and reform of the intellectual property system in this context. We have two interesting perspectives to offer: a philosopher's perspective and a politician's perspective.

Professor Sigrid Sterckx, who specializes in ethics at the Department of Philosophy and Moral Science of the University of Ghent, looks in Chapter 11 at the promises and realities of the WTO TRIPs patent regime after the Doha declaration. This analysis leads her to the following conclusions:

> Economic research shows that the nature of technology transfer and the utility of intellectual property rights follow a kind of 'technology ladder'. However, in the continuous process of the 'strengthening' of patents, little or no attention is paid to the economic circumstances in poor countries. The fact that the patent system has

very diverse effects in different *industries* – and this is also true in industrialised countries – is also ignored. A strongest-possible and long-lasting patent protection is pursued in all countries and all fields of industry – a 'one size fits all' (viz. extra large) approach.

I would not go as far as Jagdish Bhagwati, one of the most prominent economists of our time, who has claimed in the *Financial Times* that: . . . [Intellectual Property Protection] is not a 'trade' issue; the WTO ought to be about lowering trade barriers and tackling market access problems. The inclusion of IPP has turned the organization into a royalty collection agency.[3]

Intellectual property rights do have trade-related aspects. But this is precisely why scientists, consumers and patients in both industrialised and developing countries should be so worried about the maximalist rights approach that is currently taken in the field of intellectual property. The urgent challenge we are facing today has been summarised in simple words, but very much to the point, in the recent report of the UK Commission on Intellectual Property Rights.

Developed countries should pay more attention to reconciling their commercial self-interest with the need to reduce poverty in developing countries, which is in everyone's interest. Higher IP standards should not be pressed on developing countries without a series and objective assessment of their impact on development and poor people. We need to ensure that the global IP system evolves so that the needs of developing countries are incorporated and, most importantly, so that it contributes to the reduction of poverty in developing countries by stimulating innovation and technology transfer relevant to them, while also making available the products of technology at the most competitive prices possible.

Intellectual property protection is not *per se* hostile to the interests of developing countries, but the system should be adapted to reflect *their* innovation and investment needs. To the extent that this is difficult or impossible, alternative models should be developed that promote the needs of developing countries at much lower social costs than the models that are currently in place.

Chapter 12 then offers a politician's perspective on the importance of intellectual property in international trade relations, but also on the need for reform if the system is to serve the needs of all communities around the world. This chapter is the speech which Minister Fientje Moerman, Deputy Minister–President and Flemish Minister for Economics, Business, Science, Innovation and Foreign Trade of the Flemish Regional Government (Flanders, Belgium) delivered in Shanghai on 24 November 2004 at the Shanghai Conference on Intellectual Property Rights (IPR) and WTO Compliance – Chinese and European Perspectives.

By way of postscript, Part V of the book and Chapter 13 set out the agenda for the future.

---

3 Jagdish Bhagwati (2002), 'Patents and the Poor', *The Financial Times*, 16 September.

# PART I

# TRIPS compliance: substantive rights

# 1. Are Chinese intellectual property laws consistent with the TRIPs Agreement?

**Guo Shoukang* and Zuo Xiaodong****

## INTRODUCTION

China joined the World Trade Organization (WTO) on 11 December 2001.[1] As a member of the WTO, China will enjoy the rights conferred by the WTO agreement and, at the same time, undertake all the obligations provided for in the WTO agreement. According to Article XVI:4 of the WTO Agreement, China undertook that, through the amendment of existing domestic legislation and enactment of new legislation, China would implement the WTO Agreement in an effective and unified manner.[2] China has honoured the commitment regarding the domestic implementation of the Agreement on Trade-Related Intellectual Property Rights (TRIPs) – an important component of the WTO Agreement. Before and since the WTO accession, China has amended basic laws of intellectual property; that is, the *Patent Law*, *Trademark Law* and *Copyright Law*, promulgated a number of administrative regulations such as *Regulation on the Protection of Layout Designs of Integrated Circuits*, *Regulation on Customs Protection of Intellectual Property* and added supplementary detailed rules for implementation, as well as judicial interpretations. These laws and regulations provide, as required by TRIPs, protection for various intellectual properties such as copyright and related rights, trademarks, geographical indications, industrial designs, patents, layout designs of integrated circuits, undisclosed information and so on. A framework of intellectual property laws as required by TRIPs has been put in place.

* Professor, Supervisor of PhD candidates, Law School of Renmin University of China, 中国人民大学法学院教授 博士生导师, Chair of UNESCO Seminars on Copyright and Neighbouring Right.

** Director and legal counsel, Legal Department, China Grand Enterprises Group.

1 Accession of the People's Republic of China, WT/L/432.

2 Report of the Working Party on the Accession of China, WT/ACC/CHN/49, 1 October 2001, paras 68, 70.

The consolidation of intellectual property laws in China in the period 2000–2001 had a clear purpose: to make Chinese intellectual property laws consistent with TRIPs. Therefore, these amendments have basically covered all issues that need to be addressed for the domestic legislation to be consistent with TRIPs. A detailed explanation will be given below, comparing basic Chinese legislation on intellectual property with corresponding provisions of TRIPs.

## Patent Law

China's first Patent Law was promulgated on 12 March 1984 and entered into force on 1 April 1985. This law has been drafted on the basis of advanced international experiences with patents and modified to suit the Chinese situation. It reflected the main principles of the Paris Convention for the Protection of Industrial Property (hereinafter Paris Convention) to which China had become a party, such as national treatment, the right of priority and independence of patents. Therefore, it is widely regarded as having a high starting point, being updated and made compatible with the Chinese situation.[3]

During the process of China regaining GATT membership, the Patent Law was amended for the first time on 4 September 1992. This amendment enabled the Patent Law to be basically consistent with the draft version of TRIPs.[4] The consistency mainly manifested itself in the scope of protection, the right of the patentee and the duration of protection. The amended Patent Law expanded the scope of patent protection to foods, drinks, spices, medicines and substances obtained through chemical methods.[5] It strengthened the right of the patentee by providing the right to import and by expanding the protection of patented process to cover products obtained directly through such processes.[6] It extended the duration of protection to 20 years for invention patents and 10 years for utility models and industrial designs from the date of application.[7]

Differences remained between the 1992 Patent Law of China and the TRIPs. Therefore, the Patent Law was amended for the second time on 25 August 2000. The guiding principle of this amendment was to make the Patent Law fully and systematically integrate with the provisions of TRIPs and any

---

3 Legal Department of the State Intellectual Bureau, *Detailed Analysis of the New Patent Law*, 2001, preface, at p. 2; Guo Shoukang (ed.) *Intellectual Property Law*, 2002年, at p. 125.

4 Dunkel Draft.

5 Article 25 of the 1992 Patent Law of the People's Republic of China.

6 Article 11 of the 1992 Patent Law of the People's Republic of China.

7 Article 45 of the 1992 Patent Law of the People's Republic of China.

issue irrelevant to that integration was not considered. This approach of rejecting 'free riders' ensured the timely completion of the amendment. The remaining inconsistencies between the 1992 Patent Law of China and the TRIPs were addressed. These include the following.

**The right of the patentee is further expanded**

Regarding inventions and utility models, the patentee's right over 'offer for sale' the patented product or the product obtained directly by the patented process was added.[8] This made the provision of the Chinese Patent Law on rights conferred consistent with Article 28 of TRIPs.

**Providing the opportunity for judicial review of final administrative decisions**

According to Articles 41 and 46 of the 2001 Patent Law, the applicant for a patent or the proprietor of an invention, utility model or industrial design may bring action in the people's court against the decision of review or revocation by the Patent Review Committee within three months of receiving such decision. This provision is fully consistent with the requirement of judicial review of final administrative decisions provided in Articles 32 and 41.4 of TRIPs.

**Improving the regime for compulsory licensing**

In this area, China has amended not only the Patent Law, but also the Detailed Rules Implementing the Patent Law. Furthermore, the Measures on Compulsory Licensing of Patents was promulgated on 13 June 2003 and entered into force on 15 July 2003. It mainly provides procedures for the grant, fee determination and termination of compulsory licences of inventions or utility models.[9] In order to implement the Doha Ministerial Declaration on the TRIPs Agreement and Public Health (the Doha declaration) and WTO Council Decision on the Implementation of Paragraph 6 of the Doha Declaration on the TRIPs Agreement and Public Health, China promulgated the Measures on Compulsory Licensing of Patents Involving Public Health on 29 November 2005.

The amendments for the purpose of falling in line with TRIPs are mainly in the area of dependent patents and the limiting of compulsory licensing. Regarding the compulsory licensing of dependent patents, the previous version of the Patent Law only required that the second (dependent) invention or utility model should involve 'a technical advantage' in relation to the first

---

8 Article 11 of the 2001 Patent Law of the People's Republic of China.

9 Order 31 of the Director of the State Intellectual Property Bureau.

one, which was very lenient[10] and differed from Article 31(L)(*i*) of TRIPs requiring 'an important technical advance of considerable economic significance'. Therefore Article 50 of 2002 Patent Law adopted the exact wording of TRIPs.

Regarding the limiting of compulsory licensing, Article 52 of the 2002 Patent Law absorbed the provisions on duration, scope and termination of the compulsory licence contained in the 1992 Detailed Rules Implementing the Patent Law. It provides that the compulsory licence shall have a prescribed scope and duration in accordance with the purpose for which it is granted. As soon as that purpose no longer exists and will not recur, upon the plea of the patentee, the patent authority of the State Council shall, after review, revoke the decision authorizing the compulsory licensing. Although the 2002 Patent Law has not imposed conditions such as the supply of the domestic market and conditions in the case of semiconductor technology, Article 72 of the Detailed Rules Implementing the Patent Law provides that the compulsory licence is granted predominantly for the supply of the domestic market. If semiconductor technology is involved, compulsory licensing shall only be allowed for public non-commercial use or to remedy a practice determined after judicial or administrative process to be anti-competitive.

There are two issues of compulsory licensing the regulation of which by Chinese Patent Law and TRIPs differ in wording but remain consistent in substance. The first one is the compensation of the compulsory licence. The Chinese Patent Law provides that the right holder shall be paid a reasonable licence fee, which is consistent in meaning with the requirement in TRIPs of adequate remuneration, taking into account the economic value of the authorization. The second one is whether the legal use without authorization is assignable. TRIPs provides that such use can only be assignable when that part of enterprise or goodwill which enjoys such use is being assigned as well. The Chinese Patent Law simply provides that the enterprise or individual granted the compulsory licence has no power to authorize others to exploit the patent, which seems to be stricter than, and therefore consistent with, the requirement of TRIPs.

### Provisional measures

Article 50 of TRIPs provides for provisional measures. In Chinese law, the order to preserve evidence before trial had been issued according to the Civil

---

10 Some argued that this condition was too easy to meet and should indeed be met by any subsequent dependent patent; otherwise, the second patent would not have been granted without a certain degree of creativity comparing to the prior patent. Li Shunde, 'TRIPS and the Intellectual Property Law of Our Country I' (2002), **58** *Survey of Scientific and Technological Achievement*.

Procedure Law which was not adequate to implement the provisions of TRIPs on preventing infringement. Therefore, Article 61 of the 2002 Patent Law was added during the amending process. It provides that, if evidence proves that the patent right is being infringed or such infringement is imminent, and where any delay is likely to cause irreparable harm to the right holder's legitimate interest, the court may, upon the plea of the right holder, adopt provisional measures before the proceedings regarding the merits of the case (*inaudita altera parte*) such as injunctions and Mareva orders. In order to supplement this provision, the Supreme Court has adopted Several Provisions of the Supreme People's Court on the Application of Law to Preventing Infringement of Patent Right before Trial which provides detailed regulations on the procedure of adopting provisional measures. Of course, the wording of Article 61 of the 2002 Patent Law has not reflected all key elements of Article 50 of TRIPs such as the notification of the provisional measure and conditions for the adoption of provisional measures. But in substance, the 2002 Patent Law is generally regarded as including all components of Article 50 of TRIPs. Furthermore, China has stated clearly that Article 61 of the 2002 Patent Law will be implemented in a way fully consistent with Article 50:1–4 of TRIPs.[11]

**Clarification of circumstances where damages shall be granted**

According to Article 62(2) of the 1992 Patent Law, unknowing use or sale of patented products which have been produced and sold without the authorization of the right holder would not constitute patent infringement. In contrast, Article 45(1) of TRIPs provides that the infringer who knowingly, or with reasonable grounds to know, engaged in infringing activity is liable to pay damages. Under TRIPs, the factor of 'actual knowledge' does not stop the infringement from being established, but only influences the form of liability, that is, whether damages shall be ordered. This differs from the 1992 Patent Law regarding the understanding of infringement. Article 62(2) of the 1992 Patent Law was annulled during amendment. Instead, Article 63 of the 2002 Patent Law provides that unknowing use or sale of patented products or products obtained directly by patented process which have been produced and sold without the authorization of the right holder, does not render one liable to pay compensation if such use or sale is for the purpose of manufacture or business operation and if the acquisition of such products can be proved through legal channels. Therefore, the Chinese Patent Law has been modified to be generally consistent with TRIPs regarding the definition of infringement. However, certain differences regarding the circumstances under which damages shall be

---

11 Report of the Working Party on the Accession of China, WT/ACC/CHN/49, 1 October 2001, para. 296.

ordered remain. TRIPs provides that the infringer who 'knowingly, or with reasonable grounds to know', engaged in infringing activities is liable to pay damages, while the Chinese Patent Law provides that the infringer is not liable to pay compensation when the infringement has been conducted 'unknowingly' and qualified with conditions such as 'for the purpose of manufacture or business operation' and proof of products being legally acquired.

## Trademark Law

China's first Trademark Law was promulgated on 23 August 1982 and entered into force on 1 March 1983. It was amended for the first time on 22 February 1993. The 1993 amendment added provisions on the protection of service marks, the duration of protection (10 years), the extension of protection and revocation of registration in the case of three years of no usage, which were consistent with TRIPs requirements. In order to meet the obligations of WTO accession, the Trademark Law was amended a second time on 27 October 2001. This amendment has basically eliminated all remaining inconsistencies with TRIPs, which manifests itself in the following points.

### Clarification of key elements that constitute trademarks

The old Trademark Law defined the key elements of a trademark as including only 'words, graphics or their combination', which differed from Article 15(1) of TRIPs which refers to 'words including personal names, letters, numerals, figurative elements and combinations of colours as well as any combination of such signs'. Following the amendment, the Trademark Law provides that the key elements constituting a trademark include 'words, graphics, letters, numerals, three dimensional signs, and combinations of colours as well as any combination of abovementioned elements'.

### Protection of well-known trademarks

Article 6*bis* (2) of the Paris Convention has already provided protection for well-known marks. If a trademark constitutes a reproduction, an imitation or a translation of a well-known mark, liable to create confusion, its registration shall be refused or cancelled and its use shall be prohibited. Article 16(2) and (3) provides further protection by, on the one hand, defining the criteria for the identification of well-known trademarks and, on the other hand, extending the protection of well-known trademarks to goods or services which are not similar to those in respect of which a trademark is registered; that is, a trademark shall be banned from use or registration when such trademark of goods or services which are not similar to those in respect of which a well-known trademark is registered, when it nonetheless constitutes a reproduction, an imitation, or a translation of such well-known mark, and use of that trademark in relation to those goods or services would indicate a connection between those goods or services and the owner of the registered well-known trademark, and the interests of the owner of the registered well-known trademark are likely to be damaged by such use.

In practice, China protects well-known trademarks according to the Paris Convention, for example, through the Provisional Regulation on the Identification and Administration of Well-known Trademarks adopted by the State Administration for Industry and Commerce in 1996.[12] The 2001 amendment of Trademark Law inserted into the Trademark Law protection of well-known trademarks in accordance with the Paris Convention and TRIPs. Article 13 of the 2001 Trademark Law provides: 'if a trademark constitutes a reproduction, an imitation, or a translation, liable to create confusion, of a well-known mark in respect of identical or similar merchandise but not yet registered in China, its registration shall be refused and its use shall be prohibited; if a trademark constitutes a reproduction, an imitation, or a translation, misleading the public, of a registered well-known mark in respect of not similar merchandise, and the interests of the owner of the registered well-known trademark are likely to be damaged by such use, its registration shall be refused and its use shall be prohibited'.

This provision has absorbed the regulation on the protection of well-known marks in the Paris Convention and TRIPs, and is clearer. At the same time, Article 14 of the 2001 Trademark Law provides the criteria for identifying well-known trademarks in correspondence with Article 16(2) of TRIPs.

**The right of priority added**

Article 4 of the Paris Convention established the right of priority. Article 11 provides that the applicant of a trademark shall be given the right of priority in respect of such trademark in respect of goods which are introduced for the first time at official or officially recognized international exhibitions held in the territory of members. Article 62(3) provides that Article 4 of Paris Convention shall apply mutatis mutandis to service marks.

Before the 2001 amendment, China's Trademark Law itself had no provision regarding the right of priority. It was found in the Provisional Regulation on the Invocation of the Right of Priority in Trademark Registration adopted by the State Administration for Industry and Commerce in 1985 and in the 1988 Implementing Measures of Trademark Law, where the right of priority was provided. However, the issue of the right of priority in respect of international

---

12 Xuezheng Wang (2004), 'WTO Accession and Trademark Protection in China', in *Frontline Issues of Protection of Intellectual Property Right in China and TRIPs*, Beijing: Law Press China, p. 146.

exhibitions was left unaddressed. The 2001 amendment incorporated the regulation on the right of priority into the Trademark Law (Articles 24, 25) which provides all aspects of right of priority, including the right on the ground of registration, that on the ground of first introduction at international exhibitions, conditions, duration and procedure of right of priority, in accordance with the Paris Convention and TRIPs.

**Judicial review of administrative decisions involving trademarks**

Article 41.4 of TRIPs requires that parties to a proceeding shall have an opportunity for review of final administrative decisions by a judicial authority. The Chinese Trademark Law had a problem on this issue before the 2001 amendment. Articles 21, 22, 29 and 35 of the 1993 Trademark Law provided that parties might appeal, before the Trademark Review Committee, against decisions of the Trademark Bureau, such as the rejection of an application, a ruling on an objection against a preliminary declaration and the revocation of a registered trademark. The decision or ruling of the Trademark Review Committee would be final. In order to be consistent with TRIPs, the 2001 Trademark Law has provided procedures enabling the parties to bring action in court.[13]

**Distinctiveness acquired through use**

Article 15(1) of TRIPs provides that, where signs are not inherently capable of distinguishing the relevant goods or services, members may make registrability depend on distinctiveness acquired through use. This provision is not the minimum requirement of the TRIPs. Members have the right to choose whether or not to adopt such regulation in their laws. During the 2001 amendment, the Chinese Trademark Law incorporated such a provision in Article 11. According to Article 11 of the 2001 Trademark Law, signs that can not inherently be used as trademarks, but have acquired distinctiveness through use, may be registered as trademarks.

**Prohibition on certain signs being used as trademarks**

Article 6*ter* of the Paris Convention provides that official signs of and hallmarks indicating control and warranty by the countries of the Union shall not be registered as trademarks. Before the 2001 amendment, the Chinese Trademark Law had contained no such prohibition, although de facto the prohibition existed in practice. During amendment, a provision was added as Article 10(1)[4] of the 2001 Trademark Law which provides that any sign

---

[13] Articles 32, 33, 43 and 49 provide that parties may bring an action in the people's court against the decision or ruling of the Trademark Review Committee within 30 days of receiving such decision or ruling.

'identical or similar to official signs or hallmarks indicating control and warranty' can not be used as a trademark except otherwise authorized, which is consistent with the Paris Convention and TRIPs.

**Provisional measures**

In accordance with Article 50 of TRIPs, the 2001 Trademark Law provides for the scheme of provisional measures on prevention of infringement and preservation of assets and evidences before trial (Articles 57, 58). In order to facilitate the implementation of this provision, the Supreme Court has adopted an Interpretation on Issues Concerning the Application of Law to Preventing Infringement of Registered Trademark Right and Preservation of Evidences before Trial on 9 January 2002.

**Clarification of circumstances in which damages shall be ordered**

Article 52(2) of the 2001 Trademark Law provides that any sale of products which is infringing rights of registered trademarks constitutes trademark infringement, which abandoned the condition of 'knowingly'. At the same time, Article 56(3) provides that any person who had unknowingly sold a product infringing a registered trademark is not liable to pay damages, provided that such person can prove that the product has been acquired through legal channels and names the supplier. This amendment corresponds to the relevant amendment to the Chinese Patent Law in 2000.

**Geographical indications**

The protection of geographical indications conferred by TRIPs is mainly requiring legal means to be provided by members to prevent the use of geographical indications in misleading the public as to the origin of a good or in an act of unfair competition. Regarding trademarks, it requires the prevention of the registration of a trademark which contains geographical indications and misleads the public as to the real geographical origin of the good. After amendment, the Trademark Law protects the geographical indications using collective trademarks or certification marks. In addition, China's Anti-Unfair Competition Law, Product Quality Law, Consumer Protection Law and relevant rules adopted by the State Administration for Industry and Commerce and the General Administration of Quality Supervision, Inspection and Quarantine, provide for the protection of geographical indications by requiring information of real geographical origin to be supplied. The provision regarding geographical indications was inserted into the 2001 Trademark Law during amendment. Article 16 of the 2001 Trademark Law defines geographical indications as 'indications which identify a good as originating in a region where a given quality, reputation or other characteristic of the good is essentially attributable to the natural or social factors of such region'. This definition is fully consistent with that in TRIPs. According to the 2001 Trademark Law, if a trademark contains certain geographical indications, but the product does not originate in the area indicated by such geographical indications, thereby misleading the public, such trademark shall not be registered and its use shall be prohibited. However, if the bona fide application for registration of such trademark has been granted, the registration shall remain valid. At the same time, the Implementing Regulation of Trademark Law provides that geographical indications may be registered as certification trademarks or as collective trademarks. Therefore, from the perspective of trademark protection, Chinese law offered the same protection as TRIPs for geographical indications.

## Copyright Law

In order to prepare for the accession to the WTO and to meet the need of economic and technological development, China amended the 1990 Copyright Law in October 2001 in accordance with the requirements of TRIPs. The amendments mainly include the following.

### Rental rights

Article 11 of TRIPs provides for rental rights in respect of computer programs and cinematographic works; that is, proprietors have the right to authorize or to prohibit the commercial rental to the public of originals or copies of their copyright works. In respect of computer programs, the rental rights do not arise from rentals where the program itself is not the essential object of the rental. In respect of cinematographic works, the rental rights may not be given, unless such rental has led to widespread copying of such works which is materially impairing the exclusive right of reproduction conferred on proprietors. Rental rights in respect of computer programs also apply in respect of phonograms. The amended Copyright Law provides for rental rights in respect of computer programs, cinematographic works, phonograms and videos. Article 10(7) of the 2001 Copyright Law provides that the 'rental right is the right to authorize, for a consideration, the temporary use of cinematographic works or works created by means similar to cinematography or computer programs, except where the computer program itself is not the essential object of the rental'. Article 41 provides that 'the author of the phonogram or video shall, in respect of his works, have the right to authorize the reproduction, publishing, rental or dissemination through information network of his work and to receive remuneration for such authorization'. These provisions are consistent with the requirements of TRIPs.

**Protection of computer programs**

TRIPs requires that computer programs shall be protected as literary works under the Berne Convention (1971).[14] China's 1990 Copyright Law provided that computer programs should be protected, but detailed protective measures were left for the State Council to adopt in a separate document. The State Council promulgated the Regulation on the Protection of Computer Software on 4 June 1990, which provided that computer software must be registered; otherwise, copyright in it can not be invoked against the third party.[15] This provision differs from the requirement of TRIPs. The new Regulation on the Protection of Computer Software entered into force on 1 January 2002 and no longer requires compulsory registration. It provides that computer software shall be protected as a literary work with no formalities required, which is consistent with TRIPs.

**Compilations of data**

Article 10.2 of TRIPs provides that compilations of data or other material, whether in machine readable or other form, which by reason of the selection or arrangement of their contents constitute intellectual creations shall be protected as such. Such protection, which shall not extend to the data or material itself, shall be without prejudice to any copyright subsisting in the data or material itself. This provision differs from the regulation on compilation of works in the Berne Convention. The 1990 Copyright Law of China only contains regulations on editing of works, which also differs from the provision of the Berne Convention. The 2001 Copyright Law annulled the provision on editing works, but provides, in Article 14, instead for the protection of compilations of works, which is fully consistent with TRIPs.

---

14 Berne Convention for the Protection of Literary and Artistic Works (Paris Act, 1971).

15 *Notice of the Supreme People's Court on Several Issues concerning the Implementation of Copyright Law* enacted on 24 December 1993 provides that the proprietor's right to sue shall not be infected by the fact whether the computer software has been registered or not. Of course, this provision only involves the right to bring an infringement action. It does not involve substantial rights. Therefore, some consider that, to enable a piece of computer software to be administratively protected, it has to be registered. See Xu, Chao (2004), Deputy Director of Copyright Department of State Copyright Bureau, 'Legal Regime of Copyright and the Amendment of Copyright Law', in *Frontline Issues of Protection of Intellectual Property Right in China and TRIPs*, Beijing: Law Press China, p. 146. Provision on the Implementation of International Copyright Treaties enacted by the State Council on 25 September 1992 provides that foreign computer programs shall be protected as literary works; the registration procedure for foreign computer programs is optional; the duration of protection is 50 years from the end of year in which the program is first published.

### Reasonable use

Article 13 of TRIPs provides for the principal requirement regarding the limitation and exception to exclusive rights: limitations or exceptions to exclusive rights shall be confined to certain special cases which do not conflict with a normal exploitation of the work and do not unreasonably prejudice the legitimate interests of the right holder. This is the overall requirement for reasonable use, the so-called 'three step test'. This approach differs from the regulation on reasonable use under the Berne Convention.[16] And Article 9(2) of the Berne Convention applies only to the right of reproduction.

Article 22 of the 1990 Copyright Law on reasonable use differed from the requirement of the Berne Convention. The 2001 Copyright Law has followed TRIPs on the issue of reasonable use. On the one hand, certain additional conditions regarding what circumstances will constitute reasonable use are provided. For example, in respect of use, for the purpose of reporting current events, of works already published by media such as newspapers, periodicals, radio or television stations, the condition of 'unavoidable reproduction or quotation' has to be satisfied. In respect of free performance of published works it is a requirement that 'the audiences have not been charged and the performer has not been paid'. On the other hand, more importantly, Article 21 of the Implementing Regulation of Copyright Law which entered into force on 15 September 2002 provides that 'according to relevant provisions of the Copyright Law, use of published works without authorization of the copyright holder shall not impair the normal exploitation of such work or unreasonably prejudice the legitimate interests of the copyright holder', which clearly is an implementation of the 'three steps examination'. This made the regulation of reasonable use under Chinese Copyright Law consistent with TRIPs.

### Right of performers and producers of phonograms

Article 14 of TRIPs provides for the rights of performers and producers of phonograms. The 1990 Copyright Law did not reflect, at least in its wording, the requirement of TRIPs in this regard. The members of the working party for China's WTO accession also felt that the rights of performers and producers of phonograms need to be clarified and made consistent with Article 14 of TRIPs.[17]

---

[16] Chengsi Zheng (1997), *Copyright Law*, 2nd edn, Beijing: Renmin University Press, p. 251 It is argued that under the Berne Convention, the reasonable use in all forms is limited to oral works such as political speeches and speeches in legal proceedings; in respect of other works, only reproduction (including extraction), translation and broadcasting can be deemed, under certain circumstances, as reasonable use.

[17] Report of the Working Party on the Accession of China, WT/ACC/CHN/49, 1 October 2001, para. 258.

The 2001 Copyright Law now clarifies the right of performers and producers of phonograms as required by TRIPs.

**Compulsory licensing**

The scope of compulsory licensing is relatively wide in the pre-amendment Copyright Law, which included newspaper reproduction, performance, sound recording, broadcasting by radio and television stations and which was in direct contradiction of the Berne Convention.[18] Compulsory licensing in respect of performances was cancelled in the 2001 Copyright Law (Article 36). The compulsory licence regarding sound recordings is limited to producing phonograms using musical works which have already been produced as phonograms by others (Article 39). The compulsory licence for the use of published works in making radio and television programmes has been absorbed into the compulsory licence for use of published works which excludes the use of cinematographic works and videos, while it includes phonograms (Articles 42, 43). After amendment, the Copyright Law is consistent with the Berne Convention except in respect of newspaper reproduction.[19]

**Provisional measures**

In order to be consistent with Article 50 of TRIPs, provisions have been inserted into the Copyright Law providing for regulations on applications, before the trial, for court orders to prevent infringement and to preserve assets and evidence. The Interpretation of the Supreme People's Court Concerning Several Issues on the Application of the Law in Hearing Civil Disputes over Copyright entered into force on 15 October 2002 and provides that the Interpretation on Issues Concerning the Application of Law to Preventing Infringement of Registered Trademark Right and Preservation of Evidences before Trial shall apply mutadis mutandis to the adoption of provisional measures in copyright cases.

**Strengthening the enforcement**

In respect of administrative procedures, it is provided that the authorities may, inter alia, confiscate and destroy pirated copies, and confiscate materials, tools and equipments used to produce the pirated copies. In respect of judicial procedures, it is provided that the courts have the authority to order any unlawful gain, pirated copy or asset used in the illegal conduct to be confiscated from the infringer of copyrights or related rights. In respect of damages, it is

---

[18] Li, Shunde (2002), 'TRIPS and the Intellectual Property Law of our country II', **59**, *Survey of Scientific and Technological Achievement.*

[19] Berne Convention for the Protection of Literary and Artistic Works (Paris Act, 1971), Art. 11bis, para. 2, Art. 13, para. 1.

provided that the infringer is liable to pay damages equivalent to the actual loss of the proprietor; in case the actual loss is hard to determine, the damages may be awarded according to the unlawful gain of the infringer and shall include the reasonable cost of the proprietor in preventing the infringement. In case neither actual loss nor unlawful gain can be ascertained, the court may, taking into consideration the circumstances of the infringing activity, order damages of no more than half a million Yuan.[20] These are all newly added provisions for the implementation of TRIPs.

## Layout Designs of Integrated Circuits

The Regulation on the Protection of Layout Designs of Integrated Circuits was enacted on 19 April 2001, and entered into force on 1 October 2001, together with the Detailed Implementation Rules for the Regulation on the Protection of Layout Designs of Integrated Circuits. This regulation is fully consistent with the requirement of TRIPs.

## Protection of Undisclosed Information

Article 39 of TRIPs requires that members shall protect undisclosed information and data submitted to governments or governmental agencies. The undisclosed information is protected in China as trade secrets in accordance with Article 10 of the Anti-Unfair Competition Law. It defines a trade secret as technical and operational information that is not in the public domain, has economic value, is practically applicable, and the secrecy of which is guarded by specific measures. This definition is fully consistent with the definition of undisclosed information in TRIPs.

Article 10 of the Anti-Unfair Competition Law also provides that the following activities will constitute infringement of trade secrets: (i) to obtain the trade secrets of a right holder through theft, enticement, coercion, or other illegitimate means; (ii) to disclose, use or allow others to use such trade secret obtained through the illegitimate means identified above; (iii) to disclose, use or allow others to use the trade secret in his possession in breach of a contractual obligation of confidence or an obligation of confidence imposed by the right holder of such trade secret; (iv) in cases where the third party knows or should know the illegal activities mentioned in the previous sections, to obtain, use or disclose other's trade secret by such third party. This is consistent with TRIPs.

Upon WTO accession, China undertook that unfair commercial use should be prevented in respect of the undisclosed test or other data submitted as a

[20] Articles 47, 48 and 51 of 2001 Copyright Law.

condition of approving the marketing of pharmaceutical or agricultural chemical products which utilize new chemical entities. This commitment has been implemented. Article 35 of the Implementing Regulation of the Law on the Administration of Pharmaceutical Products which entered into force on 15 September 2002 provides as follows:

> The State shall protect undisclosed test or other data submitted by the producer or seller of a pharmaceutical chemical product which utilizes new chemical entities and the production or sale of which has been approved, provided that such data have been obtained by the producer or seller autonomously.
>
> The unfair commercial use by any person of such undisclosed test or other data shall be prohibited. Within six years from the date on which the certificate of approval was received by the producer or seller, the authority in charge of the supervision and administration of pharmaceutical products shall reject any application, supported by the existing test or other data submitted by such producer or seller but without their consent, for the approval of the production or sale of any pharmaceutical product which utilizes new chemical entities, except if the data submitted have been obtained autonomously by the applicant.
>
> The authority in charge of the supervision and administration of pharmaceutical products shall not disclose such data except where necessary to meet the public interests, or unless steps are taken to ensure that the data are protected against unfair commercial use.

## Protection of New Varieties of Plants

TRIPs requires members to provide protection for new varieties of plants through patent, an effective specific regime or the combination of the two. China's Regulation on the Protection of New Varieties of Plants entered into force on 1 October 1997. China joined the International Convention for the Protection of New Varieties of Plants (1978 Act) in August 1998. The Supreme People's Court promulgated the Interpretation on Several Issues Concerning the Hearing of Disputes over New Varieties of Plants on 25 December 2000. The Ministry of Agriculture and the State Forestry Administration, as the policy makers for the protection of new varieties of plants, have also adopted supplementary rules on the implementation of the regulation. China has provided the protection for new varieties of plants in a way consistent with the requirement of TRIPs.

## Other Issues Regarding the Enforcement of Intellectual Property Law

China's well-established judicial system and intellectual property laws are the guarantee for the proprietor to receive adequate remedies. Explanations have been given above in various sections regarding civil and administrative procedures, remedies and provisional measures. This section will only briefly mention border controls and criminal procedures.

**Border measures**

The Regulation on Customs Protection of Intellectual Property was promulgated on 5 July 1995 and entered into force on 1 October 1995 and it provided the border measures for the protection of intellectual property. According to this regulation, China Customs has the authority to impound imported products infringing trademarks, patents or copyright protected under Chinese law. In order to be consistent with TRIPs, the new Regulation on Customs Protection of Intellectual Property was promulgated by the State Council on 26 November 2003 and entered into force on 1 March 2004. The new regulation has implemented, article by article, Articles 51–60 of TRIPs, and honoured China's commitment that 'China would provide holders of intellectual property rights with procedures related to border measures that complied fully with the relevant provisions of the TRIPS Agreement (Articles 51 to 60)'.[21] No further explanation will be given here.

**Criminal procedures**

Articles 213–20 of the Criminal Law of the People's Republic of China provides for crimes of infringing intellectual property right. Any act seriously infringing the right holders' registered trademarks, patents, copyrights or trade secrets may be punishable by imprisonment and fines.

In respect of trademark counterfeiting, Article 213 of the Criminal Law provides: 'Whoever, without permission from the owner of a registered trademark, uses a trademark which is identical with the registered trademark on the same kind of commodity shall, if the circumstances are serious, be sentenced to not more than three years of fixed-term imprisonment or criminal detention, and shall also, or shall only, be fined; if the circumstances are especially serious, he shall be sentenced to fixed-term imprisonment of not less than three years but not more than seven years and shall also be fined'. Article 214 provides: 'Whoever knowingly sells commodities bearing counterfeit registered trademarks shall, if the amount of sale is relatively large, be sentenced to not more than three years of fixed-term imprisonment or criminal detention, and shall also, or shall only, be fined; if the amount of sales is huge, he shall be sentenced to fixed-term imprisonment of not less than three years but not more than seven years and shall also be fined'.

In respect of copyright piracy, Article 217 provides: 'Whoever, for the purpose of making profits, engaging in any of the following activities infringing the copyright shall, in cases where the amount of illegal gains is relatively large, or there are other serious circumstances, be sentenced to fixed-term

21 Report of the Working Party on the Accession of China, WT/ACC/CHN/49, 1 October 2001, para. 302.

imprisonment of not more than three years or criminal detention in conjunction with, or be independently subject to, a statutory fine; in cases where the amount of illegal gains is huge or there are other especially serious circumstances, be sentenced to fixed-term imprisonment of not less than three years but not more than seven years in conjunction with a statutory fine: (1) reproducing and distributing a written work, musical work, motion picture, television programme or other visual works, computer software or other works without permission of the copyright owner; (2) publishing a book of which the exclusive right of publication is enjoyed by another person; (3) reproducing and distributing an audio or video recording produced by another person without permission of the producer; or (4) producing or selling a work of fine art with forged signature of another painter.' Article 218 provides: 'Whoever is, for the purpose of making profits, knowingly selling works reproduced by infringing the copyright of the owners as mentioned in Article 217 of this Law shall, if the amount of illegal gains is huge, be sentenced to fixed-term imprisonment of not more than three years or criminal detention in conjunction with, or be independently subject to, a statutory fine'.

The above-mentioned provisions of the Criminal Law are fully consistent with the requirement of TRIPs. The Supreme People's Court and the Supreme People's Procuratorate jointly adopted the Interpretation on Several Issues Concerning the Application of Law in the Trial of Criminal Cases Involving Infringement of Intellectual Property Right on 8 December 2004, which has lowered dramatically the threshold for offences against intellectual property right to be punishable by the Criminal Law: for example, illegal activities involving more than 50 000 Yuan will be punishable under Articles 213 and 214, compared to the previous threshold of 100 000 Yuan for individuals and 500 000 Yuan for units; illegal gains of more than 30 000 Yuan will be punishable under Article 217 compared to the previous threshold of 50 000 Yuan for individuals and 200 000 Yuan for units.

## CONCLUSION

To sum up, China's intellectual property law offers protection basically consistent with the requirement of TRIPs. It will be made clear that the existence of infringement of intellectual property rights does not necessarily mean that the intellectual property law or its enforcement has a problem. Attention will be paid to whether effective remedies have been provided in respect of activities infringing intellectual property rights. China's intellectual property protection regime is being improved; its enforcement is being strengthened. In the process of implementing international treaties, China has demonstrated the credibility of a responsible super nation.

Besides meeting the requirement of TRIPs, China's intellectual property laws also need to be adjusted to the requirement of the development of society and to technological advance. In such process, certain regulations of China's intellectual property law have exceeded the requirement of TRIPs. For example, in order to meet the need of developing information technology, the right of dissemination through information networks is provided in the 2001 Copyright Law. And the 'Interpretation of the Supreme Peoples Court on Several Issues concerning the Application of Law in the Trial of Cases in Relation to Copyright Disputes over Computer Network'[22] was adopted by the Supreme People's Court. The Regulation on the Protection of the Right of Dissemination through Information Network is being drafted at the time of writing and is presumably going to be promulgated soon.[23] This will pave the way for China to join the WIPO Copyright Treaty (WCT) and the WIPO Performances and Phonograms Treaty (WPPT). At the moment, a new wave of amendments of China's intellectual property laws is being prepared in order to meet the need of social, economic, technological and cultural development and the challenge of emerging new issues. Along with the development and advance of the society, economy and technology, the protection of intellectual property in China will be continuously improved and strengthened.

---

22 Adopted 22 November 2000, amended 2 January 2004.

23 It is also translated as Regulations on the Protection of the Right of Communication through Information Network. However, it is the view of the translator that the Chinese term '传播' is better represented by the word 'dissemination' than by 'communication'. The draft can be found in http://www.chinaiprlaw.com/english/laws/laws22.htm. (Note by the translator).

# 2. Substantive law issues in Europe a decade after TRIPs

**Paul Torremans***

## INTRODUCTION

The TRIPs Agreement is Annex 1C of the Marrakesh Agreement Establishing the World Trade Organization, signed in Marrakesh, Morocco on 15 April 1994.[1] It is therefore part of the compromise deal that saw the emergence of the WTO at the end of the Uruguay Round of trade negotiations. This already raises an important point to which we shall have to return later on in this chapter. TRIPs is not a stand-alone agreement on intellectual property and it is therefore not guaranteed that each of its provisions strikes the perfect balance for all countries and economies in terms of intellectual property protection. It is quite possible that certain provisions reflect a deliberately distorted balance in terms of intellectual property rights in order to compensate for other concessions or necessary imbalances in other areas, such as agriculture or textiles.

But before we can analyse this in more detail it is necessary to examine more closely each of the provisions of the TRIPs Agreement in their own right. Only a detailed understanding of each of these provisions will allow us to draw broader conclusions for the agreement as a whole. Owing to its position in this book, the present chapter will deal only with substantive intellectual property rights provisions and in essence the focus will be on copyright, trade marks and patents. All this will be looked at from a European perspective.

The broader judgment which will be derived on the basis of this detailed analysis of the substantive intellectual property provisions cannot be made in splendid isolation. Not only is there the relationship between TRIPs and the rest of the WTO agreement, to which we have already referred, but TRIPs itself also sets out certain objectives and principles which it aims to achieve and put into practice, respectively. An important aspect of the broader judgment will therefore be to check whether TRIPs has managed to achieve its

---

* Professor, School of Law, University of Nottingham, UK and Faculty of Law, University of Ghent, Belgium.

1 See http://www.wto.org/english/tratop_e/trips_e/t_agm0_e.htm.

objectives, or whether it has at least enabled the member states of the WTO to achieve these by making their national intellectual property legislations TRIPs-compliant. In either case such an approach should also have respected the principles set out in the TRIPs Agreement.

We will need to look at options for the improvement of the TRIPs Agreement. A decade of experience has given Europe a good idea of what TRIPs means in practice and where there is room for improvement. To some extent it is hoped that our experiences will allow countries such as China, which joined a bit later, to avoid some of the problems and mistakes that were made in the early days.

There is little need to repeat here that the TRIPs Agreement works on a basis of national treatment. For intellectual property lawyers this is almost a given and the cornerstone of the existing international intellectual property framework. As a trade agreement, 'TRIPs' stands after all for Trade Related aspects of Intellectual Property Rights; the cornerstone of free trade agreement, which is the most favoured nation treatment, has been added.[2]

Let us therefore first of all turn to the substantive intellectual property law provisions in the TRIPs Agreement and the way in which they have been implemented in Europe.

## COPYRIGHT IN THE TRIPS AGREEMENT

The TRIPs Agreement deals with copyright and related rights in a single section under Part II of the Agreement. We have said above that we are concerned with substantive intellectual property rights. In the terminology used in the Agreement, Part II is concerned with 'standards concerning the availability, scope and use of intellectual property rights'. Owing to the narrow links between copyright and related rights the two are put together in section one, but there is no overlap between the articles of the Agreement in this respect. Articles 9 to 13 deal with copyright and only article 14 deals with related rights.

TRIPs was conceived in part as an answer to the inability of the international community to agree a revision of the Berne Convention after 1971. New types of work as well as new supports to carry works on had emerged and the economic environment in which the commercial exploitation of copyright took place had changed almost beyond recognition. There was therefore a need to adapt the existing international legal framework to allow it to cope with these changes, but member states had very different views on the direction in which

---

2 Articles 3 and 4 of the TRIPs Agreement, respectively.

these changes should go. The unanimous view that was required for a revision of the Berne Convention had therefore not been found since 1971.[3] On top of that, certain countries had not adhered to the Berne Convention at all, or had been reluctant to ratify the latest versions of the Convention. Some of them were not bound at all and others were therefore only bound by older versions of the Agreement.

## The Link with the Berne Convention (1971)

It should therefore not come as a surprise that, in its Article 9, TRIPs contains an explicit reference to the Berne Convention. The article appears under the heading 'Relation to the Berne Convention', but essentially only its first paragraph deals with that relationship. According to the text:

> 1. Members shall comply with Articles 1 through 21 of the Berne Convention (1971) and the Appendix thereto. However, Members shall not have rights or obligations under this Agreement in respect of the rights conferred under Article 6bis of that Convention or of the rights derived therefrom.

This is not an attempt to update the Berne Convention, but the idea is to create a level basis from which to start. The latest revision of the Berne Convention will be the starting point for all member states. This resolves the problem that some countries had only ratified an older version of the Convention and were only bound by that version in relation to other Berne members. The way this level basis has been created is also interesting. No-one will have to become a member of the Berne Union if they were not already one and there is also no need to ratify any version of the Convention. All that is asked is that WTO members behave as if they were bound by the latest revision of the Berne Convention. Articles 1 to 21 have been chosen for this operation. This should not come as a surprise, as these deal with substantive law issues. There was no need to include also those Berne articles dealing, for example, with the Berne Union, meetings, voting rights and so on.

That leaves us with the, at first glance, somewhat curious omission of article 6*bis* of the Berne Convention from the list of articles that need to be implemented.[4] Why would one single out the Berne provision on moral rights for omission? The argument that was put forward initially was that moral rights are not trade-related and have as such no place in a free trade agreement. This

---

3 See S. Ricketson and J. Ginsburg (2006), *International Copyright and Neighboring Rights: The Berne Convention and Beyond*, OUP.

4 See D. Gervais (2003), *The TRIPs Agreement: Drafting History and Analysis*, Sweet & Maxwell, 2nd edn, pp. 124–6.

argument does not hold water though, as the absence of a minimum norm on moral rights leads to discrepancies between the laws of different countries, which in turn can become an impediment for free trade in copyright goods. Heavily modified copyright goods that originate in a country with minimal integrity right protection could be an infringement in another country with very strict integrity right protection that sees any unauthorized modification as an infringement. The free trade flow in that kind of goods is therefore heavily affected. A minimum norm would at least reduce the number of those cases of conflict and guarantee all rightholders also a minimum guarantee in terms of paternity and integrity rights when their works are exploited globally. In that sense moral rights are even more trade-related than the issue of the term of certain rights which was also included in the TRIPs Agreement. One has the clear impression that there were other reasons for the exclusion of moral rights. The US arguably failed to implement article 6*bis* in a comprehensive way when it joined the Berne Convention in 1986. While this is not a problem under Berne, as there is hardly a realistic possibility that one will be sued for non-implementation due to the arcane and complicated provisions on that point, TRIPs has an effective enforcement mechanism amongst member states and the threat of a WTO panel dealing with the non-implementation of moral rights by the US may have been sufficient to seek and obtain the omission of article 6*bis* Berne Convention from the list of articles that needed to be complied with. Be that as it may, the omission of a minimalist provision on moral rights from the TRIPs Agreement is a missed opportunity. A balanced copyright system needs minimalist protection for the personality of the author and, by not providing it in what is seen as an agreement setting international minimum standards, one creates the wrong impression.

Paragraph 2 of article 9 TRIPs Agreement is of a slightly different nature. In the eyes of copyright experts it repeats a basic principle of copyright, that is, the idea–expression dichotomy. It does something more though. There was not really a clear text on this idea–expression dichotomy which was very much implied in and read between the lines of the treaty provisions. Stating it clearly in the following terms makes it explicit and has the merit of clarifying what everyone already understood to be the position:[5] '2. Copyright protection shall extend to expressions and not to ideas, procedures, methods of operation or mathematical concepts as such.'

In a sense, article 9 sets the basic minimum level. It brings all member states to the same starting line. What it does not do is cover the gaps due to the lack of updating since the last revision of the Berne Convention, in 1971. Articles 10 and 11 set about achieving that update.

---

5 See C. Massouye (1978), *WIPO Guide to the Berne Convention*, WIPO, p. 12.

## Updating Copyright

Two new types of works have appeared since the 1970s: computer programs and databases. Various countries had already protected these in their national copyright laws, but at international level there were no specific provisions yet. The solution for computer programs is very simple. Even if they are not necessarily the typical example of a literary work and even though they present many atypical characteristics, the decision has been made to protect them as literary works.[6] For copyright purposes computer programs are put in the category of literary works and as such they are entitled to copyright protection. The only additional information that is given in article 10 is that protection applies both to these programs in source code and in object code. The TRIPs Agreement does not oblige member states to accommodate by means of special provisions in their copyright legislation the atypical characteristics of computer programs. One can simply treat them as any other literary work, even if they do not really fit that regime of protection perfectly well. It may well be advisable, though, for member states to go beyond their minimal obligations under TRIPs and to provide for specific rules, for example to deal with problems related to the need for interoperability of computer programs (such as between operating software and applications) and to allow reverse engineering for that purpose (as is common practice in the software industry). In the EU we had already gone down this path in the Software Directive[7] before the adoption of the TRIPs Agreement. Article 10 was therefore not a step forward for Europe, but offered less protection as a minimum norm for computer programs. It is often argued that the 'decompilation' and reverse engineering provisions of the Directive are not used in practice. It is submitted, though, that it would be wrong to conclude on that basis that they are superfluous. The fact that they are there to enable the potential imposition of a solution if there is no voluntary agreement between the parties is sufficient to persuade the parties to be reasonable on this point. The dissuasive effect of these provisions should not be underestimated and they may therefore usefully be seen as a model and be copied by other countries, despite the fact that they did not find their way into the minimum norm in TRIPs.[8]

TRIPs also introduces copyright protection for databases at an international

---

6 See J.H. Reichman (1995), 'The Know-How Gap in the TRIPS Agreement: Why Software Fared Badly, and What Are the Solutions', **17** *Hastings Communication and Entertainment Law Journal*, 763.

7 Council Directive 91/250/EEC on the Legal Protection of Computer Programs of 14 May 1991 [2001] OJ L122/42.

8 See also P. Torremans (2005), *Holyoak and Torremans Intellectual Property Law*, 4th edn, OUP, pp. 527–35.

level. Paragraph 2 of article 10 deals with this point, but, by simply looking at the whole article 10, one sees immediately that this provision is slightly more complicated than the simple provision on computer programs, even if it has the same basic structure.

## ARTICLE 10 COMPUTER PROGRAMS AND COMPILATIONS OF DATA

> 1. Computer programs, whether in source or object code, shall be protected as literary works under the Berne Convention (1971).
> 2. Compilations of data or other material, whether in machine-readable or other form, which by reason of the selection or arrangement of their contents constitute intellectual creations shall be protected as such. Such protection, which shall not extend to the data or material itself, shall be without prejudice to any copyright subsisting in the data or material itself.

Whilst everyone understands what amounts to a computer program, there was a need to be more specific about databases. The term 'databases' is avoided and it is made clear that we are essentially dealing with a compilation of data or other materials, whether in electronic, digital, machine-readable, paper or any other form. The data do not have to be copyright works and neither do the other materials, even if the latter will often be copyright works, such as poems, photographs and so on. Even more importantly, any protection for the database leaves the copyright protection for the data or other materials unaffected. Copyright for the database will not create copyright in otherwise unprotected data, nor will it abolish, shorten, extend or change the form of protection or the authorship and ownership of any existing copyright in the data or other materials. What is created, though, is a form of protection for the added value of bringing together the data or other materials. For this to happen in a specific case, there has to be an intellectual creation (read 'originality'[9]), which is found in either the selection or the arrangement of the contents of the database. What is protected is that original structure of the database, that selection or arrangement. The protection does not extend to the contents of the database as such, but the provision does not go beyond the need to distinguish between structure and content. There is no more specific agreement on the format of protection. More importantly, often the most valuable database will not have an 'original' structure. The commercial value of

---

[9] See Gervais (2002), ' "Feist Goes Global": A Comparative Analysis of the Notion of Originality in Copyright Law', **49** *Journal of the Copyright Society of the USA*, 949.

these is often determined by the fact that they comprehensively cover the data in a certain area and that these have been arranged in a standard format (such as alphabetically for names). TRIPs does not offer protection for these kinds of databases, but member states are free, but not obliged, to offer additional protection such as the sui generis protection offered in the EU's Database Directive.[10] That protection specifically protects the economic investment in the creation of the database.[11] It is not clear, though, whether that protection really encourages the creation of databases in the same sense that copyright ought to stimulate literary and artistic creation, and the Directive clearly cannot be seen as an ideal model that can be recommended to other countries.[12] There simply is not yet enough evidence to support such a move and, for example, in the US there is strong resistance against the adoption of a similar model.

Article 11 is also part of the update.[13] It does not deal with new types of works, though. Instead it takes account of a new way in which certain types of works are exploited commercially. In the past works were exploited through the sale of hard copies of the work. For example, when I wanted to watch a video I went out to buy it. Copyright took that into account by levying a small royalty per copy sold. Nowadays it is more likely that I do not buy a copy of the video, but that I rent it for the night. A single copy sold to a videoshop is therefore rented out dozens of times. Article 11 takes account of this new way of exploitation and creates a rental right on the basis of which a royalty can be levied for each rental of the video, which effectively replaces a sale. The concept is that the reward for the copyright owner will remain at the same level.

Article 11 only imposes such a rental right in relation to computer programs and cinematographic works.[14] For the latter there is only such an obligation if there is evidence that rental has led to widespread copying, which affects the right of reproduction of the right holder. Or in terms of Article 11 itself:

---

10 Directive 96/9/EC of the European Parliament and the Council on the Legal Protection of Databases of 11 March 1996, [1996] OJ L77/20.

11 See J. Gaster (1999), *Der Rechtsschutz von Datenbanken. Kommentar zur Richtlinie 96/9/EG*, Carl Heymanns Verlag and Gaster, 'The EC sui generis right revisited after two years: a review of the practice of database protection in the EU Member States', [2000] 5 Communications Law 87.

12 See also P. Torremans (2005), *Holyoak and Torremans Intellectual Property Law*, 4th edn, OUP, pp. 535–42.

13 See D. Gervais (2003), *The TRIPs Agreement: Drafting History and Analysis*, 2nd edn, Sweet & Maxwell, pp. 139–40.

14 See J. Reinbothe and A. Howard (1991), 'The State of Play in the Negotiations on TRIPS', EIPR 158.

## ARTICLE 11 RENTAL RIGHTS

> In respect of at least computer programs and cinematographic works, a Member shall provide authors and their successors in title the right to authorize or to prohibit the commercial rental to the public of originals or copies of their copyright works. A Member shall be exempted from this obligation in respect of cinematographic works unless such rental has led to widespread copying of such works which is materially impairing the exclusive right of reproduction conferred in that Member on authors and their successors in title. In respect of computer programs, this obligation does not apply to rentals where the program itself is not the essential object of the rental.

Finally, there is also no rental right in respect of computer programs in those cases where the program itself is not the essential object of the rental. This at first sight somewhat unclear exception is based on pure pragmatism. Most items we use nowadays have some bit of software in them. If I rent a car, I also rent the bit of software that controls the engine, the air-conditioning and the hi-fi system, to name just these. It would hardly be feasible to give the right holders in all these bits of software a minimal share in the rental of the car. It would be impossible to identify them all and the proportional share of each of them would no doubt be lower than the overhead costs involved in collecting and distributing the money. The rental right has therefore been restricted to those cases where the software itself is the essential object of the rental, that is, where I set out to rent the software, irrespective of whether it comes on a support or together with an accessory bit of equipment.

From a European perspective, article 11 is only a humble beginning. Council Directive 92/100/EEC on Rental Right and Lending Right and on certain Rights Related to Copyright in the Field of Intellectual Property[15] had already created a much broader rental right that applies to all authors, as well as to performers and producers of phonograms and films. In part the need for a broader measure is no doubt explained by the fact that rental has de facto become commonplace in the European market, whereas it is still more of an exception in certain other parts of the world. This may, however, no longer be the case in the near future and at that stage a broader rental right will become a necessity. Once more the legal system may need to react to economic and social change and article 11 may soon become a minimalist provision from a previous era.

---

15 [1992] OJ L346/61.

**Term of Protection, Limitations and Exceptions**

Articles 12 and 13 of the TRIPs Agreement do not really update copyright. Instead they harmonize certain provisions that had been partially dealt with only in the existing international texts. The Berne term of protection is often summarized as 50 years *post mortem auctoris*. This highlights also its shortcoming. It is not very good at harmonizing those terms of copyright protection that are not based on the life of the author. Article 12 transposes the basic rule to these cases by replacing the death of the author by the end of the calendar year of authorized publication and, in order to avoid an unreasonably long term of protection through publication a long time after the work was made, it adds that, if the work was not published in the 50 years after making the copyright; it shall expire 50 years after the end of the calendar year in which it was made. No doubt the maximum of 50 years between making and publication is there to guarantee in practice a term of protection that is somewhat longer than 50 years, which corresponds to the reality that the author normally does not die immediately after the work was made and therefore also benefits from a somewhat longer term of protection.[16] Article 12 spells the rule out as follows:

## ARTICLE 12 TERM OF PROTECTION

> Whenever the term of protection of a work, other than a photographic work or a work of applied art, is calculated on a basis other than the life of a natural person, such term shall be no less than 50 years from the end of the calendar year of authorized publication, or, failing such authorized publication within 50 years from the making of the work, 50 years from the end of the calendar year of making.

The exception for works of applied art and photographs is explained easily by the fact that many national legislations already have shorter terms of protection for them, as they were originally not seen as proper copyright works at the same level as literary works, paintings, sculptures and so on. That historical perspective may well no longer apply, but there was clearly no consensus to raise the term of protection for these works to the same minimum level.

Article 13 is probably one of the key provisions of the TRIPs Agreement. It deals with limitations and exceptions in the following way.

---

16 See H. Wager (1996), 'Substantive Copyright Law in TRIPS', in H. Cohen Jehoram et al. (eds), *Trade Related Aspects of Copyright*, Kluwer, p. 34.

## ARTICLE 13 LIMITATIONS AND EXCEPTIONS

> Members shall confine limitations or exceptions to exclusive rights to certain special cases which do not conflict with a normal exploitation of the work and do not unreasonably prejudice the legitimate interests of the right holder.

This three-step test to which limitations and exceptions need to conform is not entirely new. It had already appeared in the Berne Convention in article 9(2). But in a Berne context it therefore only applied to the right of reproduction and exceptions and limitations to that right. The main step forward in article 13 TRIPs is that the three-step test standard now applies to all limitations and exceptions, irrespective of the exclusive right to which they apply. Apart from the reproduction right the right of communication to the public and the distribution right are now, for example, also covered.[17]

The fact that it is not new does not mean that the three-step test is necessarily easily understood. The first step talks about special cases. In essence this means that exceptions and limitations that apply across the board in all circumstances will not pass this hurdle. But exceptions that apply only to visually impaired people or for the purposes of private study will pass the first hurdle. A broad exception such as 'fair use' is not an obvious candidate in this respect, as the special case is not clear in advance, but a strict definition of the concept of fairness, when taken in combination with the two other steps, allows us to draw the conclusion that in practice the 'fair use' exception will only apply to certain special cases, even if the latter are not perfectly defined in advance.

The second step, which applies of course cumulatively, as does the third step, makes it clear that, even though the exception or limitation applies only to a special case, normal exploitation of the work must remain possible. Copying exceptions given to students, for example, should not make a normal commercialization of a periodical through subscriptions and sale of individual copies impossible. The exception must never in commercial practice replace the commercial exploitation of the work.

The third step emphasizes the point that there should not be as a result of the limitation or exception any unreasonable prejudice to the legitimate interests of the rightholder. These legitimate interests of course include a return on the exploitations of the work as well as respect for its economic and moral rights. One should not, however, see too much of an overlap with step two. Here one accepts that the limitation and exception will cause prejudice. The right holder will in most cases lose money, for example because private copies are not paid for and may in certain cases replace sales of the work. What is

---

[17] See D. Gervais (2003), *The TRIPs Agreement: Drafting History and Analysis*, 2nd edn, Sweet & Maxwell, pp. 144–52.

made clear, though, is that prejudice should not be unreasonable: it should be proportional to the aims the exception sets out to achieve. The prejudice must be justifiable in terms of the benefit achieved by (the policy behind) the exception and, by definition almost, a balance must be struck between the rights of the beneficiaries of the limitation or exception and those of the owner of the copyright that is affected.

It is clear that the application of the three-step test to each national limitation or exception will not be easy and straightforward. There has already been one panel report[18] on the basis of Article 13[19] and, whilst it helped to clarify the issues, it clearly did not represent the end of the discussion.[20]

## RELATED RIGHTS IN THE TRIPS AGREEMENT

Article 14 shifts the emphasis from copyright to related rights. Historically, related rights had been dealt with at international level in the Rome Convention 1961.[21] However, this convention never attracted a number of ratifications coming anywhere near to those of the Berne Convention. The TRIPs Agreement therefore does not specifically refer to the Rome Convention 1961. Instead Article 14 starts afresh and sets out the basic minimum standards in relation to related rights. It does so as follows:

> Article 14 Protection of Performers, Producers of Phonograms (Sound Recordings) and Broadcasting Organizations
>
> 1. In respect of a fixation of their performance on a phonogram, performers shall have the possibility of preventing the following acts when undertaken without their authorization: the fixation of their unfixed performance and the reproduction of such fixation. Performers shall also have the possibility of preventing the following acts when undertaken without their authorization: the broadcasting by wireless means and the communication to the public of their live performance.
> 2. Producers of phonograms shall enjoy the right to authorize or prohibit the direct or indirect reproduction of their phonograms.
> 3. Broadcasting organizations shall have the right to prohibit the following acts when undertaken without their authorization: the fixation, the reproduction of fixations, and the rebroadcasting by wireless means of broadcasts, as well as the communication to the public of television broadcasts of the same. Where Members

---

18 J. Ginsburg (2002), 'Towards Supranational Copyright Law? The WTO Panel Decision and the "Three-Step Test" for Copyright Exceptions', **187** RIDA, 3.

19 United States – Section 110(5) of the Copyright Act, Panel Report WT/DS160/R (2000).

20 See M. Ficsor (2002), 'How Much of What? The "Three-Step Test" and Its Application in Two Recent WTO Dispute Settlement Cases', **192** RIDA, 111.

21 See C. Massouye (1981), *Guide to the Rome Convention and to the Phonograms Convention*, WIPO.

> do not grant such rights to broadcasting organizations, they shall provide owners of copyright in the subject matter of broadcasts with the possibility of preventing the above acts, subject to the provisions of the Berne Convention (1971).
> 4. The provisions of Article 11 in respect of computer programs shall apply *mutatis mutandis* to producers of phonograms and any other right holders in phonograms as determined in a Member's law. If on 15 April 1994 a Member has in force a system of equitable remuneration of right holders in respect of the rental of phonograms, it may maintain such system provided that the commercial rental of phonograms is not giving rise to the material impairment of the exclusive rights of reproduction of right holders.
> 5. The term of the protection available under this Agreement to performers and producers of phonograms shall last at least until the end of a period of 50 years computed from the end of the calendar year in which the fixation was made or the performance took place. The term of protection granted pursuant to paragraph 3 shall last for at least 20 years from the end of the calendar year in which the broadcast took place.
> 6. Any Member may, in relation to the rights conferred under paragraphs 1, 2 and 3, provide for conditions, limitations, exceptions and reservations to the extent permitted by the Rome Convention. However, the provisions of Article 18 of the Berne Convention (1971) shall also apply, *mutatis mutandis*, to the rights of performers and producers of phonograms in phonograms.

These related rights are granted to three groups of beneficiaries: performers, producers of phonograms and broadcasting organizations. Performers get the right to authorize the fixation and the reproduction of such fixation of their performances and their live performances can only be broadcast by wireless means or communicated to the public with their permission. In the next step producers of phonograms that have fixation, such a performance in an authorized way receives their own right to authorize or prohibit the reproduction of their phonograms. These rights are granted for at least a term of 50 years from the end of the calendar year in which the fixation was made or the performance took place.[22] Broadcasting organizations are also given a separate right in relation to their broadcasts. It covers essentially the fixation and reproduction of these, as well as rebroadcasting or communication to the public. The rights of the broadcasters are restricted to a term of 20 years from the end of the calendar year in which the broadcast took place. Producers of phonograms also receive a rental right along the lines of the model in Article 11.

In terms of related rights, TRIPs does not get very far.[23] All one finds is a series of minimum standards. The fact that there was at least agreement on

---

22 A further step forward for the rights of performers and producers of phonograms was taken soon afterwards in 1996, with the conclusion of the Wipo Performances and Phonograms Treaty (WPPT).

23 See D. Gervais (2003), *The TRIPs Agreement: Drafting History and Analysis*, 2nd edn, Sweet & Maxwell, pp. 156–62.

these is in itself already a step forward. This is again obvious when looking at the current difficulties in improving on article 14 by concluding an international agreement on rights for broadcasting organizations. These negotiations failed at WIPO in 1996 and at the time of writing (June 2006) there was still little optimism that the next attempt would be concluded successfully in the near future. Individual countries in Europe have gone beyond the minimum in article 14, though.[24]

## TRADE MARKS IN TRIPS

Weird as it may sound, the Paris Convention had never offered a precise definition of a trade mark or of the requirements a sign must meet in order to be registered. This is an essential point in terms of international harmonization in the light of global branding practices in a worldwide market. Defining the protectable subject matter was therefore a first priority, which was addressed in Article 15.

### Definitions

> Article 15 Protectable Subject Matter
> 1. Any sign, or any combination of signs, capable of distinguishing the goods or services of one undertaking from those of other undertakings, shall be capable of constituting a trademark. Such signs, in particular words including personal names, letters, numerals, figurative elements and combinations of colours as well as any combination of such signs, shall be eligible for registration as trademarks. Where signs are not inherently capable of distinguishing the relevant goods or services, Members may make registrability depend on distinctiveness acquired through use. Members may require, as a condition of registration, that signs be visually perceptible.
> 2. Paragraph 1 shall not be understood to prevent a Member from denying registration of a trademark on other grounds, provided that they do not derogate from the provisions of the Paris Convention (1967).
> 3. Members may make registrability depend on use. However, actual use of a trademark shall not be a condition for filing an application for registration. An application shall not be refused solely on the ground that intended use has not taken place before the expiry of a period of three years from the date of application.
> 4. The nature of the goods or services to which a trademark is to be applied shall in no case form an obstacle to registration of the trademark.
> 5. Members shall publish each trademark either before it is registered or promptly after it is registered and shall afford a reasonable opportunity for petitions to cancel the registration. In addition, Members may afford an opportunity for the registration of a trademark to be opposed.

---

[24] For an example, see the discussion of the UK model in P. Torremans (2005), *Holyoak and Torremans Intellectual Property Law*, 4th edn, OUP, pp. 268–74.

Most of these provisions are straightforward, but some of them require additional comments. The definition of a trade mark which article 15 offers contains two main requirements. First, in order to secure registration the applicant must put forward a sign or a combination of signs. The term 'signs' is not defined, but a list of examples is given, which includes personal names, letters, numerals, figurative elements and combinations of colours. The latter example hints at the fact that TRIPs has a slightly more restrictive minimum norm in mind than, for example, the European Trade Mark Directive under the provisions of which single colours[25] and sounds[26] can be registered under strict conditions. Or it may all of course just have been a particular choice of examples, which has no binding force as the list is open-ended. Maybe all that can be said is that the sign must at least be able to convey information of any nature.[27] But if that is not the case the sign will not be distinctive anyway. So the sign requirement maybe only indicates that anything that can convey information is potentially a valid trade mark if it meets the other requirements. Explicitly excluding certain types of signs such as smells may therefore be a breach of article 15. Secondly, a sign must be distinctive as to origin. It must be able to distinguish between goods or services produced or rendered by the applicant and identical goods or services produced or rendered by a competitor. Certain signs are inherently capable of distinguishing and give rise to no additional problems. Certain other marks can become distinctive through use, but are not inherently so, for example because they contain a descriptive element. Many modern trade mark systems also allow the registration of these marks that are only capable of distinguishing without imposing additional requirements and leave it to the market to weed out marks that are not effective in distinguishing.[28] The TRIPs Agreement permits a slightly more restrictive approach and allows member states to require proof of distinctiveness acquired through use before registering signs that are only capable of distinguishing and that are not inherently distinctive.

A third requirement that is found in article 15 is not mandatory. Members have a choice either to require as a condition of registration that signs be visually perceptible, or not to do so. This requirement may be effective in ruling

[25] Case C-104/01 *Libertel Groep BV* v. *Benelux-Merkenbureau* [2003] ECR I-3793, [2004] FSR 65.

[26] Case C-283/01 *Shield Mark BV* v. *Joost Kist h.o.d.n. Memex* [2004] Ch 97, [2004] RPC 315.

[27] *Philips Electronics BV* v. *Remington Consumer Products Ltd* [1998] RPC 283, per Jacob J (as he then was).

[28] E.g. First Directive 89/104/EEC of the Council, of 21 December 1988, to Approximate the Laws of the Member States Relating to Trade Marks [1989] OJ l40/1, see Case C-299/99 *Philips Electronics NV* v. *Remington Consumer Products Ltd* [2002] ECR I-5475, [2003] Ch 159, [2003] RPC 14.

out, for example, sound trade marks and olfactory trade marks. Member states that wish to rule out these kinds of signs are therefore well advised to implement this optional requirement, rather than to try and define the sign requirement restrictively. A number of countries, particularly in Europe,[29] do not require that marks be visually perceptible, but instead they require that marks be capable of graphical representation. The European Court of Justice has held that the latter requirement does not correspond to the former. Marks can be capable of graphical representation in an indirect way, even if they are not themselves visually perceptible.[30] A sound, for example, can be represented graphically through full musical notation, even if the sound itself cannot be perceived visually.[31] It is submitted, though, that this approach does not cause problems for article 15 TRIPs. Article 15 is a minimum norm and represents the most restrictive approach allowed. Capability of graphical representation is a more liberal requirement: more marks will pass the test, and it is therefore not a breach of article 15 TRIPs.

Once the requirements for registration and hence the definition of a trade mark have been established, the TRIPs Agreement can move on to define the rights that are conferred by a trade mark. Article 16 deals with this next aspect as follows.

> Article 16 Rights Conferred
> 1. The owner of a registered trademark shall have the exclusive right to prevent all third parties not having the owner's consent from using in the course of trade identical or similar signs for goods or services which are identical or similar to those in respect of which the trademark is registered where such use would result in a likelihood of confusion. In case of the use of an identical sign for identical goods or services, a likelihood of confusion shall be presumed. The rights described above shall not prejudice any existing prior rights, nor shall they affect the possibility of Members making rights available on the basis of use.
> 2. Article 6*bis* of the Paris Convention (1967) shall apply, mutatis mutandis, to services. In determining whether a trademark is well-known, Members shall take account of the knowledge of the trademark in the relevant sector of the public, including knowledge in the Member concerned which has been obtained as a result of the promotion of the trademark.
> 3. Article 6*bis* of the Paris Convention (1967) shall apply, mutatis mutandis, to goods or services which are not similar to those in respect of which a trademark is registered, provided that use of that trademark in relation to those goods or services would indicate a connection between those goods or services and the owner of the

[29] See First Directive 89/104/EEC of the Council, of 21 December 1988, to Approximate the Laws of the Member States Relating to Trade Marks [1989] OJ 140/1.

[30] Case C-273/00 *Ralf Sieckmann* v. *Deutches Patent – und Markenamt* [2002] ECR I-11737, [2003] Ch 487, [2003] RPC 685.

[31] Case C-283/01 *Shield Mark BV* v. *Joost Kist h.o.d.n. Memex* [2004] Ch 97, [2004] RPC 315.

> registered trademark and provided that the interests of the owner of the registered trademark are likely to be damaged by such use.

The right holder shall have the exclusive right to use the mark, but that right does not extend to all goods or services. What is offered is a negative definition. The focus is put on the right holder's right to stop the use of the mark in relation to certain goods or services. As a preliminary point it is made clear that that right applies in relation both to signs that are identical to the registered trade mark and to signs that are similar to it. When such a sign is used in relation to identical or similar goods or services the right to stop such use will apply if the right holder can demonstrate that the use will give rise to a likelihood of confusion. In a single case, the use of an identical sign in relation to identical goods or services, the likelihood of confusion is assumed and need not be proven. A number of points are left open by this definition of rights. First of all, there is no definition of the concept of similarity. As this concept delimits the scope of protection, varying national concepts of similarity may give rise to wider or narrower protection and they can hence affect the level of harmonization achieved by article 16 in a negative way. Secondly, there is no definition of the concept of likelihood of confusion. Some national systems stick to a narrow concept of likelihood of confusion as to origin; that is, the consumer thinks the sign indicates that the goods or services originate from the owner of the trade mark registration. Other national systems have moved away from origin and accept different forms of confusion. The most striking development here is the adoption of the concept of association or dilution.[32] In Europe this has been said to involve the perception by the consumer that there is an economic relationship between the parties where there is none,[33] or a simple link in case of trade marks with a reputation.[34] All these options remain possible under article 16 and no single solution is imposed, as all of them involve some form of confusion, be it about origin, the existence of a link or the existence of an economic relationship, on the part of the consumer that is confronted by the mark as well as with the allegedly infringing sign. On top of that the special treatment for famous trade marks in Article 6*bis* Paris Convention (1967) is extended to services[35] and to goods or

---

[32] See P. Torremans (2005), *Holyoak and Torremans Intellectual Property Law*, 4th edn, OUP, pp. 398–412.

[33] Case 251/95 *Sabel BV* v. *Puma AG* [1997] ECR I-6191 and [1998] 1 CMLR 445.

[34] Case C-408/01 *Adidas-Salomon and Adidas Benelux BV* v. *Fitnessworld Trading Ltd* [2004] Ch 120, [2004] FSR 401 and [2004] 1 CMLR 448.

[35] See H. Rangel-Ortiz (1995), 'Trademarks, NAFTA and TRIPS – An Update', **29** *Trademark World*, p. 31.

services which are not similar to those in respect of which the trade mark has been registered.[36]

## Exceptions and Limitations

These rights that are conferred on the owner of a trade mark are not unrestricted. Exceptions are possible, but Article 17 TRIPs imposes conditions on these exceptions in the national laws of the member states.

> Article 17 Exceptions
> Members may provide limited exceptions to the rights conferred by a trademark, such as fair use of descriptive terms, provided that such exceptions take account of the legitimate interests of the owner of the trademark and of third parties.

The terminology that is used reminds one of the three-step test in relation to copyright exceptions.[37] The exception needs to be limited in scope and cannot apply across the board. In other words it deals with special cases only, such as the example of the fair use of descriptive terms that form part of a mark that is given in article 17 itself. In addition the exception needs to strike a balance between the interests of the owner of the trade mark and, as third parties, the consumer and the competitor. This must again leave the owner the possibility to exploit the trade mark, while at the same time accepting some prejudice, albeit not an unreasonable one. As a trade mark always has the protection of the goodwill of the right holder as well as the information value of the consumer in relation to which that goodwill necessarily exists in mind, these elements should not be undermined by an exception. The competitor has in principle very few legitimate interests in using the mark or a confusingly similar sign, as it can always pick another mark. However, there may be reasons to use a descriptive element in order to inform the consumer of the kind of product or service available, or there may be reasons, particularly in certain trades, to use one's own name[38] even if the name is similar or identical to a registered trade mark. Exceptions can therefore play a useful role in this context while at the same time meeting the requirements of article 17.

---

[36] See M. Blakeney (1994), 'Well-Known Marks', EIPR, 481.

[37] See D. Gervais (2003), *The TRIPs Agreement: Drafting History and Analysis*, 2nd edn, Sweet & Maxwell, pp. 176–7.

[38] See e.g. Section 11(2) Trade Marks Act 1994 in the UK.

## Term of Protection

In terms of the term of protection, article 18 harmonizes the minimum term and speaks for itself:

> Article 18 Term of Protection
> Initial registration, and each renewal of registration, of a trademark shall be for a term of no less than seven years. The registration of a trademark shall be renewable indefinitely.

## Use and Other Requirements

Articles 19 and 20 deal with issues that arose in the past in the context of the international use of trade marks. Companies that trade internationally often registered their marks in each country even though they did not immediately use them everywhere. The risk then existed that national laws required use in the short term and that *mala fide* competitors applied for these marks to be cancelled in order to be able to use confusingly similar names on that market, thereby relying on the fact that the consumer knows the international reputation of the mark and will therefore be misled. Article 19 now imposes a minimum term of three years of non-use before such cancellation can intervene and even then the right holder can avoid cancellation by showing a good reason for the non-use.[39]

> Article 19 Requirement of Use
> 1. If use is required to maintain a registration, the registration may be cancelled only after an uninterrupted period of at least three years of non-use, unless valid reasons based on the existence of obstacles to such use are shown by the trademark owner. Circumstances arising independently of the will of the owner of the trademark which constitute an obstacle to the use of the trademark, such as import restrictions on or other government requirements for goods or services protected by the trademark, shall be recognized as valid reasons for non-use.
> 2. When subject to the control of its owner, use of a trademark by another person shall be recognized as use of the trademark for the purpose of maintaining the registration.

Article 20 looks mysterious at first glance and its heading of 'other requirements' does not help at all to dispel the mystery.

> Article 20 Other Requirements
> The use of a trademark in the course of trade shall not be unjustifiably encumbered by special requirements, such as use with another trademark, use in a

---

[39] See D. Gervais (2003), *The TRIPs Agreement: Drafting History and Analysis*, 2nd edn, Sweet & Maxwell, pp. 178–9.

> special form or use in a manner detrimental to its capability to distinguish the goods or services of one undertaking from those of other undertakings. This will not preclude a requirement prescribing the use of the trademark identifying the undertaking producing the goods or services along with, but without linking it to, the trademark distinguishing the specific goods or services in question of that undertaking.

In essence, some national laws insisted on additional requirements, such as the use in combination with another trade mark to combat certain abuses by foreign right holders. The latter sometimes concluded licensing agreements when entering a new market whereby the licensee was taking all the risks of setting up a production and distribution network and of advertising, all this while simply using the licensed trade mark. The licence was then concluded for a short term only and when successful the licensor did not renew it and set up its own company, always using the trade mark which was the only identifier for the consumer. The former licensee was then left without anything, as they had to change the trade mark and start afresh. The public did not appreciate that they were the former licensee and the driving force behind the mark in that country. The mandatory use of another mark, owned by the licensee, in combination with the foreign licensed mark, avoids that problem. The licensee will always retain a mark known by the public and the licensor cannot take over the market without dropping at least part of the mark known to the consumer. Article 20 of TRIPs now prohibits all these remedies and practices.[40] Foreign rightholders should not be hindered in the exploitation of their trade mark on a global market. The solution according to TRIPs should be a contractual one. The licensee should seek the inclusion of safeguards in the contract. This may well work between equal parties, but this is not always the case. Abuses can therefore not be ruled out altogether and article 20 is a rather one sided solution that primarily takes account of the right holders' interests.

## Licensing and Assignment

Finally, article 21 allows the licensing and the assignment of trade marks. It rules out compulsory licensing, but, more importantly, it also scraps the mandatory requirement that still existed in some national laws and according to which a trade mark could only be transferred in combination with the underlying business. Now, under TRIPs, the trade mark has become a tradable

---

40 See A. Kur (1996), 'The Right to Use One's Own Trade Mark: A Self-Evident Issue or a New Concept in German, European and International Trade Mark Law?', EIPR, 198.

commodity in its own right.[41] Any transfer is also based on the free contractual agreement that is reached between the parties. Or as Article 21 summarizes:

> Article 21 Licensing and Assignment
> Members may determine conditions on the licensing and assignment of trademarks, it being understood that the compulsory licensing of trademarks shall not be permitted and that the owner of a registered trademark shall have the right to assign the trademark with or without the transfer of the business to which the trademark belongs.

## Patents in TRIPs

Patents were another big issue in the TRIPs negotiations. This is easily understood if one looks at the financial issues involved. Many countries had no patents for certain types of inventions or for certain types of technologies. Compulsory licensing also existed in various forms. On top of that, the international framework was not very detailed. The most widely ratified international agreement, the Paris Convention, did not contain a clear definition of a patentable invention or the requirements for patentability. The TRIPs approach to patents is therefore similar to that to trade marks and the starting point is again the definitional aspects. Article 27 not only provides a definition of the requirements for patentability, but it also circumscribes the inventions which member states may exclude from patentability. In doing so in the following terms it fills the definitional lacuna and at the same time it addresses the problem of the very different exclusions that existed in the member states.

## Patentable Subject Matter

> Article 27 Patentable Subject Matter
> 1. Subject to the provisions of paragraphs 2 and 3, patents shall be available for any inventions, whether products or processes, in all fields of technology, provided that they are new, involve an inventive step and are capable of industrial application. Subject to paragraph 4 of Article 65, paragraph 8 of Article 70 and paragraph 3 of this Article, patents shall be available and patent rights enjoyable without discrimination as to the place of invention, the field of technology and whether products are imported or locally produced.

The starting point is very simple. There are, according to TRIPs, three requirements for patentability. First, the invention must be new in the sense that the information concerned had not yet been put in the public domain. Secondly,

---

[41] For an example, see article 8, First Directive 89/104/EEC of the Council, of 21 December 1988, to Approximate the Laws of the Member States Relating to Trade Marks [1989] OJ 140/1.

the invention must also involve an inventive step; that is, it should not be an obvious step forward in the eyes of a person skilled in the relevant field. Thirdly, the invention must at least be capable of industrial application. In American jargon this is called 'usefulness' and it is the potential we are looking for. That usefulness must be found at an industrial level. One off uses are not what we are looking for.[42]

Even more important than this harmonization of the basic requirements for patentability, though, is the fact that patents must be made available in all fields of technology. It will therefore no longer be possible to exclude, for example, pharmaceutical products from qualifying as patentable inventions, irrespective of whether they are new, inventive and capable of industrial application. On top of that one can no longer make a distinction between patents for processes and patents for products. Both need to be patentable and one cannot exclude one category from patentability. This represents a sea change for many countries and provides a very broad scope of patentability.[43] Discrimination as to the place of invention is also no longer possible.[44]

That broad scope called for some essential restrictions. Exceptions needed to be maintained one way or another, otherwise the sea change would be too important. This is exactly what the second and third paragraphs of article 27 set out to resolve.

> Article 27 Patentable Subject Matter
> [. . .]
> 2. Members may exclude from patentability inventions, the prevention within their territory of the commercial exploitation of which is necessary to protect *ordre public* or morality, including to protect human, animal or plant life or health or to avoid serious prejudice to the environment, provided that such exclusion is not made merely because the exploitation is prohibited by their law.
> 3. Members may also exclude from patentability:
> (a) diagnostic, therapeutic and surgical methods for the treatment of humans or animals;
> (b) plants and animals other than micro organisms, and essentially biological processes for the production of plants or animals other than non-biological and microbiological processes. However, Members shall provide for the protection of plant varieties either by patents or by an effective *sui generis* system or by any combination thereof. The provisions of this subparagraph shall be reviewed four years after the date of entry into force of the WTO Agreement.

---

42 For a more detailed example of an analysis of the exact meaning of the three requirements for patentability, see, in a UK context, P. Torremans (2005), *Holyoak and Torremans Intellectual Property Law*, 4th edn, OUP, pp. 52–81.

43 See R. Barry (1996), 'The Effect of GATT and TRIPS on U.K. Patent Law', **81** *Patent World*, 13.

44 See T. Miller (1996), 'Inventions Made in USA: Foreign "Equality" Under Applicable International Treaties', **5**, IIC, 587.

We will deal first with the broad exception in the second paragraph. Reasons of *ordre public* or morality may allow a member state to refuse to grant a patent. The emphasis is however on the word 'may'. At first the scope of the exception seems to be rather broad, because *ordre public* and morality are said to include the protection of human, animal or plant life as well as serious prejudice to the environment, on top of their obvious meaning. But then the restrictions come in. It is only the exploitation with the territory of the member state that must have such consequences that concerns of *ordre public* or morality make it necessary that such consequences be prevented. At that stage a patent can be refused, even if on its own that only stops exploitation on an exclusive basis and not exploitation as such unless such exploitation is not viable from an economic point of view without the exclusivity of a patent. The member state needs to bring the proof, though, that, if the particular application were allowed, the patent, when exploited, would offend against *ordre public* or morality. A case-by-case examination is therefore obligatory, especially when one reads this provision in combination with the one in the first paragraph that patents are allowed for 'any inventions [. . .] in all fields of technology'. Excluding a category of inventions or a certain type of technology is therefore not possible under Article 27(2). Only individual applications can be refused after an individual examination. That brings us to the question of the definition of the concepts of *ordre public*[45] and morality. Member states are given a significant degree of freedom to fill in these concepts, but there is one important guideline. One cannot artificially create broad concepts of order public or morality by simply voting a law in parliament. Simply prohibiting the exploitation by law is not sufficient. This reflects the idea that *ordre public* and morality are based on deeply held views and convictions by a (majority in) society. It is these views that the exploitation of the patent applied for must offend against, even if of course they are reflected in the legal provisions or the latter refer to them.[46] In conclusion, though, this is a very restrictive exception with a rather narrow scope.

Paragraph three of article 27 first of all reflects the provision that is found in many national patent laws and which excludes diagnostic, therapeutic and surgical methods for the treatment of humans and animals from patentability. These should be freely available to any surgeon and treatment should not be postponed or hindered by the need to obtain authorization or a licence first.

---

[45] See P.H. Mendes da Costa (1992), 'Patent Harmonization through GATT: TRIP or trap?', **45** *Patent World*, p. 25.

[46] For a European example of the way these provisions and this link between patent law, ethics and morality can work, not without difficulty, see the report of human embryonic stem cell patents at http://www.nottingham.ac.uk/law/StemCellProject/project.report.pdf.

Plants and animals other than micro-organisms, and essentially biological processes for the production of plants or animals other than non-biological and microbiological processes, may also be excluded, but note the restrictions in the wording. The parts that may not be excluded are the most important ones in modern science. Plant varieties need in addition to be protected. On that point there was no agreement on how to do this. Europe favoured the *sui generis* right, the UPOV Convention,[47] whilst the US preferred patents.[48] Article 27(3) leaves member states the choice, but doing nothing is not an option as the exception does not cover plant varieties.[49]

## Rights and Exceptions

Having laid down the conditions for patentability, the TRIPs Agreement moves on to set out the rights to which the patentee is entitled. Paragraph one of article 28 does so in straightforward terms.[50]

> Article 28 Rights Conferred
> 1. A patent shall confer on its owner the following exclusive rights:
> (a) where the subject matter of a patent is a product, to prevent third parties not having the owner's consent from the acts of: making, using, offering for sale, selling, or importing for these purposes that product;
> (b) where the subject matter of a patent is a process, to prevent third parties not having the owner's consent from the act of using the process, and from the acts of: using, offering for sale, selling, or importing for these purposes at least the product obtained directly by that process.

However, in practice, these provisions are only easy to apply if the allegedly infringing product or process is an exact copy of the patented product or process. The real difficulty arises when a variant is used that differs from the patented product or process but is nevertheless similar to it. The difficulty of interpreting the patent and its scope is a major issue in patent law, but TRIPs does not address it and no harmonized solution is available.[51] Paragraph 2 adds that patent owners shall also have the right to assign, or transfer by

---

47 See http://www.upov.int/index.html.

48 For the perspective of developing countries, see S.K. Verma (1995), 'TRIPS and Plant Variety Protection in Developing Countries', EIPR, 281.

49 S. Crespi (1992), 'Patents and Plant Variety Rights: Is there an Interface Problem?', IIC, 168.

50 See D. Gervais (2003), *The TRIPs Agreement: Drafting History and Analysis*, 2nd edn, Sweet & Maxwell, pp. 236–7.

51 For an example of the European approach in the context of the European Patent Convention, see P. Torremans (2005), *Holyoak and Torremans Intellectual Property Law*, 4th edn, OUP, pp. 37–152.

succession, the patent and to conclude licensing contracts. Patents are therefore a tradable commodity in their own right.

Article 29 then deals with sufficiency.[52] An applicant for a patent shall disclose the invention in a manner sufficiently clear and complete for the invention to be carried out by a person skilled in the art. This is part of the essential compromise in patent law. Society accepts a limitation on competition at the production level in furtherance of competition at the innovation level by granting an exclusive right as a reward to the patentee and in exchange gains access to the technology involved, not only because a better product or process becomes available, but also because the patentee puts the technological information involved in the public domain. That technological information is the key, as it can be used for further developments and research. Some countries add that the patentee should also disclose the best way known to it to work the patent. Other countries no longer do so, as the obligation is very hard to enforce. One cannot easily identify what the patentee knows at a certain point in time if the latter does not volunteer the information. Article 29 allows the member states to continue their current practice on this point and does not impose a harmonized solution.[53]

Also in relation to patents, the rule that there are no rights without exceptions applies. Article 30 deals with these exceptions in much the same restrictive way as the three-step test in relation to copyright. There can be limited exceptions. These limitations very much refer to certain special cases only, such as use for research or teaching purposes. In the patent version there is then a proviso that 'such exceptions [must] not unreasonably conflict with a normal exploitation of the patent and [must] not unreasonably prejudice the legitimate interests of the patent owner', but effectively this proviso repeats the by now well-known two additional requirements. For example, the research exemption does not unreasonably conflict with the normal exploitation of the patent, because it leaves the commercial use of the product or process untouched and, while it causes some prejudice due to the fact that the right holder will not be paid for the research use, such prejudice is not unreasonable. The legitimate interests of third parties also need to be taken into account and can therefore not only be the basis for an exception: they can also be used to determine in a balancing act what level of interference with the normal exploitation and which level of prejudice will be justifiable and acceptable.[54]

---

[52] See D. Gervais (2003), *The TRIPs Agreement: Drafting History and Analysis*, 2nd edn, Sweet & Maxwell, pp. 239–40.

[53] For a European interpretation, see decision/opinion of the Enlarged Board of Appeal of the EPO in cases G 2/93 and G 2/98.

[54] See D. Gervais (2003), *The TRIPs Agreement: Drafting History and Analysis*, 2nd edn, Sweet & Maxwell, pp. 241–4.

## Other Use Without Authorization of the Right Holder

Exceptions limit the scope of the right proper and carve out a free use. However, in patent law there is another way to allow the use of the patented invention without the authorization of the right holder. Here there is no exception and one accepts that the use is covered by the exclusive right. But, where normally the right holder should authorize any use of the patented invention, here the authorization is compulsorily imposed on the right holder by means of a legal provision. The right holder will therefore still be entitled to compensation for the use, but it will not enter freely into the licence and the fee also will not be determined freely. The developed countries saw this system of compulsory licensing as a tool that was essential for emergency situations only and that was abused by many other countries that gave it a wide scope and used it frequently. Article 31 therefore sets out to slam the door shut. It provides that such use without authorization will only be possible if a whole series of very restrictive conditions have been met. Only in cases of anti-competitive practices are a number of these conditions not applicable. It would lead too far for our current purposes to discuss each of these conditions in detail. Let us just refer to the text of article 31.[55]

> Article 31 Other Use Without Authorization of the Right Holder
> Where the law of a Member allows for other use[56] of the subject matter of a patent without the authorization of the right holder, including use by the government or third parties authorized by the government, the following provisions shall be respected:
> (a) authorization of such use shall be considered on its individual merits;
> (b) such use may only be permitted if, prior to such use, the proposed user has made efforts to obtain authorization from the right holder on reasonable commercial terms and conditions and that such efforts have not been successful within a reasonable period of time. This requirement may be waived by a Member in the case of a national emergency or other circumstances of extreme urgency or in cases of public non-commercial use. In situations of national emergency or other circumstances of extreme urgency, the right holder shall, nevertheless, be notified as soon as reasonably practicable. In the case of public non-commercial use, where the government or contractor, without making a patent search, knows or has demonstrable grounds to know that a valid patent is or will be used by or for the government, the right holder shall be informed promptly;
> (c) the scope and duration of such use shall be limited to the purpose for which it was authorized, and in the case of semi-conductor technology shall only be for public non-commercial use or to remedy a practice determined after judicial or administrative process to be anti-competitive;

---

55 See S. Ford (2000), 'Compulsory Licensing Provisions Under the TRIPS Agreement: Balancing Pills and Patents', **14** *American University International Law Review*, 941.

56 'Other use' refers to use other than that allowed under article 30.

> (d) such use shall be non-exclusive;
> (e) such use shall be non-assignable, except with that part of the enterprise or goodwill which enjoys such use;
> (f) any such use shall be authorized predominantly for the supply of the domestic market of the Member authorizing such use;
> (g) authorization for such use shall be liable, subject to adequate protection of the legitimate interests of the persons so authorized, to be terminated if and when the circumstances which led to it cease to exist and are unlikely to recur. The competent authority shall have the authority to review, upon motivated request, the continued existence of these circumstances;
> (h) the right holder shall be paid adequate remuneration in the circumstances of each case, taking into account the economic value of the authorization;
> (i) the legal validity of any decision relating to the authorization of such use shall be subject to judicial review or other independent review by a distinct higher authority in that Member;
> (j) any decision relating to the remuneration provided in respect of such use shall be subject to judicial review or other independent review by a distinct higher authority in that Member;
> (k) Members are not obliged to apply the conditions set forth in subparagraphs (b) and (f) where such use is permitted to remedy a practice determined after judicial or administrative process to be anti-competitive. The need to correct anti-competitive practices may be taken into account in determining the amount of remuneration in such cases. Competent authorities shall have the authority to refuse termination of authorization if and when the conditions which led to such authorization are likely to recur;
> (l) where such use is authorized to permit the exploitation of a patent ('the second patent') which cannot be exploited without infringing another patent ('the first patent'), the following additional conditions shall apply:
> (i) the invention claimed in the second patent shall involve an important technical advance of considerable economic significance in relation to the invention claimed in the first patent;
> (ii) the owner of the first patent shall be entitled to a cross-licence on reasonable terms to use the invention claimed in the second patent; and
> (iii) the use authorized in respect of the first patent shall be non-assignable except with the assignment of the second patent.

It will in practice be very hard to find a licensee that wants to invest in setting up a production and distribution system without the possibility of exportation and with the risk that the licence can be revoked at any time if the situation that gave rise to its imposition no longer exists, especially as the latter may be under the control of the patentee. Be that as it may, the system can only work if each country that wishes to apply it has local production capacity. This may well not be a problem for the developed world, but developing countries may lack it, as was shown in the crisis surrounding access to HIV/AIDS medicines. Article 31 is therefore not suitable for all countries in its current form and even the US came close to breaching it when it needed an Anthrax drug during the emergency situation following the events of 11 September 2001. The AIDS crises gave rise to the Doha declaration that alleviates the problem somewhat and call for a flexible application of article 31. We will not go into this issue at this stage, as Professor Sterckx deals with it in detail in her contribution to this book. Suffice it to say that article 31 remains problematical and that a redraft will be required when TRIPs is amended in the future.[57]

### Other Provisions

Three further articles of the TRIPs Agreement deal with patents. Article 33 imposes a minimum term of protection of 20 years from the filing date for patents. Articles 32 and 34 are of a procedural nature.[58] Article 32 guarantees the rights of the patentee in case of revocation or forfeiture of the patent, by guaranteeing the availability of an opportunity for judicial review. Article 34 instead is concerned with infringement claims in relation to process patents. The right holder does not have access to the premises of the alleged infringer and is therefore often unable to bring complete proof of the infringement of the patented process. Article 34 starts from the idea that, at the end of the process, a product is obtained that is identical to the one obtained by using the patented process. Having established this on the basis of the evidence of the patentee, the judicial authorities of the member state concerned shall have the authority to order the defendant to prove that the process to obtain an identical product is different from the patented process. Article 34 then enters into the detail of the options that are in this respect open to the member states, but in essence the provision operates as a reversal of the burden of proof.

## A CRITICAL ANALYSIS

### TRIPs in a Broader WTO Context

In our introduction we mentioned the fact that the TRIPs Agreement contains perhaps not a perfect balance between the interests of the member states at their various stages of development. TRIPs is indeed not a stand-alone agreement on intellectual property and it is therefore not guaranteed that each of its provisions strikes the perfect balance for all countries and economies in terms of intellectual property protection. It is quite possible that certain provisions reflect a deliberately distorted balance in terms of intellectual property rights

57 Th. Haag (2002), 'TRIPS Since Doha: How Far Will the WTO Go Toward Modifying the Terms for Compulsory Licensing?', **84** *J. Pat & Trademark Off. Society*, 945.

58 See D. Gervais (2003), *The TRIPs Agreement: Drafting History and Analysis*, 2nd edn, Sweet & Maxwell, pp. 254–61.

in order to compensate for other concessions or necessary imbalances in other areas such as agriculture or textiles. Later on we mentioned that problems with article 31 concerning certain uses of the patent without authorization arise because the provision is based entirely on the interests of developed countries and does not take account of the lack of local manufacturing capacity, for example for pharmaceutical products in developing countries. Article 27 also contains a very wide definition of patentable subject matter, coupled with very narrow exceptions that do not necessarily allow for adequate protection for the biological resources of the developing countries. It is also not guaranteed that the TRIPs system protects local inventions in certain countries, the level of inventiveness of which is perhaps somewhat lower. In these countries there may not be an immediate ability to develop fully fledged inventions, but these inventions with a lower level of inventiveness could be a stepping stone. On this point TRIPs once more protects fully the interests of the developed countries, while not offering the same panoply of tools to cover the interests of developing countries. The fact that the balance needs to be restored by taking account of rights and obligations under other parts of the WTO agreement does little to convince those working in intellectual property-related areas and that are not involved with these other parts of the agreement. They do not see the direct effect of these balancing effects, whilst they are directly affected by the negative impact of the unbalanced provisions of TRIPs.

## Objectives and Principles of TRIPs

Another point which we need to address is the fact that, in its articles 7 and 8, the TRIPs Agreement itself sets out objectives and principles that create certain expectations for the member states but also for its citizens that are affected by the TRIPs Agreement. We need to analyse these objectives and principles in a little more detail before we can check whether they have been implemented and achieved in practice. Article 7 sets out the objectives which the implementation of the TRIPs Agreement in a liberalized global trading environment should achieve.[59]

> Article 7 Objectives
> The protection and enforcement of intellectual property rights should contribute to the promotion of technological innovation and to the transfer and dissemination of technology, to the mutual advantage of producers and users of technological knowledge and in a manner conducive to social and economic welfare, and to a balance of rights and obligations.

---

[59] See D. Gervais (2003), *The TRIPs Agreement: Drafting History and Analysis*, 2nd edn, Sweet & Maxwell, pp. 116–20.

These objectives are ambitious. Intellectual property protection and enforcement is first of all expected to make a significant contribution to the promotion of technological innovation.[60] There is indeed an element of truth in the idea that the availability of a reward for the innovator or creator in the form of a patent or copyright, to name just these rights, must encourage and stimulate investment in research and development or in the creation and development of literary and artistic works. Without certain exclusive rights some of these would not have been developed, in part because their exploitation may well not have been economically viable. On the other hand one can ask certain questions. The immediate effect of TRIPs is to expand protection for innovations and creations from the developed world globally. These innovations and creations had taken place anyway and one merely expands their market. In the developing world the additional protection benefits primarily foreign inventors and creators and may result in the local market being flooded by foreign products. Local production may suffer and it is not clear that there is an overwhelming benefit in terms of the promotion of new technological innovation. It is true that in the long term local as well as international levels of innovation will pick up, but this effect is more limited than one would expect at first glance and in developing countries other additional tools and initiatives will have to be deployed in order to achieve this improved level of innovation. A mere implementation of TRIPs will not be sufficient.

Secondly, the TRIPs Agreement has the objective of contributing to the transfer and dissemination of technology. Indeed, the availability of protection and enforcement measures may well convince right holders to exploit their technology in more countries. Patent filings then grant access to the technological information. But, in order for there to be a real transfer of technology, the reader must also be capable of understanding the information and of putting it into practice. The latter is not guaranteed by the simple filing of the patent document. They may not contain enough information to enable by themselves a transfer of technology. Local manufacturing and the training of local staff would add that element, but the TRIPs Agreement does not impose it. Local needs can be met by importation. Making the product or process available is indeed a benefit, but in itself it does not necessarily lead to the transfer and dissemination of the technology involved.

Achieving these two objectives should be done 'to the mutual advantage of producers and users of technological knowledge'. This suggests that there should be a balance between the rights and obligations of the two sides,

60 See M. McGrath (1996), 'The Patent Provisions in TRIPS: Protecting Reasonable Remuneration for Services Rendered – or the Latest Development in Western Colonialism?', EIPR, 398.

producers and users. It is not difficult to see that the broader scope of protection and the improved minimum standards enhance the position of the producers. Exceptions and limitations on the other hand benefit the users, but here a very restrictive approach has been adopted. Also only enabling (restrictive) provisions, along the lines of article 13, have been included. TRIPs contains very few specific measures to the benefit of the users. One could argue that the deficit before TRIPs was primarily found in the protection of the producers and that TRIPs needed to focus on that aspect in order to achieve a better balance, but the absence of specific user oriented provisions that go into practical detail must lead to the conclusion that TRIPs itself only achieves one side of the balancing act. The member states will have to work hard within the restrictive framework of TRIPs to really achieve the full balance.

Finally, according to the text of article 7, the achievement of these objectives should work 'in a manner conducive to social and economic welfare, and to a balance of rights and obligations'.[61] These are nice intentions, but they highlight the major deficit of article 7: it has no teeth. There are no instruments to enforce the objectives that are set out, whilst the specific obligations to protect and enforce intellectual property rights can be enforced and have teeth. As far as the objectives go, one can only hope that they will be achieved almost as a side-effect of the specific provisions of the TRIPs Agreement. This is not very satisfactory.

Article 8 then continues down a slightly more practical path and adds principles[62] to these objectives in the terms below.

> Article 8 Principles
> 1. Members may, in formulating or amending their laws and regulations, adopt measures necessary to protect public health and nutrition, and to promote the public interest in sectors of vital importance to their socio-economic and technological development, provided that such measures are consistent with the provisions of this Agreement.
> 2. Appropriate measures, provided that they are consistent with the provisions of this Agreement, may be needed to prevent the abuse of intellectual property rights by right holders or the resort to practices which unreasonably restrain trade or adversely affect the international transfer of technology.

Paragraph 1 seems to offer room for manoeuvre to member states in the execution of other of their important duties, such as the protection of public health

---

61 See G.R. Stewart, M.J. Tawfik and M. Irish (1995), *International Trade and Intellectual Property: The Search for a Balanced System*, Westview Press.

62 See D. Gervais (2003), *The TRIPs Agreement: Drafting History and Analysis*, 2nd edn, Sweet & Maxwell, pp. 121–2.

and nutrition, as well as the public interest in sectors of vital importance to their socio-economic and technological development. Measures that are necessary to secure these important issues can be taken, or so it seems. The logic would indeed be that these are higher interests and that, insofar as is necessary, intellectual property should yield when these issues are at stake. The proviso at the end of paragraph 1, however, comes to exactly the opposite conclusion. The intellectual property provisions of TRIPs need to be respected first and only any room within or beside these provisions can be used to protect the issues listed in article 8, paragraph 1. Article 8(1) is therefore useless. Insofar as TRIPs does not impose specific measures, member states were already free to make their own decisions. Once more, article 8 is a mere statement, rather than an instrument to balance intellectual property rights and other vital interests.

Paragraph 2 adopts the same approach. First of all, member states need to respect the provisions of the TRIPs Agreement and only afterwards can they take measures that are needed to prevent the abuse of intellectual property rights by right holders or the resort to practices which unreasonably restrain trade or adversely affect the international transfer of technology. At least there is a recognition that abuse of rights is also possible when it comes to intellectual property rights and that such abuse needs to be eradicated. Unreasonable restrictions on trade or transfer of technology fall into the same category. It is unfortunate, though, that TRIPs itself does not offer more specific measures to address these problems.

Articles 7 and 8 are therefore far more restrictive than they may seem at first sight, and even within that restrictive scope they offer no option to enforce the objectives and principles which they list. In conclusion they are more political declarations than legal provisions. It is also clear that the rest of the TRIPs Agreement does not necessarily achieve these objectives or implement these principles. The intellectual property strengthening exercise is given absolute preference and the other interests come afterwards and need to be dealt with by member states on an individual basis outside the TRIPs implementation context. The objectives and principles in articles 7 and 8 are therefore by no means able to restore the somewhat distorted balance which we found in the substantive provisions of TRIPs. If anything, they confirm that distortion.

## Suggestions for Reform

One could of course enter into a detailed discussion of each of the articles of the TRIPs Agreement which we mentioned above, but that would lead too far. Instead, it is suggested that what is essentially needed is a more in-depth change. Article 7 should be allowed to play its proper role. It should set out the objectives which the member states are hoping and striving to achieve. Intellectual property and the substantive provisions of TRIPs are then a tool to achieve these objectives. The latter provisions can therefore not override the objectives. By integrating article 7 in the core of the agreement one allows it to take centre stage. The substantive intellectual property rights that are granted need to be balanced against the interests of users if these objectives are to be obtained. The tool to balance these rights, and to authorize exemptions and limitations on these rights, is thus article 7. Both the rights and the exemptions and limitations only have a place in a modern intellectual property system if they contribute to the achievement of these objectives.

What is therefore proposed on top of the comments that were made in the discussion of each article of TRIPs is a strengthening of article 7 and the deletion of the TRIPs articles that deal with limitations and exemptions.[63] The criteria set out in the latter articles could not guarantee a completely equitable balance between the interests of users, right holders and any other stakeholders. That balance is now achieved through article 7, that takes a wider perspective and that takes all the higher values behind the intellectual property system into account. The revised Article 7 could read as follows:[64]

**Objectives**

The protection and enforcement of intellectual property rights should:

(a) contribute, in a manner conducive to social and economic welfare;

  i. to cultural development and the enhancement of creativity, taking due account of the larger public interest, particularly in education, research and access to information and knowledge for all;

  ii. to the promotion of innovation and technological progress, to the transfer of technology and to the dissemination of information and knowledge;

  iii. to the promotion of fairness in trade in the interests of producers, traders and consumers;

(b) ensure, to the advantage of society as a whole, a balance of rights and obligations so that, in particular, the effect of the protection conferred by an intellectual property right corresponds to the contribution made to creativity and innovation;

(c) prohibit abusive use of intellectual property rights, which harms the objectives set out under (a).

---

63 Articles 13, 17 and 26(2) respectively.

64 The suggestions made in respect of Article 7 and its revised wording have benefited heavily from my discussions during a 'Friends of the Project' seminar of the Intellectual Property in Transition Research Programme in Stockholm in November 2005. However, they do not necessarily represent the final conclusions reached by that research programme on this point.

## CONCLUSION

Europe has for a long time had well-developed intellectual property laws. The TRIPs Agreement was therefore no sea change. However, there have been changes, even if the implementation focused more on enforcement and litigation. There were more details to be fine-tuned in these areas and the European integration effort was also less advanced in these areas.

A decade of experience in TRIPs has however highlighted a series of problems with the agreement. Some of these were known from the start and resulted from issues on which no complete agreement had been reached and that had been buried in the text of the TRIPs Agreement. Some of these problems also proved to be more serious and substantial than had originally been expected. Other problems were new problems that had not been foreseen when the TRIPs Agreement was drafted.

It is therefore clear that the TRIPs Agreement cannot be the final stage of development in this area. Even after Doha, major reforms are necessary. In this chapter we have highlighted many problems and suggestions for improvement in relation to individual TRIPs articles, but we have focused on the need to redraft article 7 and give it the central role it deserves if the system is to work in a proper balanced way.

It is hoped that these comments and suggestions may make a modest contribution to the discussion on TRIPs reform. What is clear, though, is that we first need to analyse the exact impact of the current provisions and the way in which they work. This needs time and the constant tinkering with the provisions as part of a TRIPs plus approach that is pursued through bilateral agreements is therefore counterproductive. Instead we should take time to reflect and properly negotiate the revision of TRIPs in an open and transparent way in multilateral fora such as the WTO.

# PART II

# TRIPS compliance: enforcement issues

# 3. The TRIPS Agreement and the changing landscape of international intellectual property

**Daniel J. Gervais***

## INTRODUCTION

The focus of this essay will be the economic, social and cultural forces at play in international intellectual property. Economics will provide us with the most useful set of analytical tools. The reason is self-evident. When US and other Western lobbies successfully arranged the marriage of IP and trade rules, it became inevitable that IP rules would be measured using an economic yardstick. After all, trade liberalization is not an end in itself. Rather, it is a means to an end, namely the promotion of economic growth. While they may interface with those rights and standards, trade rules do not protect either environmental or labour standards, nor do they protect human rights as part of their core mission. Thus, by setting the IP table in the house of trade, the cloak of IP as a simple variation on the classic theme of property[1] or even as a human right – notions essentially developed in the eighteenth and nineteenth centuries – was bound to fall.

The linkage between IP and trade also points to a different method of making policy analysis and recommendations. The raw public choice approach may not be ideal. If one concedes that making a proper policy analysis is impossible or inherently unreliable because theoretical models are inadequate or valid empirical data are unavailable, then perhaps that is the best way to proceed. I am not yet prepared to throw in the policy towel, however, and neither did the UK Commission on Intellectual Property Rights ('UK IPR Commission').[2]

---

* Acting Dean, Vice-Dean (Research) and Osler Professor of Intellectual Property Law, Faculty of Law (Common Law), University of Ottawa (Canada).

1 See generally William M. Landes and Richard A. Posner, *The Political Economy of Intellectual Property Law* (2004).

2 Commission on Intell. Prop. Rights, Integrating Intellectual Property Rights and Development Policy (2002), available at http://www.iprcommission.org/papers/pdfs/final_ report/CIPRfullfinal.pdf hereinafter UK IPR Commission Report.

Against this backdrop, I will examine, first, the emergence of the World Trade Organization ('WTO') Agreement on Trade-Related Aspects of Intellectual Property Rights ('TRIPS').[3] TRIPS was negotiated as part of the Uruguay Round of Multilateral Trade Negotiations. TRIPS was an effort both to increase (for most WTO members) the level of IP protection and to reduce differences among national rules. TRIPS added a significant level of comfort for multinational corporations deciding when and where to export to new markets or expand research and development efforts; some of the more important factors those corporations tend to consider include the tax structure and available subsidies, the availability of qualified workers and the labour relations environment, the protection of investments, the quality of the legal and judicial systems, and law enforcement.[4] I will also consider briefly the Doha Ministerial Declaration of November 2001 and follow-up work on access to medicines.

In my concluding remarks, I will address the current push for a 'balanced' approach and suggest ways in which such a balanced IP regime could be constructed as part of a broad, knowledge-oriented economic strategy.

# 1 TRIPS

## 1.1 The Emergence of the TRIPS Agreement

The TRIPS Agreement was negotiated as part of the Uruguay Round of Multilateral Trade Negotiations. In fact, TRIPS is Annex 1C of the Agreement Establishing the World Trade Organization.[5] As such, it was part of a package. Its negotiators came from an initial group of about 20 countries, increased to approximately 30; nearly half of the negotiators came from industrialized nations; the remainder hailed from developing countries. The representatives of developing nations were often trade negotiators with little or no prior exposure to IP law and few even had advanced legal training in IP.

---

3 Agreement on Trade-Related Aspects of Intellectual Property Rights, 15 April 1994, Marrakesh Agreement Establishing the World Trade Organization, Annex 1C, Legal Instruments – Results of the Uruguay Round, **33** I.L.M., 1197 (1994) [hereinafter TRIPS].

4 See Keith E. Maskus (2000), *Intellectual Property Rights in the Global Economy*, Institute for International Economics, pp. 199–205.

5 Final Act Embodying the Results of the Uruguay Round of Multilateral Trade Negotiations, 15 April 1994, **33** I.L.M. 1125, 1144–53 (1994) [hereinafter Results of the Uruguay Round]. For a detailed negotiating history, see Daniel Gervais (2003), *The TRIPS Agreement: Drafting History and Analysis*, 2nd edn, London: Sweet & Maxwell.

This dissymmetry arguably put them at a disadvantage when discussing detailed and arcane drafting points, especially those linked to the specific history of existing treaties such as the Berne and Paris Conventions.[6]

The negotiating process was also interesting. In the first few months of 1990, a number of industrialized countries tabled, with little advance notice, draft legal texts of what they saw as the future TRIPS Agreement. Prior to the tabling of these texts, the discussions had focused on identifying existing norms and possible trade-related gaps therein, but the emerging outline of a possible TRIPS result had essentially been at the level of principles, not legal texts. The draft legal texts, which emanated from the European Community, the United States, Japan, Switzerland and Australia,[7] foreshadowed a detailed agreement covering all IP rights then in existence, even the seldom used *sui generis* protection for computer chips. The proposals also included detailed provisions on the enforcement of those rights before national courts and customs authorities and a provision bringing future TRIPS disputes under the General Agreement on Tariffs and Trade ('GATT')/WTO dispute-settlement umbrella. These proposals were far from obvious in light of the limited mandate of the TRIPS negotiating group.[8]

As a reaction, more than a dozen developing countries[9] proposed another 'legal' text, much more limited in scope, with few specific normative aspects. They insisted on the need to maintain flexibility to implement economic and social development objectives. The Uruguay Round Secretariat then prepared a 'composite' text, which melded all industrialized countries' proposals into what became the 'A' proposal, while the developing countries' text became the 'B' text. The final agreement mirrored the 'A' text. As such, it essentially embodied norms that had been accepted[10] by industrialized countries. The concerns of developing countries were reflected in large part in two provisions

---

6 See Berne Convention for the Protection of Literary and Artistic Works, 9 September 1886, 25 U.S.T. 1341, 828 U.N.T.S. 221 [hereinafter Berne Convention]; Paris Convention for the Protection of Industrial Property, 20 March 1883, 21 U.S.T. 1583, 828 U.N.T.S. 303 [hereinafter Paris Convention]; see also Paul J. Heald (2003), Mowing the Playing Field: Addressing Information Distortion and Asymmetry in the TRIPS Game, **88** *Minn. L. Rev.*, 249.

7 See Gervais, *supra*, note 6, at 16–17.

8 See World Trade Organization, Ministerial Declaration of 20 September 1986, MIN(86)/W/19, 25 I.L.M. 1623 (1986), available at http://www.sice.oas.org/trade/Punta_e.asp. (Punta del Este Declaration, launching the Uruguay Round).

9 Argentina, Brazil, Chile, China, Columbia, Cuba, Egypt, India, Nigeria, Peru, Tanzania, and Uruguay. Pakistan and Zimbabwe joined later on.

10 For example, the United States ratified the Berne Convention in 1989. See Berne Convention Implementation Act of 1988, Pub. L. No. 100–568, §§7–9, 102 Stat. 2853, 2857–59 (codified as amended at 17 U.S.C. 101 (2000)).

– articles 7 and 8 and in part of the preamble (where, for example, it is stated that IP rights are 'private rights').

In most cases, TRIPS negotiators incorporated existing international norms by reference. Those norms were altered only to the extent that there was a 'consensus' that they should be updated.[11] This is true of the Paris, Berne and Washington treaties, which deal with copyright, industrial property (patents, designs and trademarks), and integrated circuits, respectively.[12] By and large, the so-called 'North' thus imposed its then most-advanced set of norms on the 'South'. In fact, major industrialized countries made relatively few concessions, despite their disagreements on some issues, except the need to submit themselves to binding dispute settlement. By contrast, developing countries accepted a package that perhaps some of them did not fully understand, and yet one which contained a complete set of IP norms they had to implement into their national law. In addition to articles 7 and 8, already mentioned, they did obtain transitional periods to implement the agreement. For most developing countries, transitional periods expired in January 2000.[13]

Some might say there is a certain degree of irony in TRIPS. The multinational companies that successfully lobbied to establish a linkage between IP and trade, first in the domestic US context and then in the WTO, did so because of their need to increase profits and markets or, to put it differently, to maximize rent extraction and increase the number of foreign territories into which they could consider expanding. Imposing this sometimes harsh medicine on developing countries created difficult situations, especially in poorer nations. However, it also created, or will lead to the emergence of, new competitors for the same companies that lobbied for TRIPS, as more developing nations at the receiving end of technology transfers and inward foreign direct investment (FDI) develop the ability to innovate and compete. Combined with a healthy dose of economic nationalism, the medium-term impacts of TRIPS and related measures, such as free-trade agreements and bilateral investment treaties, the purpose of which are to bring developing

---

11 See Gervais, *supra*, note 6, at 68.

12 The Paris and Berne Conventions were mentioned in note 7 *supra*. The Washington Treaty is the Treaty on Intellectual Property in Respect of Integrated Circuits, 26 May 1989, **28** I.L.M., 1477 (1989), available at http://www.wipo.int/treaties/en/ip/washington/pdf/trtdocs_wo011.pdf (it never entered into force but was used nonetheless as a foundation for TRIPS).

13 The transitional period for pharmaceutical patents has been extended until 2016 for least-developed countries in the Doha Declaration. Countries that did not protect pharmaceutical products (or other areas) by patent at the time of entry into force had until January 2005 to do so. However, 'exclusive marketing rights' as well as a mailbox application procedure (to preserve novelty) had to be introduced in the interim period (see TRIPS, Articles 70.8 and 70.9).

countries into the Western IP system, are certainly worth pondering.[14] Consider Japan after the Second World War and now, or China in 1990 and China *circa* 2020. Under pressure to increase profits and shareholder value, the multinational companies that sowed the TRIPS seed are encouraging this process. While, in the short term, those companies may consider developing countries primarily as new export markets and lower-cost production centres, will they maintain the technological superiority of the 'West' in research and development and, hence, continued economic dominance.[15] If research and development at a level comparable to that of Western laboratories can be developed in developing countries, there will be little incentive to keep those activities in higher price environments. This highlights even more the need for developing countries to develop a knowledge-optimization strategy. Once unleashed, and if properly supported, the powers of innovation may cut the present dominance of the West short.[16] For now, however, large exporting firms are the clearest TRIPS winners.[17]

## 1.2 Doha and Public Health

As of this writing (i.e. June 2006), we are in the midst of the Doha Development Round, which started in Qatar in November 2001 and may end in 2007.[18] The language of the Declaration adopted in Doha is a measure of the change (at the multilateral level at least) since 1994. In the three paragraphs concerning TRIPS, there is no hook on which to hang demands to increase IP protection.

---

[14] See Ruth L. Okediji, The International Relations of Intellectual Property: Narratives of Developing Country Participation in the Global Intellectual Property System (2003), **7** *Sing. J. Int'l & Comp. L.*, 315; and Kenneth J. Vandevelde, The Political Economy of a Bilateral Investment Treaty (1998), **92** *Am. J. Int'l L.* 621.

[15] See Suzanne Scotchmer (2004), *Innovation and Incentives*, Cambridge, Mass: MIT Press, p. 29.

[16] See Michael P. Ryan (2002), 'Knowledge-Economy Elites, the International Law of Intellectual Property and Trade, and Economic Development', **10** *Cardozo J. Int'l & Comp. L.*, 271.

[17] See Evelyn Su (2003), 'The Winners and the Losers: The Agreement on the Trade-Related Aspects of Intellectual Property Rights and Its Effects on Developing Countries', **23** *Hous. J. Int'l L.*, 169.

[18] World Trade Organization, Ministerial Declaration of 14 November 2001, WT/MIN(01)/DEC/1, 41 I.L.M. 746 (2002), available at http://www.wto.org/english/thewto_e/minist_e/min01_e/mindecl_e.htm [hereinafter 'Doha Declaration']. On the Doha process generally, see Gervais, *supra*, note 6, at 43–51. See also L. Danielle Tully (2003), 'Note, Prospects for Progress: The TRIPS Agreement and Developing Countries After the DOHA Conference', **26** *Bos. Coll. Int'l & Comp. L. Rev.*, 129).

First, paragraph 17 states that TRIPS should be implemented 'in a manner supportive of public health, by promoting both access to existing medicines and research and development into new medicines'. In the following paragraph, the Declaration addresses a mostly North–North issue, the completion of the negotiations on geographical indications on wines and spirits. The third and perhaps most well-known of the paragraphs instructs the TRIPS Council to 'examine, inter alia, the relationship between the TRIPS Agreement and the Convention on Biological Diversity, the protection of traditional knowledge and folklore', and other new developments. In undertaking this work, the Declaration says, 'the TRIPS Council shall be guided by the objectives and principles set out in Articles 7 and 8 of the TRIPS Agreement and shall take fully into account the development dimension'. In other words, apart from the possible increase in protection of names of wines and spirits, the Doha Declaration essentially reflects the concerns of developing countries.

The separate Declaration on the TRIPS Agreement and Public Health,[19] also adopted at Doha, emphasizes what had already been said in the Declaration itself – that the TRIPS Agreement should not prevent WTO members from taking measures to protect public health. Such an interpretation means that the TRIPS Agreement should be interpreted in light of its objective and purpose, as expressed in the agreement itself: 'Each Member has the right to grant compulsory licenses and the freedom to determine the grounds upon which such licenses are granted'; 'each member has the right to determine what constitutes a national emergency or other circumstances of extreme urgency' (where public health crises may represent national emergency); and 'The effect of the provisions in the TRIPS Agreement that are relevant to the exhaustion of intellectual property rights is to leave each Member free to establish its own regime for such exhaustion without challenge, subject to the [Most Favored Nation] and national treatment provisions of Articles 3 and 4'.[20]

While the purpose of the Declaration is rather self-evident, the importance of patents in preventing or reducing access to life-saving pharmaceuticals is not. Patents may be more a part of the problem than of the solution for certain developing countries coping with HIV or other epidemics, and the Declaration may help them overcome that obstacle. Yet, while a compulsory licence should reduce patent (royalty) costs, it does not eliminate the

---

19 World Trade Organization, Ministerial Declaration on the TRIPS Agreement and Public Health of 14 November 2001, WT/MIN(01)/DEC/2, 41 I.L.M. 755 (2001), available at http://docsonline.wto.org/.

20 Ibid., para. 5.

production costs or the problems associated with distribution and timely administration of the medicines.[21]

After intensive and difficult negotiations, the WTO General Council adopted the Implementation of Paragraph 6 of the Doha Declaration on the TRIPS Agreement and Public Health in 2003.[22] This allows, under certain conditions, WTO members to export generic versions of drugs used to treat diseases such as HIV/AIDS to countries that can neither afford nor manufacture these pharmaceuticals. The Declaration has now been turned into a formal amendment to TRIPS, which will be added as an Article 31*bis*, together with an Annex and an Appendix, thus preserving the format of the 2003 Decision.[23] The Declaration and amendment are imperfect,[24] but my point here is to draw attention to the process, which was designed to take the needs of developing countries into account, not to criticize the result.

## 1.3 TRIPS and Traditional Knowledge

The protection of traditional knowledge has been discussed in international fora over the last few years;[25] however, the Doha declaration put it at centre stage. There are several reasons for the sudden move of this issue to the forefront.

---

[21] See, for example, Amir Attaran and Lee Gillespie-White (2001), 'Do Patents for Antiretroviral Drugs Constrain Access to AIDS Treatment in Africa?', **286** *J. Am.Med. Ass'n.* 1886; Srividhya Ragavan (2004), 'The Jekyll and Hyde Story of International Trade: The Supreme Court in PhRMA v. Walsh and the TRIPS Agreement', **38** *U. Rich. L. Rev.*, 777.

[22] World Trade Organization, Decision of the General Council of 30 August 2003, WT/L/540 (2003), available at http://www.wto.org/english/tratop_e/trips_e/implem_para6_e.htm; see also Carlos M. Correa (2004), 'Supplying Pharmaceuticals to Countries Without Manufacturing Capacity: Examining the Solution Agreed Upon by the WTO on 30th August, 2003', **1** *J. Generic Meds.*, 105–19.

[23] WTO General Council, 'Amendment of the TRIPS Agreement', Decision of 6 December 2005. WTO Document WT/L/641 of 8 December 2005.

[24] See Bryan C. Mercurio (2004), 'TRIPS, Patents, and Access to Life-Saving Drugs in the Developing World', **8** *Marq. Intell. Prop. L. Rev.*, 211; K.M. Gopakumar (2004), 'The WTO Deal on Cheap Drugs: A Critique', **7** *J. World Intell. Prop.*, 99.

[25] For WIPO activities in this area, see generally WIPO, http://www.wipo.int/tk/en/ (last visited 7 March 2006). See also Aaron Cosbey (1999), 'The Sustainable Development Effects of the WTO TRIPS Agreement: A Focus on Developing Countries', available at http://www.tradeobservatory.org/library.cfm?RefID=24624 (last visited 7 March 2006); Chakravarthi Raghavan, 'ASEAN for Protecting Indigenous/Traditional Knowledge, Third World Network', 5 May 2000, available at http://www.twnside.org.sg/title/asean.htm; John Mugabe, Intellectual Property Protection and Traditional Knowledge: An Exploration in International Policy Discourse, November 1998, http:// www.wipo.int/tk/en/hr/paneldiscussion/papers/pdf/mugabe.pdf (last visited 7 March 2006).

First, a large number of countries believe that, until now, they have not derived great benefits from 'traditional' forms of IP, yet they find themselves rich in traditional knowledge, especially genetic resources and folklore. They would like to exploit these resources, and several major companies share this interest. The second reason is the growing political importance of aboriginal communities in several countries. While pharmaceutical and biotechnological companies are examining ways to exploit indigenous medicinal knowledge, plants and other resources that are often found in developing countries, the Internet is progressively allowing creators of folklore or folklore-based copyrighted material to disseminate their material worldwide at a very low cost.

The protection of traditional knowledge, folklore and genetic resources is far from obvious, and raises fundamental questions about the current IP framework, itself exclusively a product of evolution in the Western world.[26] In addition to posing questions about notions of authorship, work, utility, novelty, public domain and the rest, certain observers suggest that the nature of the exclusive rights and the underlying economic theories based on incentive and reward are misplaced. Traditional knowledge, they argue, is centred on respect, not innovation. It is non-commercial in nature and does not seek to expand the public domain.[27] And while existing legal rules may be used to protect certain forms of traditional knowledge, important potential conflicts remain.[28]

This explains why the debate on these issues is essentially twofold. It consists, first, of a criticism of current rules and, second, of proposals for specific, *sui generis* protection of traditional knowledge. In the latter case, in addition to the development of treaty provisions under the aegis of WIPO[29] – which could serve, at least initially, on a regional basis – work in the Doha Round might lead to political recognition of the validity of some of the demands made by developing countries rich in traditional knowledge.

---

26 See Daniel Gervais (2003), 'Spiritual But Not Intellectual? The Protection of Sacred Intangible Traditional Knowledge', **11** *Cardozo J. Int'l & Comp. L.*, 467.

27 See Michael H. Davis (2003), 'Some Realism About Indigenism', **11** *Cardozo J. Int'l & Comp. L.*, 815.

28 See Paul Kuruk (2004), 'Bridging the Gap Between Traditional Knowledge and Intellectual Property Rights: Is Reciprocity an Answer?', **7** *J. World Intell. Prop.*, 42; Jean Raymond Homere (2004), 'Intellectual Property Rights Can Help Stimulate the Economic Development of Least Developed Countries', **27** *Colum. J.L. & Arts*, 277; see also Daniel Gervais (2002), 'The Internationalization of Intellectual Property: New Challenges from the Very Old and the Very New', **12** *Fordham Intell. Prop. Media & Ent. L.J.*, 929.

29 See, e.g., World Intellectual Prop. Org. (2005), 'Draft Provisions on the Protection of Traditional Knowledge', available at http://www.wipo.int/tk/en/consultations/draft_provisions/draft_provisions.html (last visited 7 March 2006).

## 2 ECONOMICS

This section examines a number of recent analyses of available empirical evidence about the impact of IP protection. Clearly, the analysis is far from exhaustive. It only tries to identify trends. It is also worth noting that, in contrast to the very large number of studies dealing with the impact of IP protection of one type or another in major industrialized nations, there is a relative dearth of empirical analyses of the nature and impact of IP in developing economies.

Studies, however, are starting to emerge.[30] They paint a complex picture of the advantages of higher IP protection in developing economies. A simple equation cannot be drawn between an increase in trade following the introduction of TRIPS-compatible IP protection, on the one hand, and economic development on the other, especially when measured in terms of welfare increases. There are, however, at least two indicators that are helpful to analyse the impact of increasing protection, namely (a) the increase of trade flows in goods that include a significant IP component (as compared to the physical value of the material and components – for example, a music CD or a patented pharmaceutical molecule; such areas may be referred to as 'intellectual property-sensitive'); and (b) the increase in FDI concerning goods or services that require a high level of IP protection. It is essential to measure both because, to a certain extent, they cancel each other out: a company in country A (export) may have the ability to send goods to country B, but it may instead opt for local production (under licence) in country B. Economic studies mentioned above, which are based on data available from 89 countries, concluded that higher levels of IP protection are useful in areas other than fuel (and, presumably, raw resources pre-value-added transformation) and, surprisingly, high technology.

The traditional view, supported by case studies in countries such as postwar Japan, is that high IP protection, especially of patent rights, will lead to higher FDI.[31] However, in a recent analysis of the FDI component and its relation to

---

30 Some of the more notable, recent, and non-country-specific efforts include 'UK IPR Commission Report', *supra* note 3; *Intellectual Property and Development* Carsten Fink and Keith E. Maskus (eds) (2004); World Bank, 'The Uruguay Round and the Developing Economies', Will Martin and L. Alan Winters (eds) (1995), available at http://econ.worldbank.org; Suzanne Scotchmer (2004), 'The Political Economy of Intellectual Property Treaties', **20** *J. L. Econ. & Org.*, 415, 435–6; Organisation for Econ. Co-operation and Dev., 'OECD Science, Technology and Industry Outlook' (2004); Org. for Econ. Co-operation and Dev., 'Patents, Innovation and Economic Performance: OECD Conference Proceedings' (2004).

31 See Keith E. Maskus (2000), 'Intellectual Property Rights and Economic Development', **32** *Case W. Res. J. Int'l L.*, 471.

IP, Professor Keith Maskus concluded that many other factors influence FDI and technology transfer decisions, including market liberalization and deregulation, technology development policies and competition regimes.[32] Foreign firms invest internationally if there are location advantages and if it is more profitable for them to produce in that country rather than licensing their IP. Firms are more apt to invest in countries that implement strong IP protections (and to bring their IP or allow for licences in such countries). Transnational firms may also choose to invest in vertical FDI (where different plants produce products that can be used by the plant 'above' it as an input to their product).[33]

In China's case, the date of TRIPS compliance coincided with its becoming a WTO member on 11 December 2001. The author of a recent study dealing with China found that there was only a weak correlation between higher IP and increased FDI in that market.[34] Another developing country-specific study that compared African countries to India and China found significantly lower FDI numbers in Africa despite higher levels of IP protection.[35]

In the specific area of pharmaceuticals, available data analysed in another study illustrates that, at least for the large Indian market, the introduction of patent protection is likely to lead to increased research and development, price increases, and related welfare effects. However, research also shows that only 10.9 per cent of the top 500 pharmaceuticals in this market are patented. Additionally, the government retained certain tools including price controls and, in cases where article 31 of TRIPS allows, compulsory licences.[36]

---

[32] Keith E. Maskus, 'Intellectual Property Rights in Encouraging FDI and Technology Transfer', in *Intellectual Property and Development*, *supra*, note 31, at 70–71; see also Carsten Fink, 'Patent Protection, Transnational Corporations, and Market Structure: A Simulation Study of the Indian Pharmaceutical Industry', in *Intellectual Property and Development*, *supra*, note 31, at 250–51, in his summary of a study by Ginarte and Park, Juan C. Ginarte and Walter G. Park, Determinants of Patent Rights: A Cross-National Study (1997), **26** *Res. Pol'y*, 283.

[33] See Carlos A. Primo Braga and Carsten Fink (1998), 'The Relationship Between Intellectual Property Rights and Foreign Direct Investment', **9** *Duke J. Comp. & Int'l L.*, 163.

[34] See Li Yahong (2002), 'Pushing For Greater Protection: The Trend Toward Greater Protection of Intellectual Property in the Chinese Software Industry and the Implications for Rule of Law in China', **23** *U. Pennsylvania. J. Int'l Econ. L.*, 637. See also Keith E. Maskus (1998), 'The Role of Intellectual Property Rights in Encouraging Foreign Direct Investment and Technology Transfer', **9** *Duke J. Comp. & Int'l L.*, 109; Mikhaelle Schiappacasse (2004), 'Intellectual Property Rights in China: Technology Transfers and Economic Development', **2** *Buff. Intell. Prop. L.J.*, 164; and Peter K. Yu et al. (2005), 'China and the WTO: Progress, Perils, and Prospects', **17** *Colum. J. Asian L.*, 1.

[35] See Ragavan, *supra*, note 22, at 789.

[36] See Fink, *supra*, note 31, at 250–51.

The UK IPR Commission Report[37] presents a picture consistent with the above findings but also stresses that it is important not to consider developing countries as a homogeneous group. In fact, a fairly well developed sequencing phenomenon exists. In an impoverished developing country, there is little rent that foreign firms can extract. Furthermore, there is little technology to copy or improve on high technology goods, and it is unlikely that the country in question can benefit from technology transfer. FDI is unlikely because of factors unrelated to IP, such as infrastructure, or absence of a viable domestic market. International firms take notice when a country becomes both a piracy threat and a potential market, even if the threat is limited to a fairly small percentage of the population. While countries that implement IP norms may benefit from increased local development and inward FDI, they may also incur job losses in established copycat industries and welfare costs associated with higher local prices. However, consumers benefit from knowing they are purchasing the genuine product, especially in areas where the quality of the goods is essential.

In sum, economic analysis tends to demonstrate that sufficient IP protection is an essential component of increased inward FDI and trade flows in IP-sensitive goods for countries above a certain economic development threshold. The trade regime (especially tariffs and non-tariff barriers), tax and competition laws are also potent influences.

## 3 NATIONAL KNOWLEDGE OPTIMIZATION

Many of the studies mentioned above insist on the fact that sufficient and adequate IP protection is but one ingredient in a complex recipe to achieve a successful economic development soufflé. Put differently, IPR protection is essential, but in itself insufficient, to ensure growth. In fact, IP rules arguably benefit mostly major owners of IP who are largely concentrated in a few Western countries and Japan. Each country needs a comprehensive knowledge optimization strategy to exploit IP successfully to maximize its economic growth in areas that are information and IP-intensive and to be able to produce goods and services with a higher ideational content (which is what IP rules tend to protect). The adequate protection of commercially or industrially relevant knowledge forms part of such a strategy.

If the above seems fair in light of recent economic studies, those studies are also illuminating in what they do not and perhaps cannot show. It is extremely difficult to isolate the importance of the IP factor in the growth of bilateral

---

[37] See *supra*, note 3.

trade flows and FDI. It is even more difficult to determine the optimal level of protection. This is partly due to the fact that the TRIPS Agreement imposes global minimum standards, and there remain very few statistically significant options to compare various levels of protection below that floor. That problem certainly has theoretical significance in assessing the validity of econometric studies and the field of available (versus ideal) field of empirical data. However, what is a problem in theory actually forms part of the solution once we shift to a policy-setting perspective.

The TRIPS Agreement is arguably the strongest normative vector in setting IP policy. WTO members cannot legislate below the TRIPS level without incurring the risk of dispute-settlement proceedings under the Dispute-Settlement Understanding ('DSU'),[38] and it is unlikely that TRIPS norms will be diluted in the Doha Round, beyond the introduction of Article 31*bis*.[39] Therefore it is pragmatically justified to take TRIPS as a given in the IP policy equation.

The available flexibility in implementing the agreement must be considered as part of a comprehensive strategy. Integrating TRIPS norms into such a strategy is tactically sound. TRIPS strikes an adequate balance if properly implemented, especially when compared to the emerging 'TRIPS Plus' norms. The strategy I outline below is not a series of measures designed nominally to implement TRIPS rules or find loopholes to shrink the protection they offer. Proposed interpretations of articles 27 and 30 of TRIPS and the fact that the agreement in many cases imposes no clear rules as to the ownership of IPRs mean that a country can formally implement TRIPS while de-implementing parts of it through such legal 'gimmickry' (though not illegitimately) and perhaps 'get away with it' as far as the WTO dispute-settlement system is concerned. My objective is rather to suggest ways to optimize knowledge and economic development using TRIPS rules as an ingredient. This may involve some flexibility in the implementation process but only as part of a comprehensive strategy.

It is difficult and probably impossible on the basis of available empirical data to determine the optimal level of IP protection. Is the best term of protection for a patent 20 years, 18, or 22? Or is it five or 35? For copyright, is it 10 years, life of the author plus 50 or 70 years?[40] One would probably conclude that, for certain forms of invention or creation (indeed for specific inventions or works) a certain term is optimal, while a different one is more adequate in a different

---

38 Marrakesh Agreement Establishing the World Trade Organization, Annex 2, Legal Instruments – Results of the Uruguay Round, **33** I.L.M., 1125 (1994), available at http://www.wto.org/english/docs_e/legal_e/28-dsu.pdf [hereinafter DSU].

39 See Gervais, *supra*, note 6, at 43–51. With respect to Article 31*bis*, see *supra*, note 24 and accompanying text.

40 See Christopher Sprigman (2004), 'Reform(aliz)ing Copyright', **57** *Stanford L. Rev.*, 485.

context.[41] This analysis could depend, for example, on the added value of the invention, which depends in turn on the size of the inventive step it embodies, and the degree to which this step overlaps the predictable industrial or commercial applicability of the invention. One could add to the equation the degree of true competition in the industrial or economic sector affected by the invention and, correlatively, whether there are dominant players by market share.

TRIPS, one could argue, is a valid standard also because it only harmonizes national laws to a degree.[42] This is not the place for a summary of the content of TRIPS. Evidently, it contains more than simple 'wishes', in contrast to many provisions of the Paris Convention. A country must provide protection of copyrights, certain related rights, trademarks, industrial designs, certain geographical indications, patents on most classes of inventions, certain forms of confidential information and, last, and in this case least, topographies of integrated circuits, in each case for a specified period of time. On the other hand, however, there is considerable flexibility in the way the rights and protected subject matter are defined,[43] owned, managed or subject to exceptions.[44] In the area of enforcement, the agreement recognizes that the implementation in a given WTO member may be affected by the availability of resources. The United Nations Conference on Trade and Development ('UNCTAD') published a detailed document on the flexibility of TRIPS.[45] Another example is the delay until 2016 in protecting pharmaceuticals by patents granted to least-developed countries.[46]

---

41 See Caren L. Stanley (2003), 'A Dangerous Step Toward the Over Protection of Intellectual Property: Rethinking Eldred v. Ashcroft', **26** *Hamline L. Rev.*, 679.

42 See Jerome H. Reichman (2003), 'The TRIPS Agreement Comes of Age: Conflicts or Cooperation with the Developing Countries?', **32** *Case W. Res. J. Int'l L.*, 441.

43 For example, while Article 27 states that WTO members must protect 'inventions, whether products or processes, in all fields of technology, provided that they are new, involve an inventive step and are capable of industrial application', the terms 'new', 'inventive step', and 'capable of industrial application' are not defined.

44 Many exceptions are only limited by the 'three-step test' contained in TRIPS articles 13, 26(2) and 30. See Daniel J. Gervais (2005), 'Towards a New Core International Copyright Norm: The Reverse Three-Step Test', **9** *Marquette Intell. Prop. L. Rev.*, 1.

45 'United Nations Conference on Trade and Dev., Dispute Settlement', World Trade Organization, 3.14 TRIPS, at 20 (2003), available at http:// www.unctad.org/en/docs/edmmisc232add18_en.pdf.

46 Council for Trade-Related Aspects of Intellectual Property Rights, 'Extension of the Transition Period under Article 66.1 of the TRIPS Agreement for Least-Developed Country Members for Certain Obligations with Respect to Pharmaceutical Products, IP/C/25' (1 July, 2002), available at http://www.wto.org/english/news_e/pres02_e/pr301_e.htm.

Admittedly, developing economies typically need a different set of rules. As UNCTAD put it:

> Experience shows that there is a need for policy instruments specifically designed with the aim of helping countries at lower stages of development to converge on the levels of efficiency and affluence achieved by the more advanced economies, and to improve the welfare of all groups of the population. Making this the principle for policy design at both the domestic and the international level requires recognition of the fact that successful development and integration of the developing countries is in the mutual interest of all countries, as longer-term growth and trading opportunities of the more advanced economies also depend on the expansion of industrial capacity and markets in the poorer economies.[47]

I would suggest that, as far as IP is concerned, there is sufficient policy-related 'room to move' within TRIPS, even though the major concession to developing countries other than least-developed ones was a set of transitional periods, which primarily ended in January 2000, and in January 2005 for pharmaceutical patents.[48] Therefore I suggest that countries should use TRIPS' built-in normative elasticity to reconcile the new norms to the extent possible with their industrial, cultural,[49] legal and economic parameters based on their determination of priorities. The purpose should not be to circumvent TRIPS, because by and large it incorporates a well-honed set of norms establishing structures of protection, the impact, use and misuse of which have been extensively analysed. In addition, local research and development efforts after years of FDI have transformed China as a major holder of domestically developed IP.

I also suggest integrating TRIPS norms in a broader strategy. As with market openness, IP rules per se are a catalyst, at best. Part of that strategy includes accepting TRIPS as a given and perhaps, as some argue, as a common reference/defence point against TRIPS-plus demands made in bilateral discussions. That being said, TRIPS is not a static bundle of norms. It evolves with each panel and appellate body interpretation. It is also not to be read in 'clinical isolation' from public international law.[50] Developing and other countries

---

47 United Nations Conference on Trade and Dev., Trade and Development Report 96 (2004), available at http://www.unctad.org/en/docs/tdr2004_en.pdf [hereinafter Trade and Development Report].

48 TRIPS, *supra* note 9, art. 65(2), (4). In the case of pharmaceutical patents, least-developed countries now have until 2016.

49 See William P. Alford (1995), 'To Steal a Book Is an Elegant Offense: Intellectual Property Law in Chinese Civilization'.

50 See Appellate Body Report, 'United States Standards for Reformulated and Conventional Gasoline', pt.III.B, WT/DS2/AB/R (April 29, 1996), available at http://docsonline.wto.org.

can thus coalesce to develop alternative sets of norms and include TRIPS and WTO rules in the broader framework of public international law.

Importing IP rules wholesale into the legislative and industrial fabric of a developing economy is unlikely to succeed. However, it is fair to assume that a country's technology imports and inward FDI are unlikely to grow without IP rules. In other words, IP rules are required. It would be counterproductive to develop independent rules, for at least two reasons. First, there is little, if any, evidence that a new form of IP or even variations on known themes would work better. Second, there would be huge transition costs and friction in convincing foreign partners of the validity of such new or customized rules. For multinational corporate investors, there is value in predictability and dealing with a known set of regulatory parameters. TRIPS partly has the flexibility needed by developing economies. By developing a comprehensive strategy, a country can limit the negative impact of transitioning to higher IP protection and increase its chances of reaping the benefits thereof, including technology-related FDI and growing domestic Internet, pharmaceutical or other technology-based industries.

Granted, the task at hand is not a simple one, yet, instead of trying to turn back the clock of extant liberalization and IP rules, I suggest that they can be put to good use. I cannot cover all aspects of a comprehensive knowledge-optimization strategy, the primary purpose of which would be to strengthen a country's economy and its growth. However, the following paths could be followed.

Developing countries wish to attract FDI and distributorships of foreign goods. They also want to retain their best students (especially those who have studied abroad in scientific or engineering-related fields). For this to happen, they need an IP policy, but that policy must form part of a broader knowledge-optimization strategy. How best to utilize foreign knowledge and develop domestic innovation and creativity will depend in part on how foreign investors and firms view the country's comfort level. That comfort level is measured in terms of IP protection and enforcement, but it also depends on a myriad other factors, including other regulatory aspects, such as competition, investment, freedom to market, employment, and cultural and political parameters. Indeed, the realization that IP rules per se do not automatically lead to an increase in inward FDI, and that much more than IP rules is required to develop domestic innovation and creativity, is perhaps what has prompted many developing countries to insist in WTO meetings on the technology transfer part of the TRIPS bargain, which is enshrined in TRIPS article 66(2), as well as capacity building under article 67.

The IP component of the comfort level perceived by US-based multinational firms as measured by Mansfield is significant, but its importance should not be overstated. As Professor Paul J. Heald aptly noted:

> All in all, a close look at Mansfield's research provides support for the proposition that American firms with significant disclosure worries are influenced by the level of enforcement of trade secrecy and contract law in making foreign direct investment decisions. Its current status as canonical evidence that maximum enforcement of all sorts of intellectual property law – and especially patent law – will stimulate investment should not remain unchallenged. Instead of blindly relying on Mansfield's research, a more rational strategy for developing countries would take into account the costs and benefits of protection in the context of their unique economic situation. Depending on the category of intellectual property subject to the TRIPS Agreement, developing countries should seriously consider minimal compliance.[51]

Implementing TRIPS entails significant costs.[52] Not only must legal regimes be brought into conformance, but officials working in various government departments, including judges, police and customs authorities, must be trained to understand the new rules. Strengthened enforcement rules and processes may impose a serious burden on the judicial and administrative system. Many commentators, even those in favour of high IP protection levels, recognize that developing countries are often hit hard when first introducing TRIPS (or *a fortiori* TRIPS Plus) norms, and significant costs may be incurred relating to prosecution, examination, infringement, litigation, enforcement, training and so on.[53] These commentators note, however, that some of these costs may be recouped by charging user fees. It is argued that a high level of IP protection is beneficial in the long run because piracy is detrimental to long-term domestic competitive strategies.[54] Copyright laws are beneficial for local authors as piracy will increase their competition by introducing foreign works at lower costs. This will inhibit the local community from developing its work in this area in both the long and short run.

It is also argued that patent protection is not detrimental to a country per se. First, patents are just a series of instructions. On their own, they will likely be useless to someone in a developing country attempting to reverse engineer the technology. Second, patented technology from other countries likely will not be the technology needed by a developing country. Technology applicable to

---

51 Paul J. Heald (2003), 'Misreading a Canonical Work: An Analysis of Mansfield's 1994 Study', **10** *J. Intell. Prop. L.*, 309, 318.

52 See Mariko Kunimi (2001), 'TRIPS Agreement, Is It Really Successful Achievement in the WTO? The Difficulty of Balancing Between Public and Private Interests', **3** *Or. Rev. Int'l L.*, 46.

53 See Keith E. Maskus and Jerome H. Reichman (2004), 'The Globalization of Private Knowledge Goods and the Privatization of Global Public Goods', **7** *J. Int'l Econ. L.*, 279.

54 Edmund W. Kitch (1994), 'The Patent Policy of Developing Countries', **13** *UCLA Pac. Basin L.J.*, 166, 169–78.

a developing country will only be developed if there are patents in place to protect the inventor. Finally, developing countries granting patents will pay less than wealthy countries for the use of patent rights.

Properly adjusting the level of compliance with international norms, from minimal TRIPS implementation with systematic use of all available 'wiggle room' to full TRIPS Plus[55] compliance and enforcement, requires an understanding of the fine points of a highly complex set of norms, developed over decades of expert-level discussions, being 'parachuted' into a legal system that may not have such checks and balances as competition law or freedom of speech or, indeed, even the necessary level of expertise to parse the new and highly complex rules without a comprehensive training programme.[56]

### 3.1 Cooperation and Coalition Building

Developing countries can, of course, coordinate. They can exchange with each other 'recipes' for success and establish coalitions and parameters for international (bilateral, regional or multilateral) negotiations involving IP rules. They can create regional industrial property offices, regional copyright collectives or technical agencies offering services to several national collectives. They also can use fora other than the WTO in cooperation with civil society groups to attempt to develop alternative norm-setting exercises.[57] The value of these exercises as potentially relevant norms of public international law has not been fully tested before WTO dispute-settlement panels.

### 3.2 Priority Setting

Based on existing industrial infrastructures, successes, education programmes, available natural and human resources and potential domestic and regional

---

55 On the return to bilateralism generally and TRIPS Plus negotiations by the US Trade Representative, see David Vivas-Eugui (2003), 'Regional and Bilateral Agreements and a TRIPS-Plus World: The Free Trade Area of the Americas (FTAA)', available at http://www.geneva.quno.info/pdf/FTAA%20(A4).pdf; Peter Drahos (2001), BITs and BIPs: Bilateralism in Intellectual Property', **4** *J. World Intell. Prop.*, 791; Ruth L. Okediji (2004), 'Back to Bilateralism? Pendulum Swings in International Intellectual Property Protection', **1** *U. Ottawa L. & Tech. J.*, 125; Peter K. Yu (2004), 'Currents and Crosscurrents in the International Intellectual Property Regime', **38** *Loy. L.A. L. Rev.*, 323.

56 See Rochelle Cooper Dreyfuss (2004), 'TRIPS-Round II: Should Users Strike Back?', **71** *U. Chi. L. Rev.*, 21.

57 See Graeme B. Dinwoodie and Rochelle C. Dreyfuss (2004), 'TRIPS and the Dynamics of Intellectual Property Lawmaking', **36** *Case W. Res. J. Int'l L.*, 95.

markets, what are the realistic areas that a country should prioritize? The primary target of a strategy should not be to obtain new imports, although they may be useful, but rather to build domestic IP-generating activities. This can be done in part through FDI (which almost always includes a knowledge and technology transfer component), but also by developing domestic innovation, creativity and industry at optimal levels.

### 3.3 Education and Institutional Capacity Building

Once priorities have been set, education and institutional capacity building are probably the most important aspects. Education, both in the country and abroad, is the cornerstone of a viable, long-term knowledge strategy and economic growth in the information society. For example, a country should pay to send some of its best students to the top foreign universities, especially in fields where the knowledge brought back can directly advance the selected priorities. This could include engineering, biology, chemistry, physics and other sciences as well as management and law, including IP law. In certain cases, financial mechanisms may be used to ensure that trained graduates will return to their countries of origin.

If a country does not have patent protection, it will have difficulty attracting technology-oriented employers and retaining nationals that have studied in these areas. A country should hold seminars and invite foreign professors and practitioners of international standing in priority areas. Once knowledge is available on a recurring basis domestically, more students will be able to acquire it at a lower cost. Training for policy makers, judges, high officials and other persons involved in economic development projects should likewise be organized.

Developing educational institutions and services is costly. Developing IP institutions such as patent and trademark offices is perhaps even more so. Yet developing countries can either delegate these roles to foreign institutions, a majority of which are located in the First World, thereby losing some of their ability to customize the services, or take the policy bull by the horns and pay the price. Ideally, more industrialized nations should fund training and establishment of local patent and trademark offices because of their educational role with local businesses and research facilities. Absent this kind of funding, another option, used in some parts of Africa, is to build regional offices.[58]

[58] See, for example, 'The African Regional Industrial Property Organization', http://www.aripo.wipo.net/index.html (last visited 7 March 2006).

### 3.4 Subsidies and Awards

Within WTO and other applicable rules, there is still room for several subsidies in the form of tax breaks or other incentives. These may also be used to attract FDI. By granting merit-based research subsidies or grants to local creators, an incentive for local innovators and creators is created. For example, by rewarding significant achievements at an annual award ceremony, successful innovators and creators are compensated and a strong social signal is sent about the value of creation and innovation. This then functions as an additional incentive for others.

### 3.5 FDI Marketing

FDI is not a panacea, but, in the game of economic growth and development, it is a better solution than simply increasing imports. FDI generally comes with formal or informal knowledge and technology transfer and creates more and better local jobs than simple distributorships. Each country should thus market its advantages bilaterally, at international fairs, through graduate students and so on. It could survey multinational companies operating in its priority areas to determine their perception of the country's strengths and weaknesses, address shortcomings identified in the survey and provide information on positive aspects that are simply not known in key interested circles.

### 3.6 Non-IP Regulatory Adaptation

Based on WTO and other rules and surveys, regulatory shortcomings should be addressed. Usually an efficient legal system, investment protections rules, a competitive tax system and access to a qualified workforce will rate fairly high in the list of FDI preconditions. In parallel, as the UK Commission on IPRs noted, articles 8 and 40 of TRIPS allow a WTO member to determine an appropriate interface between IP and competition law. However, many countries that implemented TRIPS recently did not, and still do not, have competition legislation.

### 3.7 Patent Mining

While patent mining is also not a panacea, patent databases have the advantage of being publicly available. By mining recent patents and giving copies to local companies with product development abilities, a number of upward technological steps may be taken fairly rapidly. Of course, the obligation to comply with TRIPS means that, if the patent is granted in a developing country, the technology cannot be used directly. But even if a reasonable licence cannot be obtained, the knowledge could be used for non-commercial research, for example.

These are of course only examples of the components of a full strategy.

## CONCLUSION

Without adequate IP protection, economic development will not occur at an optimal level, although it is unclear whether IP rules have any positive effect on the development of the truly poorer nations. In addition, we now know that, while IP is an essential ingredient, it does not, by itself, make an economic plan. Many more elements are required. I argue that, for both practical reasons and on the basis of available empirical data, TRIPS should be seen, and accepted, as a given. Further, it may be defended as an appropriate reference point for developing nations in the context of TRIPS Plus bilateral trade discussions. Indeed, post-TRIPS developments have been going in two (arguably diverging) directions. On the one hand, TRIPS-related development within WTO, as well as recent developments in WIPO, have tried to be more responsive to the perceived needs of developing countries and the interests of users in securing access to protected content and material on terms they consider reasonable. This even includes broad exceptions to obligations to obtain permissions and licences. On the other hand, IP developments in bilateral and regional trade agreements mirror the so-called 'maximalist' approach. This latter trend to regulate IP rights through bilateral regimes may not immediately threaten the balanced approach of WTO and WIPO, but these bilateral initiatives likely will have a significant impact in the long run.

TRIPS contains a number of rules that WTO members must implement, but it also affords a fair margin of 'policy flexibility'. Thus implementing TRIPS may and should be viewed as part of a broader knowledge strategy resting on priority setting, education and institutional capacity building, regulatory adaptation, FDI 'marketing' and patent mining. Finally, if TRIPS were defended as the 'correct' international norm, it would have the effect of buttressing the position that TRIPS Plus is inadequate at this juncture for many, and perhaps most, developing countries.

# 4. The fight against piracy: working within the administrative enforcement system in China

**Kristie Thomas***

## INTRODUCTION

The system of intellectual property (IP) protection in China is frequently the focus of criticism for China's trade partners. Following China's accession to the World Trade Organization (WTO) in December 2001, China must now comply with the Agreement on Trade-Related Aspects of Intellectual Property Rights (TRIPS). As a result, China undertook a radical overhaul of its intellectual property legislation, beginning before accession in the late 1990s, including major revisions of the Patent Law in August 2000 and the Trademark Law and Copyright Law in October 2001. The substantive legal provisions are now widely judged to be of 'international standard'.[1]

However, there are still various criticisms made of the intellectual property system in China, but the focus of these criticisms has now shifted to the structures that exist to enforce the substantive rights provided by the legislation. It is commonly concluded that 'protection for intellectual property remains closer to rhetoric than reality'.[2] In order to understand these criticisms of the enforcement system in China, it is necessary first to understand the nature of the IP enforcement system in China and the continuing prevalence of administrative enforcement within that system.

This chapter will begin with an overview of the IP enforcement system in China, in order to show the difficult choices facing rights holders trying to protect their IP in China and the central role of administrative enforcement

* Teaching Fellow, University of Nottingham in Ningbo.

1 Mary L. Riley (1997), 'The Protection of Business Secrets and Other Intellectual Property in China', in Mary L. Riley et al. (eds), *Protecting Intellectual Property Rights in China*, Hong Kong and London: Sweet & Maxwell Asia, p. 63.

2 William P. Alford (1995), *To Steal a Book Is an Elegant Offense: Intellectual Property Law in Chinese Civilization*, Stanford, California: Stanford University Press, p. 1.

within this framework. The process of taking an action for trademark infringement through the administrative enforcement system will then be outlined. The third section will highlight the strengths and weaknesses of administrative enforcement and propose possible reasons for these perceived weaknesses. The impact of the TRIPS Agreement on the enforcement structure generally, and on the administrative enforcement process specifically, will then be outlined. The chapter will conclude with a look at approaches to protecting IP within the unique Chinese system of enforcement and assess how TRIPS has and will continue to affect the administrative enforcement process in the future.

## 1 OVERVIEW OF THE IP ENFORCEMENT SYSTEM IN CHINA

The current IP enforcement system in China is often characterized as a dual system incorporating 'parallel forms' of enforcement (judicial machinery and administrative measures).[3] The Chinese Government itself characterizes the system as consisting of 'two-way parallel protection mode, namely, administrative and judicial protection'.[4] It is evident that a clear distinction is thus drawn between *private* enforcement, through civil actions in the courts, and *public* enforcement, through various government agencies. Furthermore, despite recent moves towards greater use of the judicial machinery, public enforcement is still the main means of enforcing IP rights in China.

Within this complex structure, incorporating both public and private enforcement processes, there are various enforcement options available to an IP rights holder seeking to protect their IP in China: (a) administrative enforcement through various agencies; (b) criminal enforcement through the Public Security Bureau (PSB); (c) civil enforcement through the courts; (d) border enforcement through the customs authorities.

Administrative enforcement is still the most prevalent form of enforcement in China, especially for trademark counterfeiting.[5] In fact, 'throughout

[3] Assafa Endeshaw (1996), *Intellectual Property in China: The Roots of the Problem of Enforcement*, Singapore: Acumen Publishing, p. 114.

[4] Information Office of the State Council of the People's Republic of China (2005), *New Progress in China's Protection of Intellectual Property Rights (2005)*, White Paper (Beijing, April) available at http://english.gov.cn/official/2005-07/28/content_18131.htm (accessed 10 November 2005).

[5] Joseph M. Johnson (2001–2), 'Solving China's Counterfeiting Problem', *Managing Intellectual Property*, Issue 155 (December 2001/January 2002), p. 4. Joseph M. Johnson was commenting in his capacity as chairman of the Quality Brands Protection Committee (QBPC).

most of the 1990s, enforcement of IP rights in China almost exclusively involved the use of administrative agencies'.[6] The continuing prevalence of administrative enforcement into the twenty-first century can be seen in Table 4.1.

As shown in Table 4.1, administrative enforcement accounted for more than seven times the number of cases dealt with by the judicial machinery in 2004. This is a significant characteristic of the IP enforcement system in China and can largely be explained by the role of administrative enforcement generally as 'the Chinese state's preferred mode of policy implementation in all fields, not just IPR protection'.[7] Administrative enforcement also has a large number of personnel devoted to pursuing infringers. According to the State Council representative on IP, 'the administrative law enforcement departments have employed a team of up to one million people to work cooperatively, including patent offices, patent management offices, administrative bureaus for industry and commerce, trade mark offices, copyright administration, customs, public security, publication, cultural, and the news media'.[8]

This quotation elicits the point that it is difficult to discuss the administrative enforcement system as a whole without recognizing the numerous different administrative agencies that handle different types of IP:

- Patent: the State Intellectual Property Office (SIPO) deals with the preliminary examination of patent applications, with the Patent Re-Examination Board (PREB) responsible for re-examination. These administrative organs also supervise patent activities and can act in cases of patent infringement.[9]
- Trademark: the Trademark Office under the State Administration for Industry and Commerce (SAIC) of the State Council is responsible for trademark issues, including infringements.[10]

---

6 Tim Browning and Carol Wang (2004), 'Ten Years of Enforcement in China', *Managing Intellectual Property*, February, China IP Focus, p. 38.

7 Donald C. Clarke (1999), 'Private Enforcement of Intellectual Property Rights in China', *National Bureau of Asian Research*, p. 35.

8 Duan Ruichun (1998–9), 'China's Intellectual Property Rights Protection Towards the 21st Century', *Duke Journal of Comparative & International Law*, **9**, p. 215.

9 Further information on the State Intellectual Property Office (SIPO) is available at http://www.sipo.gov.cn/sipo_English/default.htm.

10 The terms SAIC and AIC are used interchangeably by many observers; AIC will be used here. Further information on the Trademark Office of the State Administration for Industry and Commerce (SAIC) is available at http://sbj.saic.gov.cn/english/index_e.asp.

*Table 4.1 Number of cases dealt with by administrative and judicial enforcement in 2004*

| | Copyright administration enforcement | Trademark administration enforcement | Patent administration enforcement | Judicial enforcement (criminal cases) | Judicial enforcement (civil cases) |
|---|---|---|---|---|---|
| | 9 691 | 51 851 | 1 455 | 385 | 8 332 |
| Total | Administrative = 62 997 cases | | | Judicial = 8 717 cases | |

*Source*: compiled from the State Council White Paper, 'New Progress in China's Protection of Intellectual Property Rights', April 2005, available online at http://english.gov.cn/official/2005-07/28/content_18131.htm.

- Copyright: the National Copyright Administration (NCA) is responsible for the nationwide administration of copyright, including the imposition of administrative sanctions in the case of copyright infringements.[11]
- Customs: rights holders can register with the General Administration of Customs in order to attempt to halt infringing goods at the border.[12]
- Product-specific agencies: in addition to the main IP agencies listed above, there are a host of other agencies which may have a role to play in the administrative enforcement of IP. For example, 'the State Drug Administration (SDA) under the State Council has the Office for Administrative Protection of Pharmaceuticals',[13] which may have an interest in dealing with IP relating to pharmaceuticals.

As Table 4.1 demonstrates, there is a wide discrepancy between the number of administrative cases handled by these different agencies. 'An informal survey of foreign companies revealed that they prefer administrative protection for trademark and patent matters, but resort to the courts for copyright infringements'.[14] This preference is confirmed by the figures in Table 4.1 above, which shows that trademark actions accounted for more than 80 per cent of the total number of administrative cases handled. The reason for this preference is that it is relatively easy to make a *prima facie* case of trademark infringement. With little training, a member of an administrative agency can identify an obvious trademark infringement, whereas identifying a patent infringement may require much more expertise. Therefore, as the majority of administrative enforcement cases are dealt with by the Trademark Office of the SAIC, the process of taking a trademark infringement complaint to the SAIC will now be outlined.

---

11 Further information on the National Copyright Administration is available at www.ncac.gov.cn and discussed by the deputy director-general of the Copyright Department in Chen Zhaokuan (1998–9), 'Administrative Management and Enforcement of Copyright in China', *Duke Journal of Comparative & International Law*, **9**, p. 249.

12 Further information on the protection of IP by customs authorities is available at http://english.customs.gov.cn.

13 Deli Yang and Peter Clarke (2004), 'Review of the Current Intellectual Property System in China', *International Journal of Technology Transfer and Commercialisation*, **3**(1), 19.

14 Ann M. Weeks (2000), 'IPR Protection and Enforcement: A Guide', *China Business Review*, **27**(6), (November/December), 29.

## 2 THE ADMINISTRATIVE ENFORCEMENT SYSTEM IN ACTION: PURSUING A CLAIM FOR TRADEMARK INFRINGEMENT

As stated above, the relevant authority for bringing an action for trademark infringement is the Administration for Industry and Commerce (AIC). This authority is granted by Article 53 of the Trademark Law 2001,[15] which states that the administrative department for industry and commerce has the power to handle disputes involving the infringements of another person's exclusive right to the use of a registered trademark. Further, 'when the said department determines that the fact of infringement is established, it shall order the infringer to cease infringing upon that right immediately, and it shall confiscate and destroy the goods involved and the tools specially used to manufacture the said goods and counterfeit the representations of the registered trademark, and may also impose a fine'. It is clear that the AIC has broad powers to deal with trademark infringements, but how does a right holder initiate an action through the AIC?

### Initiating an Action

The first stage of the administrative enforcement process is the preliminary collecting of evidence with which to instigate an action. In any country, a right holder must seek evidence of possible infringement before resorting to legal action. This is true nowhere more than in China because of the lack of investigative resources and manpower in the administrative system, which in practice means that rights holders must begin an administrative action by collecting evidence of infringement.[16] Furthermore, this initial investigation is usually carried out by a private investigation agency, 'including locating factories, equipment, existing stock of counterfeit goods, and identifying when and where the counterfeit goods are being produced or sold'.[17] This preliminary collection of evidence is necessary to prompt the enforcement agencies to act.

---

15 Selected provisions of the Trademark Law 2001 taken from *Patent Law, Trademark Law, Copyright Law of the PRC, (Chinese–English edition)*, Beijing: Law Press, 2002.

16 Simon P. Cheetham (1999), 'Protection of Intellectual Property Rights in Luxury Goods', in Mark A. Cohen, A. Elizabeth Bang and Stephanie J. Mitchell (eds), *Chinese Intellectual Property Law and Practice*, London: Kluwer Law International, p. 386.

17 Daniel C.K. Chow (2002), *A Primer on Foreign Investment Enterprises and Protection of Intellectual Property in China*, The Hague, the Netherlands: Kluwer Law International, p. 228.

The importance of collecting good quality evidence has been stressed for several reasons: firstly, that administrative agencies are short-handed and lack the necessary resources to carry out long-term operations; secondly, that, if evidence is provided of an infringement, the authorities are usually willing to investigate any further infringements; and finally, that providing good quality evidence can encourage more active participation by the enforcement authorities.[18]

In terms of the evidence needed to commence an action, a right holder must provide copies of any relevant trademark certificates. In addition, 'in order to show that an infringement is occurring, the complainant should provide all evidence of the suspected infringement. If a private investigator has been engaged, the investigator's report, together with any samples obtained, should be submitted. In addition, the complainant should certify that any samples that have been obtained are counterfeit'.[19] The right holder should then file a formal complaint with the local AIC, comprising a short document outlining the complaint and the supporting evidence.

## Making Contact with the AIC

Under Article 51 of the Implementing Regulations of the Trademark Law 2002, in cases where the exclusive right to use a registered trademark is infringed, 'each and every person may lodge a complaint with or report the case to the authority of administration for industry and commerce'.[20] In practice, however, most actions are initiated by the brand owner. Once contact is made with the administrative authorities, a brand owner will then seek an enforcement action in the form of a raid or seizure:

> In many instances, the plaintiff or complainant can obtain authorization for a raid action within minutes of filing papers and other documentary support with administrative authorities. Where a brand owner has established a relationship with local authorities, often a phone call is sufficient to initiate a raid. The authorities then proceed immediately to the suspect premises accompanied by representatives of the trademark owner and in many instances seize all counterfeit products, machinery, and equipment found on site.[21]

---

[18] Mary L. Riley (2002), 'Enforcement of Intellectual Property Rights in China (And the Trouble You Face If You Don't)', ICCLR, Issue 12, p. 458.

[19] Henry J.H. Wheare (1998), 'Enforcement', in *IP Protection in China: Practical Strategies*, 2nd edn, Hong Kong: Asia Law & Practice, p. 36.

[20] Trademark Office of the SAIC, *Implementing Regulations of the Trademark Law* (2002), available at http://sbj.saic.gov.cn/english/show.asp?id=53&bm=flfg, accessed November 2004.

[21] Daniel C.K. Chow (2002), *A Primer on Foreign Investment*, p. 208.

Details of the exact administrative process of registering a complaint of trademark infringement are also given by the Trademark Office of the AIC:

> According to the relevant provisions of the Trademark Law, anyone can complain to the local administrations at or above the county level where the infringer resides or the infringement took place. The complaints shall be put in the written form usually, noting relevant information and evidence, such as the name, address of the infringer, the place where the infringement took place or was found, and relevant marks which are suspected to have infringed registered trademarks or stuff like photos and so on. Meanwhile, the interested party can also make a complaint on the phone. Where the trademark registrant complains to the administrative authority for industry and commerce, requesting protection of the exclusive right to use a registered trademark, the written form shall be handed in with effective certification. Once the administrative authority decides to deal with the case, it shall notify the complainant of the result.[22]

Therefore it is clear that the process of registering a complaint of trademark infringement with the AIC should be relatively straightforward, with either a written or oral complaint sufficient to commence an action in most cases.

## Powers of the AIC

Article 55 outlines the powers available to the administrative department for industry and commerce investigating a suspected trademark infringement:

- questioning the parties concerned to find out the facts regarding the infringement of another person's exclusive right to the use of a registered trademark;
- checking and reproducing the parties' contracts, invoices, account books, and other materials relating to the infringement;
- conducting an on-the-spot investigation of the premises where the suspected party carries out activities infringing upon another person's exclusive right to the use of a registered trademark; and
- inspecting articles involved in the infringement; sealing or seizing the articles that are proven to have been used for infringing upon another person's exclusive right to the use of a registered trademark.

Once the AIC has concluded the action, the parties will be provided with a copy of the decision. The AIC also has the power to impose a fine for infringing an

---

22 Trademark Office of the Administration of Industry and Commerce, 'Application for Trademark Registration', available at http://sbj.saic.gov.cn/english/registration/registration.asp, accessed November 2004.

exclusive right to use a registered trademark under article 53 of the Trademark Law. Under article 52 of the Implementing Regulations, this fine 'shall be not more than three times the volume of the illegal business. If it is impossible to calculate the volume of the illegal business, the amount of the fine shall be not more than 100 000 yuan'.

In addition to the power to impose a fine, the AIC has the further power under article 53 of the Trademark Law to 'mediate a settlement on the amount of compensation for the infringement of the exclusive right to the use of the trademark'. Despite these provisions, compensation is rarely paid to rights holders as the AIC can only mediate compensation negotiations, not impose a compensation order. In the few cases where compensation is paid, it is usually a derisory amount. The administrative department for industry and commerce should also transfer to the judicial authorities any case where a crime is suspected to have been committed under article 54 of the Trademark Law 2001.

### Fees Payable

Article 63 of the Trademark Law, supplemented by article 58 of the implementing regulations, states that 'applicants for trademark registration and persons having other trademark matters handled shall pay a fee'. The amount of fees to be paid is not a transparent issue, with official and unofficial fees varying widely from case to case. If a foreign trademark owner initiates a case through a trademark agency, as is common practice, 'these agencies charge a $1000–5000 fee per complaint. By contrast, local trademark owners are permitted to file complaints directly with the TADs [trademark and advertising divisions of the Trademark Office of the SAIC], although in practice they are also encouraged to make donations to the TADs as a condition of obtaining cooperation'.[23] Therefore the cost of pursuing an action through the administrative agencies can be more expensive than it originally appears.

Other estimates of case fees range from RMB1000 to RMB5000, but can be as high as RMB100 000, depending on the number of targets. It has even been reported that 'a common practice among local enforcement officials is to ask for payments, case fees, or gifts, such as computers and mobile phones, from trademark owners in exchange for conducting enforcement actions'.[24] Many foreign trademark owners are uncomfortable with paying

---

23 Joseph T. Simone (1999), 'China's IPR Enforcement Mechanisms', *China Business Review*, **26**(1), (January/February), 14.

24 Daniel C.K. Chow (2002), *A Primer on Foreign Investment*, p. 215.

these 'fees', as they can be seen as falling into a grey area between bribes and legitimate official fees. However, it is essential to maintain good relations with local officials to expedite future enforcement actions. Having outlined the main stages and features of pursuing an administrative enforcement claim through the AIC, this system of administrative enforcement will now be analysed.

## 3 EVALUATING THE STRENGTHS OF THE ADMINISTRATIVE ENFORCEMENT SYSTEM

On the basis of the outline of the administrative IP enforcement system given above, it is clear that the system itself is not uncomplicated. So why do so many IP rights holders still choose to pursue this avenue of enforcement?

### Cost-effectiveness

Clearly, the main reason why so many rights holders choose to pursue infringers through administrative means is a pragmatic one. Overall, there is a consensus that administrative enforcement 'has generally proven more effective than private enforcement'[25] and has even been described as 'in essence the only realistic means of IP rights enforcement'.[26] Administrative enforcement is seen as the most cost-effective option and as much quicker than pursuing the infringer through the courts. According to some estimates, action can be taken within a matter of two or three days and 'in a properly run case the action can be disposed of in two to three months in total'.[27]

Administrative enforcement has a number of further benefits for rights holders: 'the attraction to foreign firms is that the administrative agencies (especially the AIC) undertake intellectual property enforcement, bearing some or all of the costs of the enforcement. The enforcement carries the weight of government support and makes use of the police's ability to gain entry and investigate premises from which private parties can be excluded'.[28] As this quotation highlights, the investigative powers that the administrative agencies can exercise is seen as a major advantage of the administrative enforcement path.

---

25 Donald C. Clarke (1999), 'Private Enforcement', p. 34.

26 Tim Browning and Carol Wang (2004), 'Ten Years of Enforcement', p. 38.

27 Henry J.H. Wheare (1998), 'Enforcement', p. 30.

28 Mary L. Riley (2002), 'Enforcement of Intellectual Property Rights in China', p. 457.

## Authority of Administrative Action

The weight of authority that an administrative action may hold with the general public is also crucial, compared to a private action against a local business, which may be negatively perceived if initiated by a foreign rights holder. Intellectual property protection is often seen as primarily benefiting foreign rights holders, which acts as a disincentive for China to enforce intellectual property rights. As China is seen as having little intellectual property of its own, intellectual property protection 'only fills the coffers of foreign IPR holders with Chinese funds'.[29] This unfounded perception that intellectual property protection only benefits foreigners creates resentment and thus foreign rights holders may choose to use administrative agencies as a veil to prevent disquiet over IP enforcement causing disruption to the local economy.

## Administrative Enforcement as Part of Wider IP Strategy

Some rights holders choose administrative enforcement as part of a wider strategy of IP protection 'because they are required to issue written penalty decisions and provide copies to complainants'.[30] These administrative decisions can then be useful in any subsequent criminal prosecutions of repeat offenders although, in practice, the transfer of evidence to the civil system is not always straightforward.[31]

## Social and Cultural Factors

There are other reasons why administrative enforcement is still preferred in the majority of infringement cases. Social and cultural factors have been highlighted as influential in the choice of public enforcement over private enforcement mechanisms. Among the social and cultural factors that have been proposed, the continuing influence of Confucianism, combined with socialism, is seen as the most influential. Confucianism is seen as encouraging compiling rather than composing and emphasizing collective rights over individual rights.[32] This lack

---

[29] Gregory S. Feder (1996), 'Enforcement of Intellectual Property Rights in China: You Can Lead a Horse to Water But You Can't Make It Drink', *Virginia Journal of International Law*, **37**(1), 253.

[30] Joseph T. Simone (1999), 'China's IPR Enforcement Mechanisms', p. 14.

[31] Daniel C.K. Chow (2002), *A Primer on Foreign Investment Enterprises*, p. 207.

[32] Peter K. Yu (2002), 'The Second Coming of Intellectual Property Rights in China', *Occasional Papers in Intellectual Property from Benjamin N. Cardozo School of Law, Yeshiva University*, No. 11, New York: Benjamin N. Cardozo School of Law, Yeshiva University, pp. 17–18.

of emphasis on individual rights may also be attributed to the impact of the socialist economic system which is based on the notion that property belongs to the state, rather than the individual. This emphasis on the collective over the individual is evident in the continuing preference for public enforcement mechanisms in the intellectual property system. Administrative authorities such as the AIC exist to protect the collective interest of the public, not to be misled by counterfeit products, rather than to protect the individual proprietary rights of an IP holder.

### Role of Public Enforcement in the Chinese Legal System

The emphasis on public enforcement mechanisms such as administrative enforcement can also be attributed to the role of law in China generally. Despite committing itself to establishing a rule of law state in a constitutional amendment in 1999, there is still evidence to suggest that China follows a rule *by* law, rather than rule *of* law approach. 'The line between law and policy is often said to be blurred', as the law is primarily seen as a mechanism for implementing policy.[33] This instrumentalist model of law leads to the prominence of administrative enforcement in intellectual property protection. The government plays a central role in IP enforcement, rather than empowering individual rights holders to enforce their own rights through the judicial system.

### Drawbacks of the Administrative Enforcement System

#### Costs

Despite the advantages of pursuing infringers through administrative agencies, there are also numerous drawbacks identified by rights holders. Although administrative enforcement is identified as a cost-effective means of protecting IP in China, this cost-effectiveness has been brought into doubt.[34] Indeed, considering the high unofficial fees often associated with compelling the local AIC's involvement, relying solely on administrative enforcement can be a frustrating and expensive method of protecting IP. Payments often include a pre-raid and post-raid meal for enforcement authorities, as well as payments to private investigation agencies and payment for legal advice; thus 'total costs for enforcement programs in China today range from several hundred thousand to several million dollars per year'.[35]

---

33 Donald C. Clarke (1999), 'Private Enforcement', p. 32.

34 Mary L. Riley (2002), 'Enforcement of Intellectual Property Rights in China', p. 459.

35 Daniel C.K. Chow (2002), *A Primer on Foreign Investment*, p. 236.

Another contributory factor to the cost of pursuing enforcement actions is the burden on the right holder to collect the preliminary evidence of infringement at their own expense before commencing an action. However, once the complaint has been made to the AIC, control over the action is removed from the IP owner because the AIC does not exist to serve the interests of IP rights holders. On the contrary, the AIC focuses on protecting public interests. Once a right holder formally complains to the administrative authorities, the action is then solely controlled by government authorities. In contrast, if an infringer is pursued through the courts, the right holder retains greater control over the process.

The burden of paying expenses to the enforcement authorities can be explained by the lack of resources allocated centrally for the cost of operating these authorities. Consequently, the enforcement authorities rely on fines and the profits from auctions of infringing goods for their revenue. Thus 'because the enforcing agencies rely heavily on fines for their operating expenses, they have a vested interest in seeing violations continue'.[36]

**Delays and local protectionism**

A further shortcoming of the administrative enforcement system in China is delay in taking action once a complaint has been received. The administrative authorities have a degree of flexibility in choosing which cases to pursue and how actively they pursue these cases. Further, the AIC also has the flexibility to delay the process of enforcement by hours, days or even weeks, during which time the infringer may simply disappear. These delays may be explained by the impact of local protectionism. Local protectionism is consistently highlighted as 'probably the single most significant problem in enforcement against counterfeiting',[37] and is caused by the role of local government in the economy. For example, AICs establish and regulate the wholesale distribution centres and markets and collect around 1 million RMB monthly from these markets. However, these markets are well-known for their trade in counterfeit goods. Therefore the AIC has conflicting roles as both entrepreneur and enforcer.

This local protectionism can affect the administrative enforcement process in several ways. Firstly, as stated above, the authorities have the flexibility to choose which cases to pursue and how quickly to conduct a raid. Thus the AIC can choose to protect local interests by not pursuing complaints at all, or by delaying a raid until the infringing goods have been removed from the site. Another example of local protectionism is that 'some local officials have been

---

36 Donald C. Clarke (1999), 'Private Enforcement', p. 34.
37 Daniel C.K. Chow (2002), *A Primer on Foreign Investment*, p. 212.

known to confiscate goods, machinery and equipment only to return these materials to counterfeiters once enforcement actions have been concluded'.[38] A further effect of local protectionism can be an extreme reluctance on the part of the AIC to impose a high fine or compensation award on infringers.[39]

**Lack of transparency**

A further criticism of the administrative enforcement system is the lack of transparency. This lack of transparency is witnessed throughout the Chinese legal system as a whole, but it is exacerbated in the administrative system by the sheer number of agencies that compete in this area. 'Though China has several government bodies and legal procedures to protect intellectual property rights, no single agency exercises day-to-day supervision and management of the various enforcement and policymaking bureaucracies. Consequently, relations among the various government departments involved in intellectual property matters at the local and national level are often characterized by bureaucratic competition and lack of communication and coordination'.[40] These numerous agencies include the Trademark Office of the SAIC which is responsible for trademarks, the National Copyright Administration which oversees copyright affairs and the State Intellectual Property Office, which, despite its all-encompassing name, is primarily concerned with patent administration. Coordinating these agencies according to an overall comprehensive enforcement strategy has proved almost impossible.[41]

**Bureaucratic tensions**

The effect of these overlapping jurisdictions is not only a lack of transparency in the system, it is also means that 'though these offices have the authority to refer matters to the People's Court, their political and bureaucratic interests tend to discourage them from doing so'.[42] This bureaucratic nightmare has been attributed to the pre-reform socialist economy which was structured in vertical sectors. Each administrative entity would have full control over its particular sector. However, as intellectual property cuts across various sectors,

---

38 Daniel C.K. Chow (2002), *A Primer on Foreign Investment*, p. 215.

39 Thomas Lagerqvist and Mary L. Riley (1997), 'How to Protect Intellectual Property Rights in China', in Mary L. Riley et al. (eds), *Protecting Intellectual Property Rights in China*, Hong Kong: Sweet & Maxwell Asia, p. 31.

40 Joseph T. Simone (1999), 'China's IPR Enforcement Mechanisms', p. 14.

41 Andy Y. Sun (2001), 'Reforming the Protection of Intellectual Property: The Case of China and Taiwan in Light of WTO Accession', *Maryland Series in Contemporary Asian Studies*, **4**, p. 25.

42 Pitman B. Potter and Michel Oksenberg (1999), 'A Patchwork of IPR Protections', *China Business Review*, **26**(1), (January/February), p. 9.

numerous agencies claim jurisdiction.[43] Therefore widespread structural reform of the bureaucratic institutions of the IP enforcement system may be necessary to ensure more coordinated and efficient administrative enforcement.

**Central-local relations**

In addition to the number of agencies that are formally involved in the administrative enforcement of IP in China, there may also be local government offices dealing with IP enforcement locally. For example, Shanghai 'established the Shanghai Foreign Invested Enterprises Anti-counterfeit Work Liaison Office to help foreign companies interact with PRC government organs'.[44] This shows the inconsistency between relatively reliable enforcement in the major cities and the non-enforcement of IP rights which still prevails elsewhere in China. This discrepancy is also due to the perceived gap between central and provincial or local governments. The central government may make commitments to comply with the international IP regime, but it is doubtful whether this same level of commitment will be made by local or provincial governments with different interests to consider. As administrative enforcement is still very much tied to these local interests, IP enforcement may not consistently meet international expectations.

**Inconsistent enforcement**

A further element to consider when analysing the administrative enforcement system is the inconsistency of law enforcement in China generally. Enforcement actions are often praised as 'waves of coordinated actions, each targeted on specific types of infringement activities'.[45] Although this follows a typically Chinese model of enforcement in 'crackdowns', it is at odds with the basic rule of law concept, and indeed IP owner expectation, that laws should be enforced consistently. The result of this is that rights holders seeking to protect their IP through the administrative enforcement mechanism may find that the authorities are much more willing to take action at certain times than at others.

Thus there are a range of weaknesses in the administrative enforcement system that inhibit effective enforcement of IP rights in China. China's entry to the World Trade Organization in December 2001 had a major impact on the legislative framework and it was predicted that WTO entry would also benefit the operation of the administrative enforcement system. The next section will

---

43 Daniel C.K. Chow (2000), 'Counterfeiting in the People's Republic of China', *Washington University Law Quarterly*, **78**(1), (Spring), 22.

44 Ann M. Weeks (2000), 'IPR Protection and Enforcement', p. 29.

45 Duan Ruichun (1998–9), 'China's Intellectual Property Protection Towards the 21st Century', p. 217.

examine the tangible impact of WTO entry and TRIPS compliance on the administrative enforcement system, to see if these predicted improvements have actually occurred.

# 4 THE IMPACT OF WTO ENTRY ON THE ADMINISTRATIVE ENFORCEMENT SYSTEM

## 4.1 The Impact of TRIPS Compliance on the IP System

The issue of intellectual property protection in China was a key issue in China's WTO accession negotiations. The importance of IP protection can be witnessed in the final Working Party Report on China's WTO accession, which devoted 55 paragraphs out of a total of 343 to China's commitments under the TRIPS regime.[46] Furthermore, China's capacity to fully implement its TRIPS commitments was 'one of the most frequently aired concerns' prior to entry in December 2001.[47] These concerns arose from the recognition that 'government commitment and a sound legal framework would not suffice to ensure enforcement, as IPRs involve millions of enterprises and hundreds of millions of individuals'.[48]

It is clear that the commitments that China has made to comply with the TRIPS Agreement have led to sweeping legislative reform of the intellectual property system, including major reforms of the Patent Law in August 2000 and the Copyright Law and Trademark Law in October 2001, as well as a range of modifications and amendments to the implementing regulations. However, it is not so easy to assess the impact of TRIPS on the enforcement system in general and the administrative enforcement process specifically.

The TRIPS Agreement is often said to add teeth to the previous international intellectual property conventions, such as the Paris Convention on Industrial Property and the Berne Convention for the Protection of Literary and Artistic Works, which lacked provisions on enforcement standards.[49] Thus

---

46 As noted by Long Yongtu (2003), 'Implications of China's Entry into the WTO in the Field of Intellectual Property Rights', in Carlos A. Magarinos, Long Yongtu and Francisco Sercovich (eds), *China in the WTO: The Birth of a New Catching-Up Strategy*, New York: Palgrave Macmillan, p. 165.

47 Angela Gregory (2001), 'Chinese Trademark Law and the TRIPS Agreement – Confucius Meets the WTO', in Deborah Cass (ed.), *China and the World Trading System: Entering the New Millennium*, Cambridge: Cambridge University Press, p. 321.

48 Long Yongtu, 'Implications of China's Entry', p. 169.

49 Andy Y. Sun (2001), 'Reforming the Protection of Intellectual Property', p. 26.

countries could comply with their previous commitments by merely passing a law, even if the law was not implemented. Consequently, 'one of the key initiatives of the TRIPS Agreement was to resolve the enforcement issues left by the existing IP protection regime'.[50]

The influence of the TRIPS Agreement on the framework of intellectual property protection in China predates WTO accession by several years. Despite not being a full member, China did participate in the Uruguay Round of negotiations as an observer and has used the TRIPS Agreement as a model law to improve the IP legislation throughout the 1990s.[51]

Besides the role of TRIPS as a model for China's legislative improvements of the IP protection system, TRIPS implementation has also raised the prospect of using the formal dispute settlement proceedings provided by the WTO to make 'an objective determination on the efficacy of enforcement measures'.[52] This possibility has further increased the emphasis on enforcement of substantive rights that was already being stressed by foreign rights holders and trade partners alike.

## 4.2 Specific Changes in the Administrative Enforcement System

### Judicial review

Specific changes that TRIPS has initiated in the IP enforcement system in China will now be examined more closely. One of the main changes that the TRIPS regime has brought to the administrative system specifically is the addition of the possibility of judicial review of final administrative decisions. Under TRIPS article 41(4), 'parties to a proceeding shall have an opportunity for review by a judicial authority of final administrative decisions'. Previously, no independent review was available for appellants from administrative decisions. The amendments of the specific intellectual property laws undertaken in 2000 and 2001 provide for judicial review of administrative decisions under articles 33, 49 and 50 of the Trademark Law; articles 41 and 55 of the Patent Law and article 55 of the Copyright Law. China is thus now in compliance with article 41(4). This has had a major impact on the administrative enforcement system overall; as all final administrative decisions are now subject to external scrutiny, authorities are less likely to resort to arbitrary decision-making.

---

50 Angela Gregory (2003), 'Chinese Trademark Law', p. 338.

51 Deli Yang (2003), 'The Development of Intellectual Property in China', *World Patent Information,* **25**(2), (2003), p. 139.

52 Antony S. Taubman (2003), 'TRIPS Goes East: Chinese Interests and International Trade in Intellectual Property', in Deborah Cass (ed.), *China and the World Trading System: Entering the New Millennium*, Cambridge: Cambridge University Press, p. 347.

### National treatment

Another key principle of the TRIPS Agreement is the principle of national treatment under article 3, 'that each member shall accord to the nationals of other members treatment no less favourable than that it accords to its own nationals with regard to the protection of intellectual property'. Although the national treatment principle does not specifically refer to the enforcement process, it is still relevant in this area. For example, article 18 of the revised Trademark Law 2001 forces foreign enterprises or individuals applying for registration of a trademark or handling other trademark matters to use a state-approved trademark agent. This is arguably in breach of the national treatment principle as domestic applicants can apply directly to the Trademark Office of the SAIC. AICs previously would only accept infringement actions from foreign rights holders through a trademark agent. Although these restrictions have now been relaxed under the influence of the TRIPS Agreement, in practice, many foreign rights holders still use the services of an agent to navigate the administrative enforcement process, which inflates the cost of bringing an enforcement action.

### Level of fines

A further area in which TRIPS implementation has had an impact is the level of fines imposed by the administrative authorities. Under article 41(1) of TRIPS, there is a general obligation that remedies should 'constitute a deterrent to further infringements'. However, fines do not appear to have increased significantly since WTO entry, as shown in Table 4.2 below. Despite a significant increase in the average fine in 2003, from 5761RMB to 7414RMB, this dropped back in 2004 to 5499RMB. It is also notable that the total number of infringement cases handled by the Trademark Office of the SAIC annually has risen significantly. This rise confirms the continuing importance of administrative enforcement in the post-WTO entry IP enforcement system.

*Table 4.2 Fines imposed by the Trademark Office of the SAIC for trademark infringements and counterfeiting (2002–4)*

| Year | Total number of cases | Total amount of fines (RMB) | Average fine (RMB) |
|---|---|---|---|
| 2002 | 23 539 | 135 612 506 | 5 761 |
| 2003 | 26 488 | 196 394 094 | 7 414 |
| 2004 | 40 171 | 220 224 500 | 5 499 |

*Source*: compiled from statistics available on the SAIC website, http://sbj.saic.gov.cn/english/tjxx/tjxx.asp.

Under the Patent Law, article 58, the administrative authorities can confiscate the illegal earnings and impose a fine of not more than three times his illegal earnings or not more than RMB50 000. The level of fines for both trademark and copyright infringement is governed by implementing regulations. Article 42 of the Implementing Regulations of the Trademark Law 2001 states that the fine imposed shall be not more than 20 per cent of the illegal business or not more than twice the profit illegally earned. Article 36 of the Implementing Regulations of the Copyright Law 2001 provides the administrative authority with the power to impose a fine not exceeding three times the amount of the illegal business gains, or a maximum of RMB100 000. Despite these generous limits for levels of fines imposed for IP infringements, there is still evidence to suggest that administrative authorities are reluctant to impose high fines and the fines imposed do not constitute an effective deterrent in line with the TRIPS provision.

**Availability of injunctions**

Under article 44 of the TRIPS Agreement, injunctions should be available 'to order a party to desist from an infringement'. Prior to WTO entry, China's intellectual property enforcement system was often criticized for non-compliance with this provision; 'for many years a glaring omission in the IP enforcement system in China was the lack of preliminary injunctions'.[53] However, the main intellectual property laws have now been amended to provide authorities with the power to issue injunctions. In China, preliminary injunctions were first permitted under the Patent Law 2000, article 61, and subsequently by the amended Trademark Law 2001, article 57, and the Copyright Law 2001, article 49.

Although these powers are granted to the People's Courts, the availability of preliminary injunctions will still have a significant effect on the administrative enforcement system in China. As these powers are still quite new, there remains some doubt about how willing the courts will be to issue preliminary injunctions. It has been suggested that there are still some teething problems in the new preliminary procedures and that the courts have so far taken a tough stance on the issuing of these orders. However, as these problems are resolved and the courts begin to become accustomed to issuing injunctions, pre-trial injunctions could offer a useful alternative to administrative actions.[54] Thus the introduction of these orders is overwhelmingly seen as a positive step for the IP enforcement system in China: 'The Supreme People's Court clarification of

---

53 Tim Browning and Carol Wang (2004), 'Ten Years of Enforcement', p. 39.

54 Matthew Murphy (2003), 'Supreme People's Court Widens Litigation Options', *Managing Intellectual Property*, November, p. 1.

these procedures should lead to civil IP cases becoming more common, either as the primary means of enforcement of rights or as an adjunct to administrative enforcement.'[55]

Consequently, the effect of the availability of pre-trial injunctions could be the increased use of civil enforcement and the rejection of administrative enforcement as the primary means of enforcing IP rights in China. It is too soon to see this effect, but, long-term, it is promising for rights holders to have more enforcement options to consider.

**Criminal prosecutions**

Article 61 of the TRIPS Agreement provides that criminal procedures should 'be applied at least in cases of wilful trademark counterfeiting or copyright piracy on a commercial scale'. It is undeniable that criminal penalties are available under the Criminal Law 1997 for *serious* trademark counterfeiting (article 213) or copyright piracy (article 217). However, the relationship between 'serious' in China's Criminal Law and 'wilful' in TRIPS is not clear. Despite a Supreme People's Court interpretation issued in December 2004, which lowered the thresholds for criminal liability, it is not certain that all cases of 'wilful' infringement would be classed as 'serious'. The administrative authorities are supposed to transfer serious infringement cases to be considered for criminal liability under article 54 of the Trademark Law 2001 and article 47 of the Copyright Law 2001, but, in practice, such a transfer is rarely made.

From Table 4.3, it is evident that the TRIPS Agreement has had a minimal impact on the number of cases transferred to judicial authorities in the first three years following WTO accession in December 2001. Despite an increase in the overall number of cases transferred, the proportion of cases transferred has not grown and has remained constant at around one in 400 cases. However, the revised thresholds for criminal liability amended in late 2004 may have an impact on the transfer of cases from administrative to judicial authorities.

For example, the much-publicised *Zippo* counterfeit case in Wenzhou was concluded after the new interpretation was issued and the infringer sentenced to one and a half years' imprisonment.[56] Under the old limits, the infringer would not have been liable for criminal prosecution as the threshold had not been reached. However, the bureaucratic rivalries between the administrative and judicial agencies still exist and may still discourage the prompt transfer of

---

55 Sara Holder, 'Preliminary Injunctions for Intellectual Property Infringements in the PRC', *Rouse & Co. International Newsletter*, 13/03/02, available online at http://www.iprights.com/publications/articles/article.asp?articleID=163.

56 Reported in the China Daily, 'In Brief', 03/06/06, p. 9.

*Table 4.3 Number of cases transferred from the Trademark Office of the SAIC to judicial organs for criminal liability (2002–4)*

| Year | Number of cases transferred to judicial authorities | Total number of cases |
|---|---|---|
| 2002 | 59 | 23 539 |
| 2003 | 45 | 26 488 |
| 2004 | 96 | 40 171 |

*Source*: compiled from statistics available on the Trademark Office website at http://sbj.saic.gov.cn/tjxx/TJTableQGCCSBQQ2004.asp.

cases for criminal prosecution. As the administrative agencies rely directly on revenue from confiscated goods to operate, they are extremely reluctant to transfer cases for criminal prosecution as they would lose the revenue associated with the case. [57]

## CONCLUSION

It is clear that, despite significant changes in the intellectual property enforcement system in China as a result of WTO accession, enforcement of IP rights through administrative means still dominates. Not only is administrative enforcement chosen by rights holders for its cost-effectiveness, availability and quick resolution, it is also the preferred choice of the state. This official preference for public enforcement mechanisms has been attributed to social and cultural factors such as Confucianism and socialism, leading to a lack of emphasis on individual rights, as well as the role of the legal system in the Chinese economy generally as a tool for policy implementation.

However, despite the key role of administrative enforcement within the IP framework, there are still various criticisms levelled at the administrative agencies. The most significant criticism is that local protectionism dominates the enforcement of IP at the local level, leading to delays in enforcement and the imposition of insignificant fines. A further observation of the administrative enforcement system is the numerous agencies that compete for dominance within the IP enforcement framework. These bureaucratic rivalries make the implementation of any comprehensive IP strategy virtually impossible, a task

---

57 Daniel C.K. Chow (2002), *A Primer on Foreign Investment Enterprises*, p. 217.

already complicated by the perceived gap in authority between central and local governments.

It is undeniable that China's WTO entry and subsequent attempts to comply with the TRIPS Agreement have had a significant effect on the protection of IP in China. The effect of TRIPS has been felt most strongly in the legislative arena, but it has also had a significant effect on the enforcement system. The main change to the administrative enforcement system has been the introduction of judicial review of final administrative decisions, which was previously unavailable. Other changes include the removal of barriers to national treatment within the administrative enforcement system, increases in the maximum fines available for IP infringements, the availability of preliminary injunctions and the lowering of thresholds for criminal liability. It is believed that these changes will have a considerable long-term effect on the IP enforcement system in China, but it is perhaps too soon to see their full impact.

It is clear that administrative enforcement remains an IP holder's main choice for enforcement, but it is also undeniable that the system is beginning to change. With judges gaining more experience of IP disputes and beginning to issue preliminary injunctions more regularly, the civil system will begin to appeal more to rights holders. However, it is unlikely that administrative enforcement will ever be abandoned; it is more likely that it will continue to play an important role in IP enforcement in China, as a fast and cost-effective method to curb infringements as part of a wider strategy of IP protection.

# 5. Problems and new developments in the enforcement of intellectual property rights in China

**Jingzhou Tao** *

## INTRODUCTION

Intellectual property rights ('IPR') protection in China has long been a sore point in its otherwise remarkable contribution to international trade and business. Enforcement is notoriously weak, and the losses to foreign companies resulting from Chinese violation cases continue to escalate. The US Government Accountability Office ('GAO') Report of October 2004,[1] which laments the weaknesses in China's enforcement of intellectual property rights, concludes that such deficiencies may have an even greater impact on trade than delays in the issuance of regulations. The Out-of-Cycle Review Results,[2] issued by the United States Trade Representative in April 2005, points out that China's inadequate intellectual property rights enforcement is leading to infringement levels at 90 per cent or more for virtually every form of intellectual property.

China itself acknowledges its problems with intellectual property rights enforcement. According to the State Administration of Industry and Commerce's ('State AIC') official statistics,[3] there were 51 851 cases of trademark-related violation in 2004, of which 40 171 were trademark infringement and counterfeiting cases. This accounts for 77.47 per cent of all trademark-related violations, up from 70.66 per cent in 2003. Intellectual property dispute cases have also dramatically increased in recent years; figures for 2004 show that the PRC courts handled 8332 cases of IP infringement that year, an

* DLA Piper Rudnick Gray Cary UK LLP.

1 To view the full text of the report, please visit www.gao.gov/cgi-bin/getrpt?GAO-05-53.

2 To view full text of the report, please visit www.ustr.gov/assets/Document_Library/Reports_Publications.

3 To view the statistics, please visit http://sbj.saic.gov.cn/tjxx/tjxx.asp.

increase of 21.1 per cent from 2003. Recent years have also witnessed several well-publicized disputes over alleged intellectual property rights infringement involving multinational companies such as Adidas, Nike, Microsoft and Kodak.

The impact of intellectual property rights infringement on businesses and society are enormous. According to a March 2004 report by the US Trademark and Patent Office, 90 per cent of business software in China is pirated, equalling USD1.5 billion in losses to software firms.[4] The Out-of-Cycle Review Results show that increased counterfeiting in pharmaceuticals has cost foreign pharmaceutical companies 10 to 15 per cent in annual revenue in China. Chinese businesses are also losing billions of RMB annually as a result of intellectual property violations. In addition to the tremendous loss of revenue to legitimate businesses, intellectual property rights infringement can also endanger human health and safety, as counterfeit products rarely meet statutory quality standards.

So what can be pinpointed in China's intellectual property rights enforcement system as the main problem areas? We consider these in turn below.

## POOR ADMINISTRATIVE ENFORCEMENT

### Weak Enforcement Teams and Poor Coordination

One of the main reasons for rampant piracy in China is, of course, the weakness of copyright enforcement organs. The enforcement of copyright and patents in particular is problematic because of the inadequacies in the organizational structure of the copyright and patent administrations, namely, the National Copyright Administration ('NCA'), the State Intellectual Property Office ('SIPO') and other provincial and municipal administrations.

At the same time, an equally serious issue is the cross-fire of multiple governmental agencies that claim overlapping responsibilities over intellectual property rights enforcement. For example, the AICs and the departments in charge of the supervision of product quality ('TSBs') both have the authority to handle trademark infringement and counterfeiting cases involving the manufacture and distribution of goods of inferior quality. Administrative enforcement authorities and judicial investigative organs, such as the Public Security Bureaus ('PSBs'), also have similar responsibilities in intellectual property cases suspected of criminal actions. Rather than ensuring that cases

4 To view the full text of the report, please visit http://www.uspto.gov/web/offices/com/speeches/2004mar23.htm.

are dealt with expediently, this political situation has led to poor cooperation and coordination among the various governmental agencies.

China has been making efforts to improve these conditions in recent years by issuing numerous rules and regulations to encourage increased coordination and cooperation among the various intellectual property rights enforcement authorities. For instance, on 13 January 2006, the State AIC promulgated a circular prescribing specific operational rules for the strengthening of cooperation and coordination between PSBs and AICs.[5] However, this is obviously just one step on the long road towards improving the enforcement system in China.

## Local Protectionism

Local protectionism constitutes the greatest barrier to intellectual property rights protection in the PRC. Part of the problem stems from certain misconceptions held by local officials that intellectual property infringement, including counterfeiting, is in fact beneficial to the local economy because it provides employment for otherwise unemployable workers. Some even believe that the imitation and counterfeiting of foreign brands is justifiable in the context of the protection of local industries from international competition.

This particular problem is difficult for the central government to address because of the current structure of the PRC government. Local officials prioritize the protection of local needs before that of national needs, and thus are less inclined to pursue vigorously strict enforcement measures that they perceive as harmful to local economic interests. They therefore assume a negative and uncooperative attitude toward complaints by rights holders against alleged intellectual property infringements, refusing to take legal action for various reasons, delaying the arrangement of site raids and neglecting to release official administrative penalty decisions in a timely manner. In areas where local protectionism is especially fierce, law enforcement officials will even impede the administrative enforcement of intellectual property rights by leaking insider information to infringers in advance. They can also adversely affect follow-up procedures in an intellectual property infringement case after enforcement actions have been initiated by imposing only minimal penalties on infringers. In some instances, local officials have been known to return confiscated goods to the infringers.

[5] *Circular Concerning the Distribution of the Provisional Rules on the Strengthening of Transfer and Coordination in the Punishment of Illegal Activities Relating to Trademark Exclusive Rights*, issued by the Ministry of Public Security and State AIC on 13 January 2006 and made effective as of the same date.

Such practices are at odds with China's obligations towards the WTO Agreement on Trade-Related Aspects of Intellectual Property Rights ('TRIPS Agreement'). Article 41(1) of the TRIPS Agreement requires members to ensure that effective enforcement procedures are available in order to remedy the infringement of intellectual property rights, and also stipulates that these procedures shall be 'fair and equitable' and 'not unnecessarily complicated or costly'. Considering the degree of discretion local authorities have in intellectual property rights enforcement, China does not seem to be holding up its end of the bargain.

## Non-deterrent Administrative Penalty

According to the Trademark Law, the maximum fine that an AIC may impose on trademark infringers is either three times the illegal profit gained or, where the illegal profit cannot be calculated, RMB100 000 (approximately USD12 000). The Copyright Law sets forth similar provisions. The PRC Patent Law separately stipulates that the maximum fine that patent authorities may impose on patent infringers who pass off others' patents as theirs is RMB50 000 (or USD6 000).

Although these penalty amounts are significantly higher than those in previous PRC intellectual property laws, they are still so mild that they do not constitute any real economic disincentive to intellectual property infringement. Since the law does not set minimum limits for fines, and because local enforcement officials have great discretion in determining the amount to be fined, the maximum penalty is very rarely imposed and imprisonment is almost unheard of. Lack of clear guidelines or rules with regard to the way fines should be calculated is also one reason why such mild penalties are imposed on infringers. Unfortunately, intellectual property owners have little recourse against these decisions.

Articles 41 and 61 of the TRIPS Agreement stipulate that remedies should constitute a 'deterrent to further infringement' and 'include imprisonment and/or monetary fines sufficient to provide a deterrent'. Clearly, this is not yet the case in China.

## The Cost of Enforcement

In China, intellectual property right owners are required to bear almost all of the costs for administrative enforcement actions. While the state provides various enforcement authorities with financial support for their law enforcement activities, intellectual property right owners still incur the costs associated with the following: (i) initiating a private investigation into infringement/infringers; (ii) hiring a domestic agent (which is required by Chinese law for foreign intellectual property rights owners) to handle an infringement case on the right owner's behalf; (iii) 'action fees'/'rewards' paid to the enforcement authorities or officials to conduct raids; and (iv) expenses incurred during the course of the transportation, storage and disposal of the seized infringing or counterfeit goods.

Furthermore, in order for Customs to detain goods suspected of infringement, the intellectual property right owners must pay for all the costs related to the storage and disposal of the goods suspected of infringement, in addition to paying Customs a deposit equal to the value of the detained export or import goods.

Possibly owing to poor administrative enforcement and the costs involved for intellectual property rights owners, only 3 per cent of the trademark cases handled in 2004 were initiated by the trademark owners themselves.

## INEFFICIENT CIVIL PROCEEDINGS

### Heavy Burden of Proof

With respect to the civil enforcement of intellectual property rights, the burden of proof in the adjudication process rests heavily on the shoulders of the intellectual property rights holders. They not only must collect evidence on the existence of the alleged IP infringement, but must also submit powerful and conclusive proof in support of their claim for compensation.

However, under the current PRC legal regime, the legal status of private investigation firms and their authority to conduct private investigation are still unclear. The courts have at times been known to challenge evidence obtained via private investigation. Intellectual property infringers and counterfeiters also grow ever more evasive, making it increasingly difficult for intellectual property rights holders to find valuable evidence and proof of the existence of intellectual property infringements. This discourages many intellectual property rights holders from seeking judicial enforcement of their intellectual property rights in the PRC.

This excessive burden of proof imposed on the plaintiff certainly does not conform to the spirit of the TRIPS agreement. Article 43 provides that the plaintiff shall present 'reasonably available evidence sufficient to support its claims' and that the court shall rely on this substantiated claim to 'order this evidence to be produced by the opposing party'. This means that, according to article 43, the plaintiff shall not be required to conduct the infringement investigation, and need only bring reasonable evidence that the infringement took place. The responsibility of conducting a thorough investigation of the infringement should be borne by the courts, and the responsibility of producing convincing evidence by the defendant.

## Insufficient Compensation

In handling intellectual property infringement cases, the courts normally order infringers to compensate the intellectual property rights holders for the actual and provable losses suffered as a direct result of the infringement, without ordering punitive damages, in addition to 'reasonable costs' for the intellectual property rights holders' investigation into the relevant infringers' infringement actions. In practice, the amount of compensation decided upon by the courts rarely covers the actual losses of those infringed upon because it is difficult for them to produce clear evidence of the losses sustained and the illegal income derived from the infringement by the infringer. The courts also lack the advanced scientific methods necessary to calculate damages and losses. In addition, the method for determining 'reasonable costs' has yet to be clarified, and so the 'statutory compensation' system has been applied to many cases since the PRC intellectual property laws were amended. However, maximum 'statutory compensation' is RMB500 000 (or around USD60 000), a rather low amount.

Article 45(1) of the TRIPS Agreement provides that, where the infringer knowingly engaged in the infringing activity, courts shall have the authority to 'order infringers to pay the rights holder damages *adequate to compensate for the injury* the rights holder has suffered because of an infringement'. The same article also provides that courts shall have the authority to order the payment of expenses incurred by the rights holder, including 'appropriate' attorney fees.

## Time-consuming Trial Process

Unlike domestic cases, the PRC Civil Procedure Law provides no time limits on the trial period for foreign-related cases. Moreover, in the short history of the PRC courts, intellectual property cases have mainly been brought to the attention of the courts in large cities such as Beijing, Shanghai and Guangzhou. Thus judges in small cities lack the expertise necessary to handle IPR infringement cases, and often require assistance from intellectual property experts. An intellectual property-related trial usually takes over a year to complete and, in difficult and complex patent cases, litigation may last two to four years, or longer.

Article 41(2) of the TRIPS Agreement provides that the procedures concerning the enforcement of intellectual property rights shall not be delayed unnecessarily. The practice in China has yet to meet this standard.

## WEAK CRIMINAL PROTECTION

### Few Infringers Receive Criminal Punishment

Although criminal enforcement of intellectual property rights is possible in China, in practice very few intellectual property infringers receive criminal sanctions. The State AIC's statistics for 2004 show that, of a total of 40 171 trademark infringement and counterfeiting cases, only 92 cases involving 82 persons were transferred to the judicial organ for review for criminal liability.

There are two reasons why so few cases are transferred to judicial authorities for assessment of criminal liabilities: (i) the administrative enforcement authorities prefer to impose fines when handling any type of intellectual property infringement case, as they are able to retain the funds. If they transfer intellectual property cases to a PSB for a review for criminal liability, the fines they receive will also have to be transferred; and (ii) PSBs do not like to accept intellectual property cases because they deal with a heavy criminal caseload of homicides, theft and robberies. They also lack experience of handling intellectual property cases and thus have little interest in them.

### Poor Coordination Between Administrative Authorities and Judicial Organs

'Double-track' protection is one of the most significant characteristics of intellectual property rights protection in China. This refers to the dual protection of administrative instruments and judicial measures, whereby intellectual property rights owners may request either the competent administrative authorities or the judicial organs to handle intellectual property rights infringement cases, or even request both authorities to handle certain cases successively in order to protect their intellectual property rights.

Unfortunately, this system has been plagued by a lack of cooperation between governmental authorities. Although the central government has issued regulations in the past few years requiring the various administrative enforcement authorities to comply strictly with legal provisions and transfer all criminal cases to the PSB or the people's prosecutors, the situation has remained largely unchanged. In 2006, in order to solve this problem, the Supreme People's Procuratorate, the National Office of the Leading Panel on Perfecting and Regulating Marketing Economy Order, the Ministry of Public Security and the Ministry of Supervision and Examination jointly issued the *Opinions Concerning the Timely Transfer of Cases of Criminal Offensive Suspicion in the Course of Administrative Enforcement*, which specifies the working norms for the transfer of cases suspected of a criminal offence.

However, it would take a certain time to obverse the effect of such regulations in improving cooperation of the authorities.

### Unfeasible Private Prosecution Regimes

The PRC Criminal Law and Criminal Procedure Law provide for a so-called 'private prosecution' regime. This means that, if an infringed intellectual property owner gathers conclusive evidence for the establishment of an intellectual property crime, it may prosecute the infringer directly before a court. However, reports of a successful private prosecution of an intellectual property infringer are extremely rare because it is difficult to gather sufficient evidence.

### Unreasonable Determination Method for Recording Criminal Intellectual Property Rights Cases

One of the thresholds for determining criminal intellectual property rights infringement is illegal business volume obtained by the infringer. However, in calculating the business volume, the price of the infringing goods, rather than the price of the legitimate goods, is used. The direct consequence of this calculation method is that the threshold is difficult to meet in many cases and some infringers escape criminal punishment. For instance, in a past State AIC raid where 40 000 counterfeit Zippo lighters were seized, the case was determined as non-criminal because the lighters were valued at a mere RMB0.5 to RMB1.2, a price much lower than that of real Zippo lighters.[6] This practice is clearly not in line with article 61 of the TRIPS Agreement, which requires that criminal procedures and penalties be applied 'at least in cases of wilful trademark counterfeiting or copyright piracy on a commercial scale. Remedies available shall include imprisonment and/or monetary fines sufficient to provide a deterrent'.

## LACK OF TRANSPARENCY

Article 63 of the TRIPS Agreement requires that laws, regulations, final judicial decisions and administrative rulings of general application pertaining to intellectual property rights enforcement be made publicly available to rights holders. Additionally, in China's WTO accession protocol, China made

---

6 Please see *Intellectual Property Enforcement High on US–China Agenda*, by Berta Gomez and Peggy B Hu, published in Usinfo.State.Gov.

specific commitments to improve transparency in the enforcement of intellectual property rights, and to put pressure on Chinese intellectual property rights enforcement administration authorities and courts to publish administrative decisions and judgments on certain cases and collect judicial judgments on intellectual property rights cases for public access.

However, lack of transparency continues to be an issue in China's enforcement of intellectual property rights. In handling intellectual property rights cases through either administrative or judicial procedures, certain regulatory documents are internally communicated within the administrative authorities or the court system. Court rules for the protection of confidentiality are also vague, and some have been voided internally. Administrative decisions and civil judgments on intellectual property cases are not made public in a regular or timely manner.

### Poor Public Awareness

The majority of infringing goods are intended for sale to the Chinese domestic market, and most Chinese consumers do not believe that piracy and counterfeiting are serious violations of law. This mindset only exacerbates intellectual property rights infringement. China has launched a national public awareness campaign on intellectual property rights protection in recent years, introducing television programmes and publishing articles in the national newspapers in an attempt to educate the public, but it is still too early to tell how effective such campaigns are.

## NEW DEVELOPMENTS IN THE ENFORCEMENT OF INTELLECTUAL PROPERTY RIGHTS IN THE PRC

### Intellectual Property Rights Customs Protection Regulations

On 20 December 2003, the State Council issued the PRC Regulations on Customs Protection of Intellectual Property Rights ('IPR Customs Regulations'),[7] and on 25 May 2004, the General Customs Administration ('GCA') issued the Implementation Measures of the PRC Regulations on Customs Protection of Intellectual Property Rights ('Implementation Measures').[8] These regulations replace those implemented in 1995, and introduce significant changes in the Customs' intellectual property rights enforcement regime.

---

7 Made effective as of 1 March 2004.

8 Made effective on 1 July 2004.

The good news is that the IPR Customs Regulations do away with the previously compulsory Customs recordal of IP rights with the GCA and extend the effective protection term of intellectual property rights recorded with GCA from seven years to 10 years. They also stipulate that, where intellectual property rights holders whose rights are recorded with the GCA request Customs to detain import or export goods suspected of intellectual property infringement, if the value of the goods is between RMB20 000 and RMB200 000, the rights holder need only provide a security equal to 50 per cent of the value of the goods. Also, under the 'general security' regime provided by the regulations, intellectual property rights holders may choose to put down a minimum RMB200 000 standing deposit with Customs for intellectual property cases in relation to these intellectual property rights holders. According to TRIPS, intellectual property rights holders are also permitted to inspect the detained goods.

On the other hand, the IPR Customs Regulations provide two basic systems for Customs' interception and detention of suspicious goods – 'positive protection' (*ex officio* detention of goods by Customs) and 'passive protection' (detention of goods at the request of intellectual property rights holders) – which are both linked to judicial procedures. Under positive protection, in the event that Customs are not able to make a decision on the relevant intellectual property case, the intellectual property rights holders should obtain a 'preliminary injunction adjudication' from a PRC court within 50 days of the goods being detained; under passive protection, the intellectual property rights holders must get the same adjudication from the court within 20 days of the detention of the goods. Ultimately, under the new regime, Customs will assume a substantially smaller and more detached role in the handling of intellectual property rights infringement cases, and may shift their responsibility for carrying out intellectual property border protection to intellectual property rights holders and judicial regimes.

The IPR Customs Regulations also still require intellectual property rights holders to bear the initial cost for the storage and disposal of the goods instead of placing such burden on the consignee or consignor, and even allow for confiscated infringing goods to be transferred to charity organizations without requiring the infringing trademarks to be removed from such goods.

## Judicial Standards to Improve Criminal Protection of IPR

Facing criticism from international businesses and pressure from other WTO members, especially the United States, China issued new legislation at the end of 2004 aimed at facilitating the criminal prosecution of intellectual property rights infringement. On 2 November 2004, the PRC Supreme People's Court and the Supreme People's Procuratorate jointly issued the Interpretations on

Several Issues of Concrete Application of Laws in Handling Criminal Cases of Intellectual Property Infringement (the 'Judicial Interpretations').[9] One important change in the Judicial Interpretations is that thresholds for the prosecution of intellectual property crimes are significantly lowered.

The Judicial Interpretations only specify the criteria for the prosecution of an individual offender in intellectual property crimes. For legal entities, they set forth that, in order to establish a criminal intellectual property action, the amount of the 'illegal business volume' or 'illegal gain' must be three times that for establishing individual intellectual property crimes (this was five times under the previous judicial interpretations promulgated before the Judicial Interpretations). For example, in copyright crimes, where an individual reproduces and distributes written works, musical works, cinematic, television and video works, software and other works without the copyright owner's authorization, or commits any criminal copyright actions stipulated by the PRC Criminal Law, and their illegal business volume is RMB50 000 (approximately USD6000) or more and their illegal gains exceed RMB30 000 (USD3600), the infringer shall be sentenced to a fixed-term imprisonment or criminal detention of no more than three years, in addition to being subject to a criminal fine. The RMB50 000 threshold was a reduction from the original RMB200 000 (approximately USD25 000), and the RMB30 000 threshold was a reduction from the previous RMB500 000. Similar significant reductions are also made for trademarks, patents and trade secrets.

The Judicial Interpretations also define certain key terms. For example, 'illegal business volume' and 'illegal amount of sales' are two important factors in establishing intellectual property crimes. According to the Judicial Interpretations, in a criminal intellectual property case, the value of the *infringing goods that have been sold* shall be calculated according to the prices at which such products were actually sold. The value of *unsold infringing goods* shall be calculated according to the labelled prices or the actual selling prices determined through investigation. Where the seized counterfeit goods lack pricing labels or where the actual prices are impossible to ascertain, their value shall be calculated according to the average market prices of the legitimate versions of the products.

Additionally, the value of in-stock counterfeit/pirated products seized in a counterfeit trademark case will now be included in the 'illegal business volume' of the infringers (this was previously excluded from the infringers' illegal business volume in considering the conviction of criminal intellectual property cases). Moreover, if an infringer had repeatedly infringed upon others' intellectual property rights but has not yet been subject to

[9] Made effective on 22 December 2004.

administrative penalties or criminal punishment, the value of the infringer's illegal business volume, illegal gains and amount of sales will be calculated cumulatively.

The Judicial Interpretations also clarify several terms in relation to crimes of passing off trademarks:

1. 'identical mark': previously, 'passing off a trademark' was interpreted strictly as the action of using a mark that is exactly the same as a legitimate trademark. The Judicial Interpretations slightly expand the scope of this term to also cover 'identical marks', that is, using a mark with no notable visual difference from a legitimate trademark to mislead the public.
2. 'use of marks': the Judicial Interpretations also introduce the definition of the 'use of marks' for establishing the criminal liability of a trademark infringement. According to these, not only does the use of counterfeited trademarks on commodities, packaging and directions for use constitute the 'passing off of trademarks', but the use of such marks in commodity transaction documents, advertisements, exhibitions and other business activities shall also be considered under the definition.
3. 'clearly know': to facilitate proper determination of the crime of 'knowingly selling counterfeits', the Judicial Interpretations also provide the exact situations under which a counterfeiter is deemed to have 'clearly known' that they are selling counterfeits. For instance, if an infringer who once received an administrative penalty or assumed civil liabilities for selling counterfeit commodities sells the same counterfeiting commodities again, its actions will be deemed to amount to 'knowingly selling counterfeits'.

Additionally, the Judicial Interpretations clarify certain terms relating to crimes of copyright infringement, including the following:

1. 'for the purpose of making profit': the direct or indirect collection of fees by publishing paid advertisements shall be considered as being 'for the purpose of making profit'. Consequently, utilizing others' copyrighted works without the express authorization of the copyright owner under such circumstances could constitute a crime of copyright infringement.
2. 'without authorization of copyright owner': pursuant to the Judicial Interpretations, this includes situations where the infringer *alters* or *exceeds* the authorization of the copyright owner in addition to actual failure to obtain the authorization of the copyright owner.
3. 'network copyright infringement': significantly, the Judicial Interpretations make clear for the first time that distributing written works, musical works, motion pictures, television programmes or other visual works, computer software or other works to the public by way of

the information network falls within the definition of 'reproducing and distributing' the copyrighted works of others, thus providing a legal basis to stop copyright infringement through the Internet in China. According to these provisions, a website providing free downloads of copyrighted music or movies could be liable for the crime of copyright infringement.

## Accomplices and Cumulative Punishment

Aiming to expand the net to catch intellectual property criminals, the Judicial Interpretations also introduce accomplice and cumulative punishment in the conviction of intellectual property crimes. Specifically, the Judicial Interpretations stipulate that, where a person or entity knowingly provides loans, funds, bank accounts, invoices, certificates, licences, area for production and operation, facilities and assistance for production and storage, or import/export agency services in relation to an intellectual property infringement, such individual or entity shall be deemed an accomplice in the intellectual property crime.

Where an individual or entity commits the crime of 'passing off' registered trademarks while knowingly selling commodities counterfeited by others, they shall be subject to a combined punishment for the two separate crimes. Similarly, if a person or entity commits the crime of infringing upon copyrights while also knowingly selling pirated products reproduced by others, they shall be concurrently punished for their involvement in both crimes.

While these are all good developments, the downside is, again, that illegal business volume is calculated using the price of infringing goods rather than the price of legitimate goods. The Judicial Interpretations criminalize copyright infringements only in cases where the activities were undertaken to make a profit, which does not take into account activities undertaken with the purpose of disseminating information. They also fail to rule on the liabilities of the end-users of pirated software.

## Administrative Measures for Internet Copyright Protection

While the rapid development of network technology provides an increasingly convenient resource to Internet users, it intensifies the risk of intellectual property infringement. Working in conjunction with the general provisions of the Copyright Law on the protection of the copyright owner's 'rights to transmit information on the network', the Administrative Measures on Internet Copyright Protection (the 'Administrative Measures') issued in April 2005[10]

10 Made effective May 2005.

by the NCA and the Ministry of Information Industry (the 'MII') specify for the first time the rights, obligations and administrative liabilities of the Internet service provider ('ISP') in cases of copyright infringements on the Internet, and also provide specific measures that the ISP may adopt in curbing copyright infringement.

Currently, the Administrative Measures are the most specific administrative rules for the prevention of copyright infringements on the Internet. Among other things, they clearly regulate the following:

1. Obligations of the ISP: according to the Administrative Measures, when a copyright owner discovers any content transmitted over the Internet which infringes his copyright, he may send a notice to the relevant ISP to request the removal of the infringing content. The ISP shall promptly remove the infringing content and retain the copyright owner's notice for six months. If, after the ISP removes such content, the Internet Content Provider ('ICP') sends a counternotice to the copyright owner stating that the removed information does not infringe upon the copyright, the ISP may restore the removed information.

   The Administrative Measures provide explicit provisions on the contents of a copyright owner's notice and an ICP's counternotice as well as the evidence that must be submitted in support of such claims. For example, a notice must include information on the copyright ownership certification, the identity certification of the copyright owner and its contact information, and exclusive evidence for the copyright infringement in question. Notices and counternotices must meet the legally provided requirements in order to be deemed valid.

   The Administrative Measures also set forth an ISP's obligation towards the preservation of the records of the alleged infringing contents; upon receiving the copyright owner's notice, an ISP must record the alleged infringing contents, the time the content was issued, and the web address or domain name, for six months. Furthermore, an Internet Access Service Provider ('IASP') must record the time of access, the user's account, the address or domain name and the dial-in telephone number of the relevant ICP and also retain this information for six months. Both ISPs and IASPs must provide such information to the administrative authorities in charge of copyright protection upon request.
2. Administrative liabilities of the ISP: if an ISP should fail to take measures to remove infringing contents upon receiving a notice from a copyright owner, and thus harms the interests of the public, the competent authority shall order it to cease the infringement activities pursuant to the provisions of the PRC Copyright Law and impose an administrative penalty including confiscation of its illegal income and a fine of up to three times

its illegal business income or, where it is impossible to calculate the illegal business income, RMB100 000.

However, the Administrative Measures also set forth certain provisions on the exemption of an ISP's liabilities. If no evidence shows that the ISP was aware of the alleged infringing contents, or if it has taken measures to remove promptly such content upon receipt of the copyright owner's Notice, the ISP shall assume no administrative liability.

Unfortunately, the Administrative Measures fail to provide a specific time limit by which an ISP must remove content suspected of infringement. By contrast, the US Digital Millennium Copyright Act of 1998 prescribes that, once a copyright owner has delivered infringement notification to an ISP, the ISP must remove the infringing content and simultaneously serve a notification to the ICP.[11] If the ICP does not raise an objection within ten days, and the copyright owner fails to lodge a lawsuit against the ICP, the ISP can republish the information suspected of infringement. Such an explicit time limit for each stage of action would be greatly beneficial in China because it would allow all parties concerned to have realistic expectations of the process.

Another shortcoming in the Administrative Measures is that an infringement action must be proved to have damaged public interests in order for administrative enforcement to take place. This rule contradicts the provisions of the Copyright Law, thus creating unnecessary barriers to intellectual property rights protection.

## Measures for the Protection of Intellectual Property Rights during Exhibitions

The Measures for the Protection of Intellectual Property Rights during Exhibitions (the 'Measures on Exhibition IPR')[12] are the first unified administrative rules in China regulating the protection of intellectual property rights in the exhibition industry, currently a particularly weak area of intellectual property rights protection.

According to these, all patents, trademarks and copyrights that may be involved in exhibitions, sales exhibitions, expositions, trade fairs and shows held in the PRC for all types of economic and technological trade are subject to protection of the Measures on Exhibition intellectual property rights.

---

[11] To view the full text of the act, please visit www.copyright.gov/legislation/dmca.pdf.

[12] Promulgated on 13 January 2006 jointly by the Ministry of Commerce, the State AIC, the NCA and SIPO, and made effective as of 1 March 2006.

Although this scope of protection has been criticized by experts in the exhibition industry as being too narrow to cover intellectual property rights such as that of integrated layout design, trade secrets and so on, it does cover the major types of intellectual property rights that are liable to be infringed upon during exhibitions.

The sponsor of the exhibition ('Sponsor'), the exhibition administrative authorities (that is, the approval or registration authorities) and the local intellectual property rights administrative authorities (that is, local trademark offices, patent offices and copyright administrations) are obliged to protect the legitimate rights of intellectual property rights owners. Specifically speaking, the Sponsor shall review the IPR status of the items on display, coordinate with local intellectual property rights administrative authorities in handling intellectual property rights-related complaints, and collate statistics on and analyse the protection of intellectual property rights during the exhibition and make reports to the exhibition administrative authorities. Exhibition administrative authorities must coordinate, supervise and examine the implementation of intellectual property rights protection during an exhibition, and if any intellectual property rights infringement is detected, it shall coordinate with the intellectual property rights administrative authorities to handle the case. The intellectual property rights administrative authorities are responsible for accepting the complaint, investigating the case and imposing penalties according to law.

There are two channels for making an intellectual property rights-related complaint where IPR infringement is suspected during the exhibition. One is through the intellectual property rights Complaint Acceptance Unit ('Unit') established in the exhibition. For exhibitions held for a period of three days or more, such a Unit can be set up by the sponsor where the exhibition administrative authorities deem it necessary. The local intellectual property rights administrative authorities at the place where the exhibition is held must send staff to join the Unit along with the Sponsor's staff and the exhibition administrative authorities. The other option, if no such Unit has been established, is to go directly to local intellectual property rights administrative authorities. The contact information of the intellectual property rights administrative authorities will be displayed in a noticeable area of the exhibition hall, as the posting of this information is mandatory according to the Measures on Exhibition intellectual property rights.

If intellectual property rights infringement is confirmed by the intellectual property rights administrative authorities, they may order the removal of the items on display, destroy the relevant marketing materials, place a notice on the display board informing others of the infringing items and punish the infringer according to the provisions of the patent, trademark and copyright laws. Where the relevant administrative authorities or the court has decided or ruled that the items on display in the exhibition did indeed infringe, the intellectual property rights administrative authorities responsible for the intellectual property rights protection of the exhibition may punish the infringer directly, on the basis of this decision or ruling.

It is worth noting that the concept of the exhibition administrative authorities is not clearly defined. This lack of a definite governing body means that many departments (PSBs, AICs and so on) have the authority to approve and register exhibitions and function as exhibition administrative authorities. This greatly hampers the enforcement of the Measures on Exhibition intellectual property rights. Moreover, although they emphasize coordination and cooperation between the sponsor, the exhibition administrative authorities and the intellectual property rights administrative authorities, there are no specific provisions in the Measures on Exhibition intellectual property rights on how such coordination and cooperation should be brought about. Many sponsors believe that too much pressure has been placed solely on them to protect intellectual property rights during exhibitions.[13]

## Other Recent Developments in IPR Enforcement

Most recent developments include the following new rules on intellectual property rights, the issuance of which indicates that the Chinese governmental authorities are still making various efforts in perfecting their intellectual property rights legislation in an attempt to improve intellectual property rights enforcement:

1. Provisions on Copyright Collective Management, promulgated by the State Council on 22 December 2004 and made effective as of 1 March 2005;
2. The Reply Concerning Relevant Issues Related to the Handling of Criminal Copyright Infringement Cases Involving Recordings and Video Products issued by the Supreme People's Court and the Supreme People's Procuratorate on 17 October 2005 and effective as of 18 October 2005;
3. Measures on the Compulsory Licensing of Patents Related to Public Health Problems, issued by SIPO on 29 November 2005 and made effective as of 1 January 2006; and
4. Measures on the Settlement of Disputes Over the Domain Name of China Internet Network Information Center, issued by the China Internet

---

[13] See 'Hot Interpretation of the Industry Circle on Measures for the Protection of Intellectual Property Rights during Exhibitions', Zhu Wenwei, *China Trade Daily*, 21 March 2006.

Network Information Center on 17 March 2006 and made effective as of the same date.

## CONCLUSION

The shortcomings in intellectual property rights enforcement in China and the sluggish pace of improvement have invited much criticism from other WTO members, in particular the US, EU members and Japan. In recent years, the US trade delegation has repeatedly visited China and negotiated with the Chinese Government with regard to intellectual property rights enticement issues. Faced with great international pressure and the risk of trade wars triggered by the dissatisfaction of the other WTO member countries, the Chinese Government's habitual reaction is to launch periodic anti-counterfeiting and anti-piracy campaigns and to issue various specific rules to show to the world that it continues to make progress in its intellectual property rights legislation. Nevertheless, such actions have thus far produced little effect. It may take decades for the Chinese Government to thoroughly eradicate rampant intellectual property rights infringement in China.

# 6. Legal protection of copyright and trademarks in cyberspace in China

**Hon. Jiang Zhipei***

## INTRODUCTION

Alongside the rapid development of the IT industry in China in recent years, IT use also increased. In December 2005, there were 111 million Internet users, 49.5 million Internet-connected computers and more than 690 000 of websites in China. Judged by the number of Internet users, China has overtaken Japan and is second only to the USA in the world. Computer networks have had a deep impact on all sections of Chinese society. At the same time, the clash of interests of different civil entities in this environment has given rise to illegal conduct, infringements and crimes which in turn have led to endless cases in Chinese courts. Among these cases, disputes regarding network copyright and trademarks are the first issues that presented themselves at centre stage and that attracted the attention of the state, society and the general public. China's Copyright Law (amended 2001) has established the right of disseminating information through networks. Although the amendment to the Trademark Law in 2001 has failed to take the Internet development into consideration, it clarifies the threshold for well-known trademarks, which provides the basis to protect well-known trademarks in cyberspace. Furthermore, a legal mechanism of protecting network copyright, trademark and domain names was established before and after the amendments of the Copyright Law and the Trademark Law. This has provided a regulatory instrument with a uniquely charming character and has allowed us to gather valuable experience for future legislation in related areas.

* Justice of the Supreme People's Court of China, Director of the Third Civil Chamber, PhD in Law.

# LEGAL PROTECTION OF COPYRIGHT IN CYBERSPACE

In 1998, the US enacted the Digital Millennium Copyright Act (DMCA) as the answer to the challenge to copyright protection posed by the Internet. A lot of comments have been made regarding this Act and related cases in American Federal courts. It is noteworthy that the Supreme People's Court of China has also promulgated the Chinese version of the 'DMCA' – the '*Interpretation of the Supreme People's Court on Several Issues concerning the Application of Law in the Trial of Cases in Relation to Copyright Disputes over Computer Network*' (hereinafter '*Interpretation on network copyright cases*') in December 2000[1] and that hundreds of cases have been tried by Chinese courts since its enactment. The legal mechanism established by the *Interpretation on network copyright cases* has been hailed by international experts as a system as good as the American DMCA. This mechanism meets the demands of the fast-developing Chinese network industry and has facilitated, to a certain extent, the formation of a legal environment suitable for the orderly development of the IT industry. Its main provisions include the following.

## Jurisdiction

'Cases of disputes over infringement of network copyright shall be subject to the jurisdiction of the people's courts at the place where the infringement is committed or where the defendant has his domicile. The places where the infringement is committed shall include the locations of such equipment as the Internet server or computer terminal by which an accused infringement act is committed. In case it is difficult to determine the place where the infringement is committed or the place where the defendant has his domicile, the locations of the computer terminal and other equipment in which the contents of infringement have been found by the claimant may be deemed as the place where the infringement act is committed' (article 1 of *Interpretation on network copyright cases*).

The reason to include the locations of network servers and computer terminals as the reference for jurisdiction is that they are relatively speaking easier to ascertain than the location of the person who committed the infringement. Therefore this jurisdiction reference is based on the characteristic of this type of case and makes it easier for the aggrieved party to initiate the litigation and for the court to exercise its jurisdiction. When it is difficult to ascertain the

---

[1] Adopted at the 1144th Session of the Judicial Committee of the Supreme People's Court on 22 November 2000, amended on 23 December 2003 and 1 July 2004. Available in English on *Lexis-Nexis*. (This footnote has been added by the translator.)

location of the equipment, the claimant may bring the lawsuit in the court of the country where equipment in which contents of infringement have been found is located. This approach not only avoids the complete destruction of the basic principle of jurisdiction in Chinese law: 'the claimant goes to the defendant', but it also offers full protection of the claimant's action rights by employing the location of equipment in which contents of infringement have been found as a reference for jurisdiction.

## The Right to Disseminate the Work Remains in the Hands of the Author

The *Interpretation on network copyright cases* makes it clear that the copyright of the digitalized work still belongs to the proprietor of the copyright. Unauthorized uploading, disseminating, copying and so on without remunerating the proprietor of the copyright will constitute infringements. The aggrieved party may sue in the court that has jurisdiction over the case or apply for various interim measures.

## Regulation Regarding the Reprinting of Works with Relevant Limitations

Article 32(2) of the Chinese Copyright Law provides that 'where the proprietor of the copyright has declared that reprinting or excerpting is not permitted, other newspaper or periodical publishers may, after the publication of the work by a newspaper or periodical, reprint the work or print an abstract of it or print it as reference material, but such other publishers shall pay remuneration to the proprietor of the copyright as required by regulations'. There have been different views on whether this provision shall be applied in cyberspace. Some argue that this provision shall not apply, and that, in order to protect copyright properly, both remuneration and explicit consent shall be required. However, this view is in direct conflict with the fact that computer networks contain enormous amounts of information, that the information concerning the author is often omitted, and that the value of the Internet relies on rapid and wide dissemination of information.

China's Supreme Court takes the view that article 32(2) of the Chinese Copyright Law shall apply to the dissemination of network works. Therefore it is provided in the *Interpretation on network copyright cases* that 'those who reprint or extract and edit through the network the works which have already been published in the newspapers and periodicals or have already been disseminated through networks, and who have paid remuneration according to the relevant provisions, and indicated the newspaper or magazine that first published the works, do not commit an infringement, unless the proprietors of the copyrights declare or the newspaper offices, the periodical offices or the

Internet Server Providers entrusted by the proprietors of the copyrights declare that no reprinting or extracting and editing is allowed. But if the works reprinted or extracted and edited exceed the scope of the works that are permitted to be reprinted, they shall be deemed an infringement' (article 3).

This article consists of three key elements: (i) the scope of works that are allowed to be reprinted or extracted in the network does not exceed the scope of the works regulated by article 32(2) of the Copyright Law, which includes mainly short literary work and excludes sound and video recording, photographic work, cinematographic work, computer software and so on; (ii) remuneration shall be paid by the user; (iii) the origin of the work shall be indicated. Therefore, unless new legislation is adopted in this regard, the reprints between network and paper media, different websites and different paper media are subject to the same legal principle. However, it is noteworthy that, as long as the proprietor of the copyright states in his work that 'no reprint is allowed', no matter whether the work is published on the net or in the newspaper, any reprint without explicit consent will be illegal.

Some do not understand the underlying rationale for this provision and are wondering why members of the Judicial Committee of the Chinese Supreme Court made this choice. During the 'Sino-American Round Table Conference on Cyberspace Law' in Philadelphia in July 2003, I addressed American experts on cyberspace law:

> Three years ago when the supreme court of China justices made the interpretation including article 3, they considered several points: (1) under article 32(2) of the Chinese copyright lawChinese judges have the power to interpret the article for handling copyright cases on the internet; (2) the balance doctrine; (3) websites are the same as newspapers or magazines etc. They are all media and should have equal rights; (4) we are concerned with a very narrow range of works and the proprietor of the copyright can choose ways to protect itself; (5) in practice this provision could decrease the number of lawsuits and let lawyers make money out of the courtroom.
>
> What is the balance doctrine? The fundamental basis of the copyright law always has been the attempt to find a balance between the necessity of protecting the right of authors in order to encourage production of all kinds of work, and the necessity of providing public access to works in order to maintain a democratic and educated society.
>
> Maintaining such a balance is easier said than done. Nowadays the balance not only operates at national but also at international level. Even though the technology is developing so fast and is so modern, the balance is always necessary.
>
> We say, perhaps, that ISP's liability is a small testcase for the balance doctrine. The protection of copyright on the Internet is a bigger test case for the balance between the rights of the author and the need for a democratic society to have access to information. Judges are the guardians and the maintenance men of the balance.[2]

2 Original script of the speech.

## Network Service Provider's Liability for Copyright Infringement

Network service provider's liability for copyright cases refers to the liability that a network service provider shall assume when an infringement of copyright was committed using its service. When the infringement is committed by the service provider itself, the liability can be ascertained in accordance with existing regulations. Based on the content of the network service, network service providers can be divided into two categories: providers of network link services and providers of network contents. The former only provides connection to the network and other physical infrastructure, the latter provides contents such as BBS (bulletin boards), newsgroups, chat rooms and so on.

Owing to their different capabilities regarding the control and manipulation of information on the web, these two categories of network service providers shall assume different liabilities. Therefore the *Interpretation on network copyright cases* is meant to serve a dual purpose regarding this issue: (i) infringement of copyright must be stopped and punished in accordance with the law; (ii) at the same time, network service providers shall be provided with a 'safe harbour' from legal liabilities. The provisions of the *Interpretation on network copyright cases* in this regard have tried, as far as possible, to make clear what exactly are the wrongdoings of network service providers. This makes it difficult for network service providers to be obliged to assume disproportional liabilities and it therefore facilitates and protects the healthy development of China's infant network industry. On the other hand, the behaviour of network service providers is regulated by the *Interpretation on network copyright cases*, which makes it clear under what circumstances service providers shall assume liability for infringement. This facilitates the self-regulation and self-protection of network service providers and it facilitates the protection of legitimate interests of proprietors of copyright. The main provisions of the *Interpretation on network copyright cases* in this regard are as follows.

1. Network service providers that only provide connection services are not liable for infringement of copyright on the network by others. This is because they do not have the capability to control or edit information published on the web. They do not have the obligation to monitor the legality of such information. Therefore, according to article 106 of the General Principles of Civil Law, in the absence of their own intent to commit such an action, these providers shall not be made responsible for others' copyright infringement.
2. Network service providers that participate in other persons' act of infringement of copyright through networks, or abet any other person to commit such an infringement or assist any other person in committing an

act of copyright infringement, shall be held liable for contributory infringement and take joint liability with the person who directly committed the infringement in accordance with article 130 of the General Principles of Civil Law (article 4).

3. As to network service providers that provide contents services, since they have a certain capability to edit and control the information on the web, they are obliged to take measures such as removing the infringing contents to stop their circulation as soon as they become aware of the incident of infringement or are given warnings coupled with concrete evidence by the proprietor of the copyright. If the service provider fails to comply with its obligations mention above, an intentional fault will be identified and the failure to conduct certain action as required will constitute contributory infringement, which makes the service provider jointly liable with the person who directly committed the infringement in accordance with article 130 of the General Principles of Civil Law (article 5).
4. Network service providers providing contents services, when required by the proprietor of the copyright, have the duty to provide network registration information concerning the person who committed the alleged infringement. The network service provider's failure to fulfil such duty without proper cause will be interpreted as showing an ill intention, and therefore constitutes contributory infringement, which makes the service provider jointly liable with the person who directly committed the infringement in accordance with article 130 of the General Principles of Civil Law (article 6).
5. Certain formalities must be followed by the proprietor of the copyright when giving warning of infringement to the network service provider or asking for the registration information of the person committing the infringement. Certain types of documents must be provided by the proprietor of the copyright: (i) certificate of identity such as an ID card, Registration of Legal Person, Business Licence and so on; (ii) documents proving the ownership of copyright such as registration certificate of copyright and the original script; (iii) documents stating the incident of infringement including the contents and location of the infringing material. If these formalities are followed, the network service provider shall act accordingly. Otherwise, and in the absence of legitimate reasons, the network service provider may ignore the warning or request for information (article 8). This approach enables the network service provider to make a judgment and prevents the network service provider from being dragged into too many law suits. If the network service provider fails to act after having been supplied with above mentioned documents, the proprietor of the copyright may apply to the court for an injunction order to stop the act of infringement, to remove any impediment or to eliminate

any influence, and the Chinese court shall grant such order in order to protect the legitimate interest of the proprietor of the copyright.

6. The measure taken by a network service provider to remove certain infringing material as requested by the proprietor of the copyright is a lawful act intended to protect the legitimate interest of the proprietor of the copyright and therefore the network service provider is exempted from any contractual liability regarding this act. If the allegation of copyright infringement is rejected subsequently, and the act of the network service provider has caused a loss to the defendant, it is the whistle-blowing proprietor of the copyright instead of the network service provider that shall pay the compensation.

As in other cases regarding intellectual property, the way to ascertain the amount of the damage in cases involving network copyright infringement shall be subject to the choice of the proprietor of the copyright. The proprietor of the copyright can normally choose from three approaches: (i) the damage is based on the actual loss of the proprietor of the copyright as a result of the infringement. This includes direct financial loss and the loss of expected benefits; (ii) the damage is based on the gains of the offender from the infringement; (iii) statutory compensation; that is, when it is difficult to ascertain the amount with the previous two approaches, the court has the discretion to set the amount of damage at a maximum of half a million Yuan. The lack of guidance on the scale of payment for network works issued by relevant authorities and associations has a negative impact on the smooth transaction of the copyright of network works and the interests of the proprietor of copyright. This has also made it difficult for the court to ascertain the amount of damages that shall be granted in cases involving network copyright infringement. We urge the relevant authorities and associations to speed up their research process, to take into consideration opinions from different interest groups and, on this basis, to adopt, as soon as possible, guidelines regarding the scale of payment for network works with a view to promoting the development of culture and the IT industry and to resolve this bottleneck issue impeding future development.

Other than previously mentioned, there are also disputes regarding network connections. The view of the Chinese court is that providing a network connection does not normally involve copyright infringement, even if deep linking may involve unfair competition. However, intentional links to websites which provide pirated materials have been identified as an infringement of copyright or neighbouring rights, and the party responsible shall assume liability for such infringement.

According to article 58 of the newly amended Chinese Copyright Law, the measures to protect the right of dissemination through the information network will be issued separately by the State Council. Chinese courts support and participate in the legislative process of this piece of administrative regulation. It is expected not only to resolve the issues already at hand, but also to find a solution for digital libraries and distance education, in order to rationalize and optimize the protection mechanism for copyright in cyberspace. This includes especially network reading and education for poor communities located in western China.

## LEGAL PROTECTION OF TRADEMARKS IN CYBERSPACE

The protection of intellectual property such as well-known trademarks in cyberspace, the regulation of the relationship between domain name users and proprietors of relevant intellectual property, and the trial of civil disputes involving domain names and network trademark infringement, have become a new challenge for the legal protection of intellectual property in the era of networks.

The Supreme People's Court adopted the '*Interpretation of the Supreme People's Court on Application of Laws in the Trial of Civil Disputes over Domain Names of Computer Network*' (hereinafter '*Interpretation on domain name disputes*') in July 2001,[3] which provides guidelines on how to apply the General Principles of Civil Law, Anti-Unfair Competition Law, Civil Procedure Law and so on in civil disputes involving the registration and use of domain names of computer networks.

Furthermore, the Supreme People's Court adopted the '*Interpretation of the Supreme People's Court Concerning the Application of Laws in the Trial of Cases of Civil Disputes Arising from Trademarks*' (hereinafter '*Interpretation on trademark disputes*') in December 2002,[4] which provides regulations for one major form of trademark infringement in cyberspace.

The enactment of these judicial interpretations marked the establishment of the judicial mechanism capable of protecting trademarks, especially well-known trademarks, business names, fair competition, domain names and so on in cyberspace. This will definitely facilitate the healthy development of electronic commerce and the IT industry in China.

---

[3] Adopted at the 1182nd meeting of the Judicial Committee of the Supreme People's Court on 26 June 2001. It came into force on 24 July 2001; available in English on *Lexis-Nexis*. (This footnote was added by the translator.)

[4] Adopted at the 1246th Session of the Judicial Committee of the Supreme People's Court on 12 October 2002, and implemented as of 16 October 2002; available in English on *Lexis-Nexis*. (This footnote was added by the translator.)

## Types of Civil Disputes Involving Domain Names in Chinese Courts

One significant characteristic of the domain name is its function of symbolizing the user of the domain name and the service attached to it in cyberspace, which is similar to the function of the trademark and business name. The registration and use of domain names further reinforces its symbolizing function, and demonstrates its economic value, which ultimately causes the conflict between the domain name and the traditional trademark and business name. Civil disputes involving the registration and use of domain names have common characteristics and shall be regulated by the same legislation. Therefore cases involving domain names in Chinese courts refer to all civil disputes involving registration and use of domain names, including disputes between domain names and well-known trademarks, common trademarks, business names, unique names of famous products, names and so on. Since the registration and use of domain names is profitable to their users, the domain name in itself is a civil right in nature. Therefore disputes between the domain names and its user are also within the scope of cases involving domain names.

## Jurisdiction in Cases Involving Domain Names

Cases involving domain names normally involve issues of infringement or unfair competition, the trial of which is difficult and requires special expertise. Therefore, following the principle of jurisdiction in tort cases set up by the Civil Procedure Law, the Supreme People's Court provides in the *Interpretation on domain name disputes* provisions on geographical and hierarchical jurisdiction and the definition and jurisdiction of cases involving domain names with foreign factors.

First of all, taking into consideration that these cases are difficult to try and specialized in nature, the Intermediate People's Court shall be the court of first instance. Secondly, these cases shall follow the basic principle of geographical jurisdiction in tort cases set up in the Civil Procedure Law, namely the court of the place of the tort or the defendant's domicile shall have jurisdiction. Owing to the characteristics of network cases and learning from the experience of network copyright cases, the location of the computer terminal through which the claimant finds out the domain name in question may be deemed to be the place of the tort.

According to the Civil Procedure Law and the relevant Interpretations of the Supreme People's Court, cases involving domain names with foreign factors refer to two type of cases: (i) at least one party to the dispute is a foreign citizen, stateless person, foreign enterprise, organization or an international organization; (ii) the registration of the domain name is made in a foreign territory, such as cases involving domain names such as '.com', '.org' and '.net' which are registered in the US. Since the establishment, amendment or termination of the legal relationship between parties occurs in a foreign territory in these cases, they shall be deemed as cases involving domain names with foreign factors.

The *Interpretation on domain name disputes* provides that 'the jurisdiction of cases involving domain names with foreign factors taking place within the territory of the People's Republic of China shall be determined according to the provisions of Chapter 4 of the Civil Procedure Law' (article 2).

### How do Chinese Courts Identify Whether the Alleged Registration and Use of Domain Names Constitutes Infringement?

The key question of the trial of a domain name dispute is to ascertain whether the conduct of the defendant such as registering or using a domain name constitutes trademark infringement or unfair competition. Therefore four prerequisites are set out in detail by the *Interpretation on domain name disputes* (article 4) in order to qualify certain registration and use of domain names as infringement or unfair competition: (i) the civil rights and interests that the claimant asked protection for are legal and valid; (ii) the domain name or the main part of the domain name of the defendant has similarities with the object that the claimant has asked protection for; (iii) the defendant does not have any legitimate reason to register or use the domain name in question; (iv) the defendant did act maliciously. When all these conditions are met, the court shall come to the conclusion that the acts of the defendant of registering or using the domain name constitute infringement or unfair competition.

It is noteworthy that one of the above mentioned conditions is whether the defendant has committed the act in question maliciously. Malice manifests itself when a person has taken a certain action knowing beforehand that such action is against the basic principles of civil law such as '*bona fides*'. However, it is often difficult to tell whether the defendant 'knew' or not at the time of action. Therefore, in order to ascertain the malicious intent of the registration or use of domain names, it is the international practice to prescribe certain circumstances under which the malicious intent of the defendant may be presumed. The *Interpretation on domain name disputes* (article 5) has set out four circumstances in this regard, under any one of which the malicious intent of the defendant will be identified by the court.

1. Registering well-known trademarks of others as domain name for commercial purposes is the first of these. These trademarks are well known to the general public and distinguish the products or services they represent from others. In this circumstance, the person who registered others' well-known trademark for commercial purposes has a clear intention of taking a free ride and his conduct is clearly against the doctrine of *bona fides*. This

provision demonstrates the guiding principle of granting special protection to well-known trademarks.

2. Registering or using a domain name which is the same as or similar to the registered trademark or domain name of the claimant for commercial purposes and thereby intentionally causing confusion with the products or services provided by the claimant or with the website of the claimant, and misleading the network users to visit his website or other online sites is the second of these. These acts also clearly demonstrate the intention of the defendant to break the principle of *bona fides* and the economic rule of fair competition. This provision accords protection for trademarks, domain names and subjects of civil rights other than well-known trademarks, and for normal business conduct in the market by civil entities.
3. Having offered to sell or rent that domain name for a high price or to transfer it by other means to get improper profits is the third of these. One important difference between good faith and malice is whether the purpose of the action is to gain improper profit. Some people register a large number of domain names related to others' rights for a normal registration fee, then offer to sell them to the proprietor in order to get an illegal profit. This kind of behaviour, which is clearly against the civil law principle of *bona fides*, shall obviously not be approved of by national law. The existence of this type of behaviour shall lead to the conclusion that the defendant has a malicious intent. Whether the price asked for is a 'high price' shall be determined on a case-by-case basis by the judge according to the evidence and reasoned statement provided by the claimant and the reply from the defendant. The judicial practice shows that the legitimate interest of the person who registered the domain name also needs to be looked after in order to respect the legal status of the domain name as a bearer of a civil right.
4. Having made no use or not even having made preparations to use the domain name after registration, and intentionally preventing the proprietor from registering that domain name is the fourth of these. A domain name is unique and is a 'rare resource'. If a person does not use the registered domain name, does not prepare to use it and prevents others from illegally using it, his malicious intent is manifested from a different angle. Of course, not all conduct involving not using registered domain names indicates a malicious intent; for example, the owner of a domain name might register domain names similar to his own to avoid confusion, which should not be deemed to be malicious.

Furthermore, since the situation is complicated in practice, the court shall identify other special incidents in which the defendant has malicious intent on a case-by-case basis according to article 5(5).

## Determination and Protection of Well-known Trademarks by Chinese Courts

In China, there have been debates about whether, in the trial of domain name and trademark infringement cases, judges can decide whether the trademark in question is a well-known mark or not. In fact, whether a trademark is well-known or not is a fact which changes in the market. The recognition of a well-known mark is actually the recognition of a changing fact. It is the international practice to let the court decide whether the trademark in dispute is a well-known mark. Chinese academics finally agreed that the court shall have the authority to recognize well-known marks. This consensus is confirmed by the *Interpretation on trademark disputes* (article 22), which provides that, while hearing a dispute regarding a trademark and a domain name, the court may, upon the plea of the party and taking into consideration the circumstances of the case, determine whether the registered trademark in question is a well-known mark or not in accordance with the law. However, the recognition by the court of a well-known mark will only be initiated through the plea of the claimant. If the claimant failed to make the plea, the court will not act on its own initiative. This provision plays an important role in strengthening the legal protection of well-known trademarks.

Article 14 of China's new Trademark Law enacted in October 2001 provides that, in determining whether a trademark is well-known, account shall be taken of (i) the knowledge of the trademark in the relevant sector of the public; (ii) the duration of the use of the trademark; (iii) the duration, extent and geographical scope of advertising, if any, of the trademark; (iv) the record of the trademark protected as a well-known trademark; (v) other relevant factors. At present, this provision is the legal basis upon which the Chinese court determines whether the trademark in dispute is well-known or not.

## Remedies

The *Interpretation on domain name disputes* provides that, after the finding of infringement or unfair competition, the court may order the defendant to desist from the infringement or cancel the registration of the domain name in question, or order the domain name in question to be registered under the name of the claimant. If injury has been suffered by the right holder because of the infringement of the defendant, the court may order the defendant to pay damages.

These remedies consist of three layers. First, the general form of remedy is to order the defendant to desist from the infringement or to cancel the registration of the domain name in question. If the defendant is ordered to cancel the registration of the domain name, the defendant should apply for the cancellation to the authority administering the registration of domain names. If the defendant fails to do so within the time limit specified, the claimant may apply for a court enforcement notice to be issued to the domain name administration authority to enforce the cancellation. Secondly, if the claimant pleads that the domain name in question shall be owned by him instead, the court may, considering the circumstances of the case, order the domain name to be registered under the name of the claimant. The claimant may then, supported by the judgment, apply for the transfer of the registration of the domain name to the domain name administration authority. If necessary, the court may issue a notice assisting the enforcement of a judgment. Thirdly, if the claimant has evidence to prove that he has suffered injury because of the infringement of the defendant, the court may order the defendant to pay damages that are adequate to compensate such injury. A lot of cases regarding domain names disputes do not involve actual injury suffered by the claimant because of the malicious registration of domain names by the defendant, in which case damages, as a remedy, shall not apply.

Article 1(3) of the *Interpretation on trademark disputes* provides unambiguously the circumstances in which trademark rights are infringed in cyberspace: 'registering the words or characters identical or similar to the registered trademark of another person as a domain name and engaging in the electronic commerce of relevant commodities via the domain name which leads to consumer deception' shall be an incident of trademark infringement provided for in article 52(5) of the Trademark Law. The infringer should be ordered to desist from the infringement or to pay damages. This provision provides effective legal protection in cyberspace for registered trademarks.

Other types of trademark infringement in cyberspace do not differ much from normal trademark infringement. Liability in respect of these will be ascertained by the Chinese courts in accordance with the relevant provisions of the Trademark Law.

## CONCLUSION

It has been more than four years since China's WTO accession. China's reform and opening up has reached the new era of building a harmonious socialist society. The reform of the Chinese judicial system has also progressed further in order to provide effective legal protection, and to fulfil the goal of building a harmonious society. The much-noticed 'professionalization of Chinese judges' has also made continuous and in-depth progress. The judicial protection of intellectual property in China will surely become fairer and more effective. This will not only facilitate the protection of intellectual property in China but also contribute to the international protection of intellectual property.

# PART III

# Non-mainstream rights and transfer of technology

# 7. Confidentiality agreements and non-competition clauses

**John Adams***

## INTRODUCTION

Although it is debated whether or not the terms 'trade secrets' and 'know-how' mean the same thing, for the purposes of the present chapter I am going to treat them as equivalent, as does UNCTAD in the following passage.

> Know-how is practical information that may give a person or company a competitive advantage. As long as it is known only to a few people, such information can be legally recognized and protected as a trade secret even though it fails to fulfil the criteria of patentability. A claim for protection of know-how as a trade secret requires that efforts be made to prevent disclosure. Law makes the taking without permission of a trade secret an illegal act, but not the discovery by proper means, i.e. by independent discovery, accidental or actual disclosure, or by reverse engineering.[1]

Article 10*bis* Paris Convention, which requires member states to afford protection against acts of unfair competition, has no express provision dealing with the protection of trade secrets.[2] However, article 39 TRIPS Agreement is clear on this. It provides as follows:

> 1. In the course of ensuring effective protection against unfair competition as provided in Article 10*bis* of the Paris Convention (1967), Members shall protect undisclosed information in accordance with paragraph 2 and data submitted to governments or governmental agencies in accordance with paragraph 3.
> 2. Natural and legal persons shall have the possibility of preventing information lawfully within their control from being disclosed to, acquired by, or used by others without their consent in a manner contrary to honest commercial practices so long as such information:

* Professor, Schools of Law, University of Sheffield (Emeritus), UK and University of Notre Dame, France.

1 Accessed 20/06/03.

2 Though misappropriation of trade secrets could be said to fall under the general prohibition on acts of competition contrary to honest practices – see AIPPI Resolution taken in Copenhagen ANNUAIRE 1995/1 pp. 38, 39.

> (a) is secret in the sense that it is not, as a body or in the precise configuration and assembly of its components, generally known among or readily accessible to persons within the circles that normally deal with the kind of information in question;
> (b) has commercial value because it is secret; and
> (c) has been subject to reasonable steps under the circumstances, by the person lawfully in control of the information, to keep it secret.
> 3. Members, when requiring, as a condition of approving the marketing of pharmaceutical or of agricultural chemical products which utilize new chemical entities, the submission of undisclosed test or other data, the origination of which involves a considerable effort, shall protect such data against unfair commercial use. In addition, Members shall protect such data against disclosure, except where necessary to protect the public, or unless steps are taken to ensure that the data are protected against unfair commercial use.

Accordingly, member states of the WTO are obliged to afford effective protection to trade secrets. This may be done either through a general law against unfair competition, or through a specific law.

The types of information which a business may wish to keep secret include the following:

a. patentable inventions or processes;
b. other novel ideas reduced to practical technical procedures;
c. 'know-how': that is, the fund of technical knowledge and experience acquired by a specialized production organization. It may be, and usually is, noted down in documents, drawings and so on;
d. ideas such as advertising schemes, and other highly confidential information of a non-technical character.

The way in which unwanted transfers of secret information are most likely to occur is through employees either moving to a competitor (or setting up their own business), or disclosing secret information to a competitor, usually in exchange for a payment. The latter is clearly conduct in respect of which member states should provide a remedy pursuant to their obligations under article 39, so that a competitor buying information this way may be enjoined from using it. It is in relation to employees moving that there is a problem. The reason for this is that there is a tension between the principle that employees must be free to use the skills they have learned in their former employment for the purposes of their new employment, and the desire of employers not to let information of the types described above fall into the hands of competitors.

## CONTRACTS IN RESTRAINT OF TRADE

By way of illustration I propose to look at the way in which this tension has been resolved in England and Wales,[3] because we have nearly six centuries' experience of dealing with the problem.[4] It is also the case that the law of the United States, which was strongly influenced by the law of England and Wales,[5] was a strong driver behind the TRIPS provisions cited above. It should also be realized that the tensions between competing policies which the law must resolve are the same in any legal system. This tension is essentially between the right of an individual to offer his or her services freely (including the body of skill and knowledge built up in a previous employment) and the right of a former employer to protect his or her business.

A contract in restraint of trade has been defined as 'one in which a party (the covenantor) agrees with any other party (the covenantee) to restrict his liberty in the future to carry on trade with other persons not parties to the contract in such a manner as he chooses'.[6] English law[7] started with the general proposition that all restraints of trade were bad, and therefore void.[8] However, exceptions were recognized, such as limited restraints given by the sellers of business, to protect their buyers.[9] It was also the case that intellectual property[10] created by an employee in the course of his or her employment belonged to the employer, and the employee could be restrained from infringing those rights, even though it was the employee who had created them.

The basis of the doctrine that restraints of trade were void was unclear. It might have been based on the view that it is desirable to preserve free competition, or it may have been based simply on the protection of a weak party

---

3 On the law of England and Wales in this area generally, see Jefferson, *Restraint of Trade*, Wiley 1996.

4 The earliest case is generally taken to be *The Dyer's Case* (1414) YB 2 H, 5 fol. 5b.

5 The first US case was *Vickey* v. *Welch* 36 Mass. 523 (1837).

6 *Petrofina (Great Britain) Ltd* v. *Martin* [1966] Ch 146, 180 per Diplock LJ.

7 Essentially, from the *Statutum Walliae* 1272, it was English law which had prevailed in Wales. Welsh law had a literature, but the law was essentially based on ancient tribal customs, and different in character from modern rational law (see Pollock and Maitland, *History of English Law*, Cambridge University Press. 1968, vol. I, p. 221; Weber, *Economy and Society*, Berkeley: University of California Press, 1978).

8 *Mitchel* v. *Reynolds* (1711) 1 P. Williams 181, 1 Smith's L.C. 458.

9 *Mitchel* v. *Reynolds* (above) at p. 190–1, 1 Smith's L.C. at p. 465; *Rannie* v. *Irvine* (1844) 7 M & Gr 969.

10 For present purposes I am using this term to include trade secrets, although it is controversial whether or not trade secrets are strictly intellectual property.

against oppression,[11] or possibly both. At all events, the rule against these restraints was relaxed over the next 200 years. The modern rules applied in England and Wales derive from the speech of Lord Macnaghten in *Nordenfelt* v. *Maxim Nordenfelt Guns and Ammunition Co Ltd*[12] and are as follows:

> All interference with individual liberty of action in trading, and all restraints of trade of themselves, if there is nothing more, are contrary to public policy, and therefore void. That is the general rule. But there are exceptions: restraints of trade and interference with individual liberty of action may be justified by the special circumstances of a particular case. It is a sufficient justification, and indeed it is the only justification, if the restriction is reasonable – reasonable, that is, in reference to the interests of the parties concerned and reasonable in reference to the interests of the public, so framed and so guarded as to afford adequate protection to the party in whose favour it is imposed, while at the same time it is in no way injurious to the public.[13]

The onus of showing that the restraint is reasonable between the parties rests upon the party alleging that it is so, that is to say, upon the covenantee. The onus of showing that, notwithstanding that a covenant is reasonable between the parties, it is nevertheless injurious to the public interest and therefore void, rests upon the party alleging it to be so, that is to say, usually upon the covenantor. But once the agreement is before the court it is open to scrutiny in all its surrounding circumstances as a question of law.

Although this formulation separates the questions 'is there a restraint of trade?' and if so 'is it reasonable?' the courts often pose the question in the rolled-up form 'does the contract unreasonably restrict?'[14] The leading modern case on restraint of trade covenants in England and Wales is *Esso Petroleum Co Ltd* v. *Harper's Garage (Stourport) Ltd*,[15] which involved a 'solus' agreement with the oil company Esso; that is, an agreement in which the proprietor of a filling station[16] agreed to buy his supplies of petrol and so on exclusively from Esso.[17] Solus agreements are obviously restraints of trade, and the House of Lords laid down a number rules in relation to these.

---

11 *Anson on Contract*, ed. Beatson, 28th edn, OUP, 2002, p. 367.

12 [1894] AC 535, 565 (HL). This was not an employee/employer case, but the rules laid down in it are an important starting point for the law governing contracts in restraint of trade.

13 [1894] AC 535, 565.

14 *Esso Petroleum Co Ltd* v. *Harper's Garage (Stourport) Ltd* [1968] AC 269, 331 per Lord Wilberforce.

15 Jbiotem (n. 14).

16 That is, 'gas station' in US usage.

17 Again, not an employer/employee case therefore.

1. The court will not merely look at the particular agreement, but will consider the trading pattern which emerges from a group of similar agreements. Thus, in this case, the House of Lords was prepared to take into account the fact that these solus agreements enabled Esso to keep down distribution costs: they needed to distribute to 7000 outlets instead of the much greater number that they would have to supply without the tie.
2. The length of the tie which will be acceptable will depend on the facts. In this case five years was considered acceptable because it was necessary to maintain a stable distribution system throughout the country, and worked to the advantage of the garage owners in that some ties would end almost every week, so that Esso would have to treat owners reasonably to secure renewals against intense competition from other oil companies. On the other hand, 21 years would stretch beyond any period for which developments were reasonably foreseeable.
3. The court will consider benefits received in return for the restraints, such as discounts on goods not given to free outlets, and financial assistance and the like received by the covenantors.
4. Provided that the agreement is otherwise reasonable, a provision that the covenantor may not dispose of the business except to a person approved by the covenantee will be reasonable on the basis that it is only by such means that the covenantee can ensure that the tie will continue for the full length of the agreement.
5. It would appear that the courts will be reluctant to interfere with covenants of the sort commonly found in leases.
6. The court will consider the relative bargaining power of the parties.[18]

Although this case was concerned with solus agreements, it is a useful illustration of the type of cost/benefit analysis courts have to try to carry out in relation to all types of restraints of trade, in addition to the unfair contract terms factor set out in paragraph (6).

For our immediate purposes, it is clear, however, that in the case of covenants between employers and employees there are special considerations which distinguish them from covenants entered into in other situations such as in the case of solus agreements, and on the sale of a business.[19] Moreover, in

---

18 As noted above, one of the two bases of the doctrine is the protection of those whose bargaining power is weak from those whose bargaining power is strong.

19 See *Nordenfelt* v. *Maxim Nordenfelt Guns and Ammunition Co Ltd* [1894] AC 535 in which a covenant in a contract between Maxim Nordenfelt, the inventor of the 'Maxim' machine gun, and an armaments company bearing his name lasting for 20 years and worldwide in extent, was upheld: the business was, after all, global.

the case of employees, another body of law can come into play, the law on the protection of trade secrets.

## COVENANTS BETWEEN EMPLOYERS AND EMPLOYEES

Provided that the employer has bought the full-time services of the employee, express restraints which operate during the currency of the employment are arguably merely an expression of the fact that the general law impliedly gives the employer the exclusive right to the services of the employee. In other words, the agreement does not restrain the employee because he or she is restrained already.[20]

Similarly, undertakings not to use otherwise than in the course of the employer's business, or disclose, an employer's trade secrets, may go no further than the obligations of fidelity imposed by the general law, and are thus not restrictive. Indeed, as we will see, the obligation of fidelity may go further than the law of trade secrets. I return to this below.

## KNOW-HOW AND TRADE SECRETS

As noted above, if information enjoys the character of a trade secret, its use may be restrained even without a covenant. Although, as I said at the outset, it is debated whether or not the terms 'trade secret' and 'know-how' are synonymous, for present purposes it will suffice to bear in mind the UNCTAD definition given above. It can be observed that secret information of this sort plays a most valuable part in modern industry. Very often know-how about the manufacturing processes involved is a necessary adjunct to the successful exploitation of a patented invention (the nature of which is necessarily public). Obviously, it is impossible to preserve a secret in this way where the information involved can easily be discovered by such things as 'reverse engineering' or gas chromatography, but it is easy to think of examples of well-known products whose formulae are secret. Coca-Cola, and well-known flower fragrances, are obvious examples which come to mind. Necessarily, however, it will be less easy to protect a *product* in this way than it is to protect a secret *process* and possibly therefore the products of the process.

In determining what action can be taken against a person who has had a trade or business secret disclosed to him in confidence, and who breaches, or threatens to breach that confidence, we must distinguish the situation of

---

20 *Lilley* v. *Elwin* (1848) 11 QB 742.

employees as confidants from that of independent parties or ex-employees. So far as independent parties are concerned, the first question is whether or not the relationship between the parties falls within any previously recognized fiduciary category, that is, whether the core duties between the parties included loyalty and fidelity.[21] Examples of such relationships are the duties of principal and agent, and or partners, to each other, and the duties owed by a company director to the company. The list of such relationships is not closed, but the courts are reluctant to find such a fiduciary duty in purely commercial relationships.

Although the extent of the employee's duty will vary in different employment situations, it will generally be broken if the employee exploits information that amounts to a trade secret in the technical legal sense[22] for his own benefit, or intends to do so. But the duty of fidelity extends beyond this. For example, memorizing marketing information such as customer lists, or copying them, with a view to canvassing customers when an employee has left his employment and set up his or her own business, will breach this duty of fidelity.[23]

If information lacks the character of confidentiality, however, and its disclosure breaches no duty of fidelity to the employer, an employee is free to disclose it. In *Service Corp International plc & anr* v. *Channel Four Television Corp & anr*,[24] an employee working undercover for the defendants who filmed events at the plaintiff's funeral homes was held not to have breached any confidence, as the film disclosed nothing confidential.[25]

After the term of employment has terminated it becomes crucial to distinguish information which amounts to a trade secret from other information. The ex-employee may not use or disclose trade secrets; that is, information which is of a high degree of confidentiality. Moreover, if information qualifies as confidential, *both the original recipient of the information, and third parties, once they get to know that the information was originally disclosed in confidence*, can be restrained from using it by the action for breach of confidence.[26] What sort of information qualifies as a trade secret?

Lord Greene MR in *Saltman Engineering* v. *Campbell & Co*[27] described

21 *Indata Equipment Supplies* v. *ACL* [1998] FSR 248.

22 What information qualifies as a trade secret in law is dealt with below.

23 *Faccenda Chicken* v. *Fowler* [1986] 1 All ER 617.

24 [1999] EMLR 83.

25 Although it did show some things about the plaintiff's business which were quite damaging.

26 *Fraser* v. *Evans* [1969] 1 QB 349, [1969] 1 All ER 8, CA: *Butler* v. *Board of Trade* [1971] Ch 680 at 690.

27 (1948) 65 RPC 203.

confidential information as something not public property and public knowledge. This is pretty vague, but suggests that relative, not total, secrecy suffices.[28] In *Lansing Linde* v. *Kerr*,[29] Staughton LJ observed that the owner of the information must limit its dissemination, or at least not encourage widespread dissemination, so that the fewer employees have access to it, the more likely it will be held to be confidential. There is also some authority for the proposition that the test of confidentiality is subjective. In *Thomas Marshall* v. *Guinle*,[30] Sir Robert Megarry VC suggested the following test:

1. the information must be information the release of which the *owner* believes would be injurious to him or of advantage to his rivals or others;
2. the *owner* [*emphasis supplied*] must believe the information is confidential or secret, that is, not already in the public domain;
3. the owner's belief under the previous two heads must be reasonable;
4. the information must be judged in the light of the usages and practices of the particular industry concerned.

It must be borne in mind, however, that Sir Robert's remarks were made in the context of an application for an interlocutory (now interim) injunction. It would be appropriate to take into account the owner's subjective beliefs in that context, whilst it might not be appropriate to do so when finally deciding the issues between the parties.

The type of information which will in general be regarded as confidential include that described at the beginning of this chapter. In general, to the extent that the information itself, independently of any skill on the part of the person using it, is original and useful, its disclosure may be restrained. To the extent that it is generally known or readily knowable or simply depends on the skill of the person using it for its utility, its disclosure or use elsewhere may not be restrained beyond the term of the agreement. This applies even though the person using it was given the opportunity to acquire the skill through the contract which purports to restrain him. In the case of *Stevenson Jordan and Harrison Ltd* v. *Macdonald and Evans*,[31] the plaintiff company's business consisted of known principles of business management applied to the problems involved in certain functions of commercial activity, with a view to isolating details of production and expenditure and fixing responsibility for their control. The plaintiffs failed to restrain publication of a book containing

---

[28] See also *Franchi* v. *Franchi* [1967] RPC 149.

[29] [1991] 1 All ER 418, 425.

[30] [1979] Ch 227.

[31] (1951) 68 RPC 190, [1951] 1 TLR 101. See also *Faccenda Chicken* v. *Fowler* [1986] 1 All ER 617, [1987] 1 Ch. 117.

a complete disclosure of their system of working. The reason was that the principles of cost accounting on which the system was based were generally known, and simply depended on the skill of their application by the plaintiff's employees for their success in any given case.

As noted above, the use of the names of customers and other learned *bona fide* by an employee in the course of his or her employment, as opposed to being deliberately memorized or copied so as to constitute a breach of the duty of fidelity, cannot be restrained.[32]

The uncertainty in this area is whether or not there is a category of information between true trade secrets and know-how (whose use can be enjoined without a contract), and generally known information of the sort involved in *Stevenson Jordan* (which cannot be the subject of a contractual restraint), whose use can be prevented by a contractual term. In *Faccenda Chicken*,[33] Goulding J thought that there was such an intermediate category.[34] In the Court of Appeal, however, Neil LJ thought that a contractual restraint would not protect an employer against use of information in this second category. He suggested that a restrictive covenant would not be enforced unless the protection sought was reasonably necessary to protect a trade secret, or to prevent some personal influence over customers being abused to entice them away.[35] This dictum caused a great deal of disquiet amongst practitioners.[36] Arguably, however, the problem he was addressing was that Goulding J had drawn his intermediate category of information too broadly, because he had said that without a restraint the ex-employee was free to use his *full* skill and knowledge (which would encompass the general skill and knowledge the use of which it has always been held that a covenant cannot restrain). At all events, clearly on the facts, a contractual restraint would not have helped. It is likely, however, that between employer and ex-employee a higher degree of confidentiality is required than between independent parties, for the reasons given above.

This is all slightly confusing, and hardly satisfactory for those trying to advise on particular cases. Fortunately, *Lansing Linde Ltd* v. *Kerr*[37] clarified

---

32 *Helmore* v. *Smith* (No 2) (1886) 35 Ch D 449, CA: *Re Irish, Irish* v. *Irish* (1888) 40 Ch D 49. Cf. *Robb* v. *Green* [1895] 2 QB 1, *Faccenda Chicken Ltd* v. *Fowler* [1986] 1 All ER 617, [1987] 1 Ch. 117 CA; *Fibrenetix Storage Ltd* v. *Davis (Tom)* [2004] EWHC 1359 (QB). See Hull (1986) 10 EIPR 319 for a helpful discussion of this.

33 [1984] ICR 589, 599.

34 In that case the plaintiff's former manager had set up a rival business using his knowledge of the customers of his former employers (which customers were fairly generally known throughout the firm).

35 [1987] 1 Ch 117, 137.

36 See Hull (1988) 12 EIPR 387.

37 [1991] 1 All ER 415; considered in *Fibrenetix Storage Ltd* v. *Davis (Tom)* [2004] EWHC 1359 (QB).

the situation somewhat. In that case Staughton and Butler-Sloss LJJ both expressed the view that 'trade' secrets were not restricted to secret formulae for the manufacture of products, but could include highly confidential information of a non-technical or non-scientific character, such as customers' names. Staughton LJ in *Lansing Linde* also expressed the view that the class of information which can justify a contractual restriction is wider than confidential information which would ordinarily be called a trade secret.[38] This view has since been approved by Bell J in *SBJ Stephenson Ltd* v. *Mandy*.[39] The practical advice, in any event, is to include express covenants where appropriate in contracts, because few people are prepared to go to court to have declared invalid what they have clearly assented to.

When a defendant is in breach of confidence, he can be restrained from using the information for a period which will prevent him from using it as a 'spring-board' to get a 'head-start' over the world,[40] but the purpose of the injunction being to prevent the defendant taking an unfair advantage, it should not be continued beyond the time the advantage may reasonably be expected to continue.

> In relation to confidential information, as opposed to real trade secrets, the Court should be concerned not to give the injured party more protection than he realistically needed or to discourage or prohibit what in the course of time becomes legitimate competition.[41]

This passage suggests that the basis of the action is *restitutionary*, and certainly some writers have argued this.[42] But the action could be purely tortious,[43] or purely equitable. There is even authority for the proposition that confidential information is property, and the action of breach of confidence is based on interference with a property right.[44]

---

38 Ibid., p. 426.

39 [2000] IRLR 233.

40 *Terrapin Ltd* v. *Builders Supplies (Hayes) Ltd* [1960] RPC 173, 177.

41 *Roger Bullivant Ltd* v. *Ellis* [1987] ICR 464, 481 per May LJ.

42 See *Goff & Jones on Restitution*, 5th edn, 1998, Ch.34; Birks 'Introduction to the Law of Restitution' 1985, pp. 343 et seq.

43 Certainly, damages are assessed on a tortious basis – *Indata Equipment Supplies* v. *ACL Supplies* [1998] FSR 248.

44 See Coleman, *The Legal Protection of Trade Secrets*, Sweet & Maxwell, 1992, Ch. 3.

## DRAFTING AN EFFECTIVE RESTRAINT OF TRADE COVENANT

If what the covenant is seeking to protect is not a true trade secret, but rather the goodwill of the former employer's business which a former employee could damage by using the knowledge of the former employer's business he or she has acquired, the following points should be borne in mind:

1. The agreements should contain a choice of jurisdiction and choice of law clause. This is very important, because the uncertain legal status even of confidential information in the strict technical sense gives rise to serious problems in relation to private international law.[45]
2. A realistic evaluation needs to be made as to whether trade secrets in the technical sense are likely to be involved. If they are, as we have seen, use and disclosure of these can be restrained both during and after the end of the term of employment. Strictly, a covenant is not necessary for this purpose, but it does serve the useful function of reminding the employee of his or her duties.
3. If the information is not technically a trade secret, but it is information about the former employer's business use of which during the course of employment would have been impressed with the obligation of fidelity, and which could be used after the termination of the employment to damage the goodwill[46] attached to the former employer's business, its use can be restrained to a limited extent. An example of such information would be customer lists deliberately copied or memorized. Obviously, the danger is that the former employee will circularize such customers to tell them of his or her new business. The restraint of trade covenant should be *explicitly* linked to the geographical extent of the former employer's goodwill, that is, the area from which the employer is likely to draw in customers. Therefore a *realistic* assessment should be made of the geographical extent of that goodwill, and thus of the geographical extent of the restraint needed, and also of the time needed for the restraint in the particular business context. For example, in the case of a highly localized business, only a very limited geographical restraint is necessary or advisable, to protect the goodwill associated with the employer's business.

---

[45] This uncertainty exists whether the underlying regime is unfair competition law or, as in England and Wales, a *sui generis* regime – see J. Fawcett and P. Torremans, *Intellectual Property and Private International Law*, Clarendon Press, 1998, p. 431 et seq.

[46] That is, the attractive force that brings in custom – *IRC* v. *Muller & Co's Margerine Ltd* [1901] AC 217.

Moreover, if the former employee has started a business which is competing with the former employer's business, in a relatively short time customers will come to learn of this new business, and they are free to take their custom to it, as is the former employee free to supply their requirements. So a relatively short restraint in terms of time is all that is likely to be upheld. On the other hand, in *Nordenfelt* v. *Maxim Nordenfelt Guns and Ammunition Co Ltd*, mentioned above, a worldwide restraint for 20 years was upheld as not unreasonable as protection for the company's goodwill.

4. A covenant restraining the covenantor from soliciting the customers of the business after the term of employment has ended is likely to be upheld, and so this should be in a separate clause from the above covenants. Non-solicitation covenants are likely to be upheld,[47] but the law cannot stop customers moving with the employee without solicitation.[48] This last consideration means that, in the case of professional services such as accountancy and law, where there is a strong personal relationship between the client and the adviser, such covenants are often of little use.

## CONCLUSION

The tension set out at the beginning of this chapter between the need to allow employees freedom to practise their trade wherever they choose to go, and the need for employers to protect their legitimate interests, will have been apparent in various parts of the above discussion. It may be helpful to conclude by reminding ourselves what an employer's legitimate interests are. These include:

1. the protection of the employer's genuine trade secrets; that is, the information has the character that the law recognizes as having the character of a trade secret;
2. the protection of the employer's goodwill;
3. similarly, protection against former employees soliciting customers of their former employers.

---

47 See, e.g., *L C Services & ors.* v. *Brown & anr.* [2003] EWHC 3024 (QB).
48 *Oswald Hickson Collier & Co (a firm)* v. *Carter-Ruck* [1984] 2 All ER 15.

# 8. Protection of know-how in Chinese enterprises and employment relationships

**Hailing Shan***

## INTRODUCTION

Under current Chinese law, know-how, with the basic characteristics of a trade secret, is an important object of the law on the protection of trade secrets.

China's current legal framework of protection of trade secrets is based upon international treaties.[1] It consists of the Anti-Unfair Competition Law as the central piece, as well as regulations contained in Contract Law, Labour Law and Criminal Law. According to the hierarchy of authority, this legal framework consists of national laws promulgated by the National People's Congress and its Standing Committee; administrative regulations promulgated by the State Council; local regulations adopted by the People's Congress and its Standing Committee at provincial, large municipal and Special Economic Zone level; ministerial (departmental) regulations adopted by various ministries and commissions under the State Council, the Central Bank, the Auditor's Office and other institutions directly affiliated to the State Council. During the period 1985–2002, more than 130 important laws and regulations related to the protection of trade secrets (including know-how) were enacted and entered into force, including 24 national laws, 15 administrative regulations adopted by the State Council, 76 ministerial (departmental) regulations and 15 local regulations. These laws and regulations have jointly formed the legal sources for the protection of trade secrets.

* Professor, School of International Law, East China University of Politics and Law.

1 China joined the WTO on 11 December 2001 and started to fulfil the obligations conferred by the treaty, including the obligation of protecting undisclosed information provided by TRIPS.

## DEFINITION AND CHARACTERISTICS OF KNOW-HOW: THE TRADE SECRET AS AN IMPORTANT COMPONENT

Current laws and judicial interpretations define trade secret and know-how as follows. Article 10 of the Anti-Unfair Competition Law enacted in 1993 provides that 'the term 'trade secret' used in this article refers to technical and operational information which is unknown to the public, capable of bringing in economic benefits for the right holder, practically applicable and the secrecy of which is guarded by specific measures adopted by the right holder'.

Article 219 of the 1997 Criminal Law provides that 'the term "trade secret" used in this article refers to technical and operational information which is unknown to the public, capable of bringing in economic benefits for the right holder, practically applicable and the secrecy of which is guarded by specific measures adopted by the right holder'.

In 2001, the Supreme People's Court promulgated the *Memorandum of Nationwide Court Working Conference of Intellectual Property Trial on Several Issues Concerning the Hearing of Disputes over Technology Contracts*, which points out that 'know-how as referred to in Ch.18 of the Contract Law means technical information which is unknown to the public, capable of bringing in economic benefits for the right holder, practically applicable and the secrecy of which is guarded by specific measures adopted by the right holder'.

Therefore, in Chinese legislative and judicial practice, know-how protected by law shares the same characteristics as trade secrets, which are as follows.

1. Know-how is unknown to the public. Article 2 of *Several Regulations on Prohibiting Activities Infringing Trade Secrets* adopted by the State Administration for Industry and Commerce provides that 'such information can not be obtained through public channels'. The Supreme Court's view is that 'such technical information, as a whole, or certain precise combination or component of it, is unknown or not easy to acquire in the relevant domain where such type of information normally circulated'.[2]
2. Know-how has economic value and practical applicability. The Supreme Court has pointed out in its document that such technical information has commercial value due to its secrecy and is capable of conferring on its holder economic benefits or competitive advantages.[3] Article 2 of *Several*

---

[2] Article 2 of *Memorandum of Nationwide Court Working Conference of Intellectual Property Trial on Several Issues Concerning the Hearing of Disputes over Technology Contracts*, adopted 19 June 2001.

[3] Ibid.

*Regulations on Prohibiting Activities Infringing Trade Secrets* adopted by the State Administration for Industry and Commerce provides that 'such information has certain applicability, is capable of bringing in for the right holder real or potential economic benefits or competitive advantages'.

3. Measures have been taken by the right holder to guard its secrecy. The fact that the right holder has taken measures to guard the secrecy of the know-how is an important condition for such know-how to be protected by law. These measures include the conclusion of the agreement on confidentiality, establishment of the enterprise internal regime on confidentiality and other reasonable measures.[4] In order to ascertain whether reasonable measures have been taken by the parties to guard the secrecy, the court will, taking into consideration the circumstances of the case at hand, determine whether measures taken by the right holder of the know-how is sufficient, in a normal situation, to maintain the confidentiality of such know-how.[5]

## BASIC MEANS TO PROTECT KNOW-HOW BY CHINESE ENTERPRISES

The main forms and means of know-how infringement in Chinese enterprises include (i) the leaking of know-how occurring during the transfer of talents among enterprises; (ii) an individual employee disclosing, without authorization, know-how to others for his personal benefit; (iii) a certain employee undertaking, without authorization and during his period of employment, a part-time job in other enterprises and disclosing know-how; (iv) the know-how being unintentionally disclosed during a tour for outside visitors; (v) retired employees being hired by competitors; (vi) the employees not having taken confidentiality seriously enough; (vii) academic papers published by employees disclosing the know-how through the introduction of the product.

In order to prevent the leaking of the enterprise's own know-how, in respect of the scenario mentioned above, a lot of Chinese enterprises have, on the strength of foreign experiences, taken the following measures: (i) ensuring the conclusion of a confidentiality agreement, including that between transferor and transferee during a technology transfer, that between the enterprise and its employees, and the non-competition promise applicable to both current and former employees in the employment contract; (ii) displaying confidentiality,

4 See Article 2 of *Several Regulations on Prohibiting Activities Infringing Trade Secrets*, adopted by the State Administration for Industry and Commerce.

5 *Supra*, note 2.

for example, using a stamp showing the confidential nature of the document and promulgating rules on confidentiality for the enterprise; (iii) clarifying the ownership of intellectual property, for example, incorporating specific provisions on the ownership of know-how subsequently acquired in technology transfer contracts, concluding intellectual property agreement with employees, defining the trade secrets of the employer and the skills of the employee in the employment contracts.

In a case of the infringement of the know-how of the enterprise, employers normally resort to legal remedies in order to cut the loss or seek compensation. The remedies available to them include the following.

### Holding the Infringer Liable for the Breach of Contract on the Ground of the Confidence Agreement in the Contract in Accordance with the Contract Law

Article 107 of China's 1999 Contract Law provides that the non-performing party or the party which has failed to fulfil its promised duties included in the contract terms shall be liable for the breach of the contract and shall continue the performance of the contract, take remedial measures, or pay damages. Article 43 provides that any trade secret learnt by parties in concluding a contract shall not be disclosed or unfairly used, regardless of the status of the contract. The party that has failed to observe such duty and caused the losses of the other party shall be obliged to pay damages. Article 60 provides that parties shall fully fulfil their contractual obligations according to the terms of the contract, including the obligation of confidence. Even after the termination of the contract, the parties shall, abiding by the doctrine of good faith, fulfil the obligation of confidence according to transaction practices.

However, to a certain extent, the contract mentioned here mainly refers to technology transfer contracts in which a confidentiality agreement has been concluded. This is because, according to current Chinese law, if contents regarding the confidentiality of trade secrets have been agreed upon by parties to an employment contract and the employee has failed to fulfil the obligation of confidence and infringed the trade secrets of the employer, such labour disputes shall be subject to arbitration by the Arbitration Committee for Labour Disputes. The Arbitration Committee shall accept the application for arbitration and make the ruling according to relevant regulations and the terms of the employment contract.[6]

---

6 *Letter on the Issue of Infringement of Trade Secrets in Labour Dispute*, promulgated by the Secretariat of Ministry of Labour and Social Security on 7 July 1999.

## Applying for Labour Dispute Arbitration by the Local Arbitration Committee for Labour Disputes on the Ground of the Employment Contract

Labour dispute arbitration refers to the scheme where labour disputes are heard and settled by the Arbitration Committee for Labour Disputes. The 1995 Labour Law of the People's Republic of China provides in its third chapter regarding employment contracts and collective contracts, that the parties to an employment contract may in the contract agree upon a clause concerning the maintaining the confidentiality of trade secrets of the employer (article 22). The obligation of confidence and the obligation of non-competition arising from the employment relationship is one aspect which gives rise to labour disputes involving trade secrets between employers and its current and former employees.

Article 77(1) of the Chinese Labour Law provides for the means to settle labour disputes: 'In cases of labour disputes between employers and employees, the parties may, in accordance with the law, apply for mediation, arbitration or initiate legal action, or settle the dispute through negotiation.' It should be pointed out that arbitration has been prioritized in settling labour disputes; that is, while mediation is only optional and not a compulsory procedure for the parties to go through, arbitration is a compulsory procedure and a prerequisite for litigation. The court will reject any law suit brought by the parties to a labour dispute which has not been subject to arbitration.[7]

However, the parties may appeal, before the court, the ruling of the Arbitration Committee for Labour Disputes (Figure 8.1) regarding disputes arising from the performance of an employment contract or from the de facto employment relationship in the absence of an employment contract, and the court shall accept such a case.[8]

## Holding the Infringer Liable for Infringement and Seeking Compensation in Accordance with the Anti-Unfair Competition Law

Article 10 of the Chinese 1993 Anti-Unfair Competition Law provides that 'Business operators shall refrain from infringing others' trade secrets using the following means: (i) obtaining a trade secret from the right holder through

---

[7] See Article 6 of *Regulation of the People's Republic of China on the Settlement of Labour Disputes in Enterprises* (State Council Order No. 117).

[8] See Article 1 of the *Interpretation on Several Issues Concerning the Application of Law in the Trial of Labour Disputes*, Supreme Court Interpretation No. 14, 2001, adopted by the Judicial Committee of the Supreme Court on 22 March 2001.

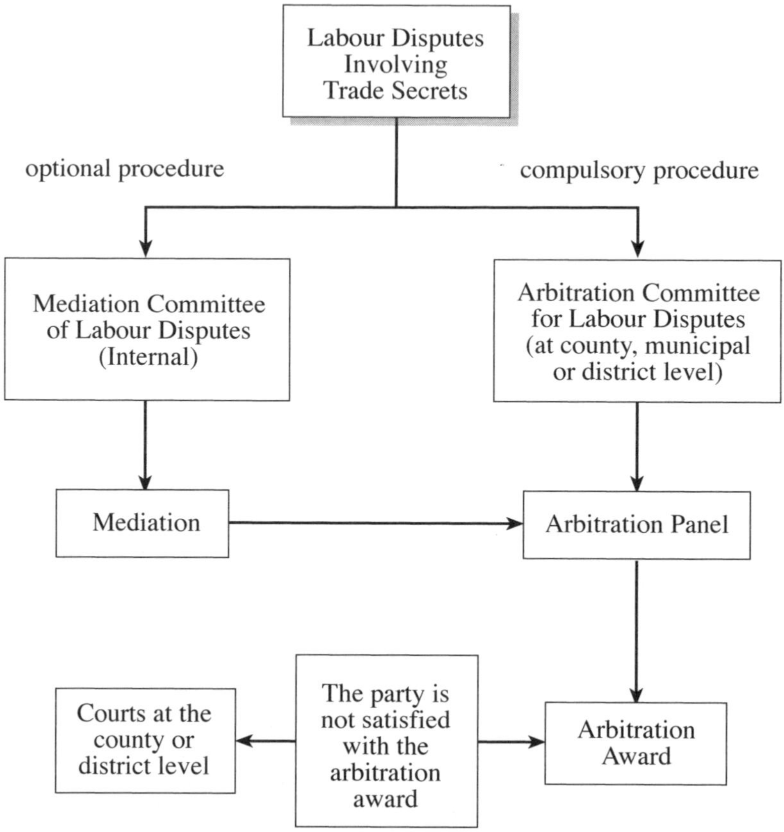


*Figure 8.1 Chinese arbitration procedure for labour disputes involving trade secrets*

theft, enticement, coercion, or other illegitimate means; (ii) disclosing, using or allowing others to use such trade secret obtained through the illegitimate means identified above; (iii) disclosing, using or allowing others to use the trade secret in his possession in breach of a contractual obligation of confidence or an obligation of confidence imposed by the right holder of such trade secret; (iv) and, for the third party, who knows or should know the illegal activities mentioned in the previous sections, obtaining, using or disclosing other's trade secret by such third party.'

The *Several Regulations on Prohibiting Activities Infringing Trade Secrets* adopted by the State Administration for Industry and Commerce in 1995 in accordance with the Anti-Unfair Competition Law has extended the scope of

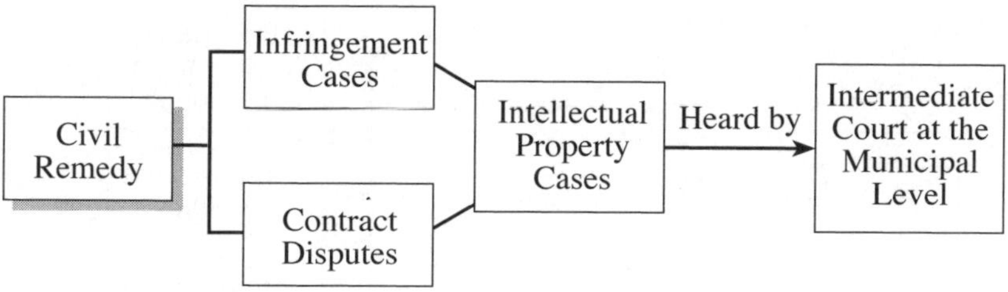


*Figure 8.2 Civil cases*

the term 'infringer' to cover not only business operators but also individuals; that is, infringement of trade secrets conducted by individuals may also be punishable by law (article 5). (See Figure 8.2.) According to the Anti-Unfair Competition Law, the business operators whose legitimate interests suffered from activities of unfair competition may initiate a civil action in the people's court and hold the infringer liable (article 20).

## Applying for Measures against Infringement to be Taken by the Administrative Authority for Industry and Commerce in Accordance with the Anti-Unfair Competition Law

Article 16 of the Chinese 1993 Anti-Unfair Competition Law provides that the administrative authority for industry and commerce at the county level, municipal level or above has the authority to inspect any activity of unfair competition within its jurisdiction. The *Several Regulations on Prohibiting Activities Infringing Trade Secrets* adopted by the State Administration for Industry and Commerce in 1995 provides that the administrative authority for industry and commerce has the authority to order the infringer engaging in the following activities infringing the trade secret to desist from infringing or to impose a fine of between 10 000 and 200 000 yuan, depending on the circumstances: (i) obtaining a trade secret from the right holder through theft, enticement, coercion, or other illegitimate means; (ii) disclosing, using or allowing others to use such trade secret obtained through the illegitimate means identified above; (iii) for the unit or individual who has a business relationship with the right holder, disclosing, using or allowing others to use the trade secret in his possession in breach of a contractual obligation of confidence or an obligation of confidence imposed by the right holder of such trade secret; (iv) for the employee of the right holder, disclosing, using or allowing others to use the trade secret in his possession in breach of a contractual obligation of confidence or an obligation of confidence imposed by the right holder of such trade secret; (v) for the third party, who knows or should know the illegal activities

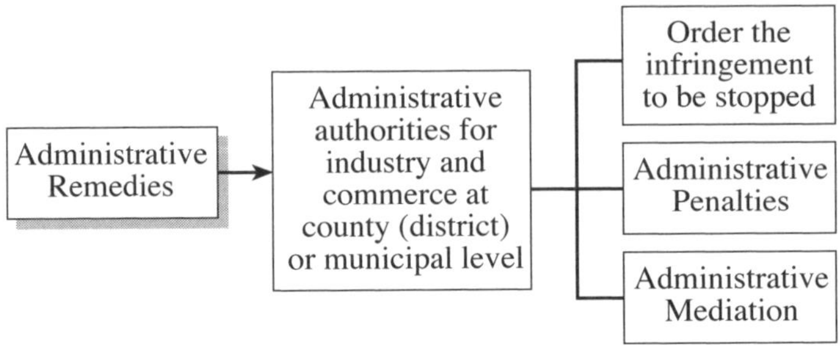


*Figure 8.3 Administrative cases*

mentioned in the previous sections, obtaining, using or disclosing other's trade secret by such third party.[9]

However, according to the Anti-Unfair Competition Law, the State Administration for Industry and Commerce and its local branches can only take administrative measures provided by the law. The aggrieved party can only resort to civil legal action for compensation if its trade secrets have suffered losses due to the infringement. The purpose for the party to apply for administrative measures to be taken by administrative authorities for industry and commerce is normally to prevent in time the infringement from happening, or to prevent any imminent or further loss. At the same time, the facts found by the state administrative authorities for industry and commerce in their inspection process are often accepted by the court during the trial, which may, to a certain extent, ease the burden of proof conferred upon the aggrieved party in the civil action.

### Informing the Police and the Prosecutor's Office Enabling the Authority to File Criminal Charges against the Infringer in Accordance with the Criminal Law

The crime of infringing trade secrets is a new crime added in the 1997 amendment of the Chinese Criminal Law. It refers to the illegal activities infringing others' trade secrets that have caused serious losses to the right holder. Article 219 of the Criminal Law provides that whoever has engaged in any of the activities listed below that infringe trade secrets and who has caused serious losses to the right holder of such trade secrets, shall, in cases where the loss suffered by the right holder is serious, be sentenced to fixed-term imprisonment of not more than three years or criminal detention in conjunction with,

---

9 Articles 3, 6, 7.

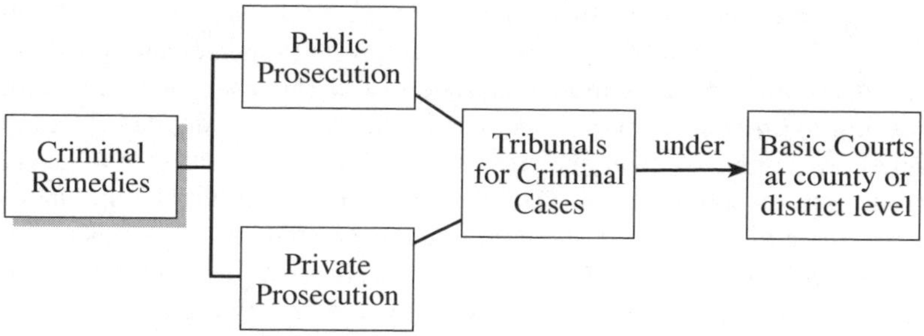


*Figure 8.4 Criminal cases*

or independently of, a statutory fine. In cases where the loss suffered by the right holder is extremely serious, such a person shall be sentenced to fixed-term imprisonment of not less than three years but not more than seven years in conjunction with a statutory fine. The activities concerned are (i) obtaining a trade secret from the right holder through theft, enticement, coercion, or other illegitimate means; (ii) disclosing, using or allowing others to use such trade secret obtained through the illegitimate means identified above; (iii) disclosing, using or allowing others to use the trade secret in his possession in breach of a contractual obligation of confidence or a obligation of confidence imposed by the right holder of such trade secret.

## LEGAL ISSUES TO BE ADDRESSED IN PRACTICE

### Current Civil Remedies Need to be Improved in Order Effectively to Prevent Further Damage to Trade Secrets

The term 'civil remedies for trade secrets' refers to the remedy acquired by the right holder applying for the interference of the public authority vested with the court. It is a type of judicial remedy and within the scope of a public remedy.[10] The right holder of trade secrets seeks civil remedies based upon the following considerations: (i) to compensate losses suffered; (ii) to prevent the imminent or further loss; (iii) to punish the infringing activity.

10 'Public remedy' refers to the means through which the right holder may, in case of infringement of his right, plead for the State, with the public authority, to remove the infringement and enable his right to be carried out; 'private remedy' refers to the means through which the right holder can, with his own power, remove the infringement and exploit his right by himself. See Liang Huixing, *General Theory of Civil Law*, Law Press, Beijing, 1996, at p. 65.

According to current Chinese law, the right holder of trade secrets may apply for interlocutory measures such as property preservation (Mareva orders), preliminary execution and so on, and the court will determine, according to procedural civil rules, whether the remedies applied for can be granted. After the trial on the merits of the case, the court will decide, according to substantive civil rules, the civil liability of the infringer including the order to desist from infringing, damages and so on, through which the right holder will gain corresponding civil remedies provided by the substantive law. However, in respect of effective prevention of trade secrets infringement and further losses, this civil remedy mechanism has serious drawbacks.

First of all, the applicability and workability of the preliminary execution scheme is weak. China's 'preliminary execution' scheme refers to the scheme under which the court may, after admitting a civil case but before giving final judgment, order the relevant party to preliminarily fulfil its obligation in order to meet the urgent need for the life or business operation of the right holder or the urgent need to stop or prevent a certain activity. Article 97 of the Civil Procedure Law of China provides that the people's court may, at the request of the parties concerned, order preliminary execution in respect of the following cases: (1) those involving claims for alimony, support for children or elders, pension for the disabled or the family of a decedent, or expenses for medical care; (2) those involving claims for remuneration for labour; and (3) those involving urgent circumstances that require preliminary execution. The judicial interpretation of the Supreme Court provides that such 'urgent circumstances' shall include those where the infringement needs to be stopped or the obstruction to be removed immediately, and where certain activity needs to be stopped immediately.[11]

However, in cases involving trade secrets and other intellectual properties, the applicability of the preliminary execution is weak and its application is very limited in such cases.[12] This is mainly because the conditions for preliminary execution are hard to meet in law suits involving trade secrets. Article 98(1) of the Civil Procedure Law provides that cases in which preliminary execution is ordered by the people's court shall meet the condition that the relationship of rights and obligations between the parties is definite, and that

[11] Article 107(1),(2) of the Supreme Court *Opinion on Several Issues Concerning the Application of the Civil Procedure Law of the People's Republic of China* adopted on 14 July 1992; article 162 of the Supreme Court *Opinion on Several Issues Concerning the Implementation of the General Principles of the Civil Law of the People's Republic of China* adopted on 24 January 1988.

[12] See Zhang Guangliang, *Civil Remedies for Intellectual Property*, Law Press, Beijing, 2003, at p. 62.

denial of preliminary execution would seriously affect the life or business of the applicant. This requires the applicant and the judge to explain, in order to support the adoption of a preliminary execution order, why, in the absence of such order, the production or business operation of the applicant will be seriously affected. However, cases involving trade secrets are often complicated. The parties have substantial disagreements on whether the trade secret of the plaintiff exists, whether the defendant's activity has been based on such trade secret or just on common knowledge, experience and skills of the defendant, and so on. The rights and obligations between the plaintiff and the defendant are not clear. Furthermore, many trade secrets cost little to form, contain little originality, are often not in use or belong to negative information, which, even if used by others, will not seriously affect the life or business of the right holder. Therefore, it is difficult for the plaintiff to apply for preliminary execution in these cases.

Secondly, the differential treatment of remedies exists. In order to be in conformity with the requirement on provisional measures contained in Part III Section 3 of TRIPS (article 50), major Chinese intellectual property laws were amended from 2000 to 2001.[13] On the foundations of remedial measures provided by the Civil Procedure Law such as preservation of assets, preservation of evidence and preliminary execution, the newly amended Patent Law, Copyright Law and Trademark Law have added to the civil procedure pre-trial restricting order and pre-trial preservation of evidence.[14] However, trade secrets have not received similar treatment. No new civil remedy measure has been added. The old regulation of the 1991 Civil Procedure Law was left unchanged. Compared with remedies against the infringement of traditional intellectual properties, the mechanism necessary for the protection of trade secrets is more demanding since the trade secret is an intangible property preserved by measures of confidentiality, which has as characteristics, for example, that it is easy to spread, transfer and then, once disclosed, it is lost forever. Should the protective measure have not been taken in a timely manner when infringement of trade secrets occurs, it would be hard for the right holder to provide evidence and it would be almost impossible for the facts to be clarified, and the trade secret would be exposed. Therefore, for the purpose of providing a timely and sufficient civil remedy to the right holder of trade secrets, it is necessary to provide in the procedural rules for certain pre-trial

---

13 The Standing Committee of the National Peoples Congress amended the Patent Law for the second time in August 2000, which entered into force on 1 July 2001; amended the Copyright Law and the Trademark Law for the second time in October 2001, which entered into force in October and December 2001, respectively.

14 Article 61 of the Patent Law, article 57 of the Trademark Law and article 49 of the Copyright Law.

(interlocutory) remedial measures in order to enable the right holder to eventually seek a material remedy.

## The Hierarchical Jurisdiction for Civil and Criminal Remedies Needs to be Improved

In the Chinese framework of judicial remedies for the protection of trade secrets, the civil remedy is a basic form and the criminal remedy is an ad hoc form. The basic characteristic of the former is that it applies to all activities infringing trade secrets, disregarding the intention of the infringer (malice or negligence) and the circumstances (serious or not). The ad hoc nature of the latter manifests itself by the fact that it is not always available to the right holder. According to the current law, only with activities wilfully infringing trade secrets and taking place in such serious circumstances that it constitutes the crime of infringing trade secrets, can the person who engaged in such activities be held for criminal liabilities.

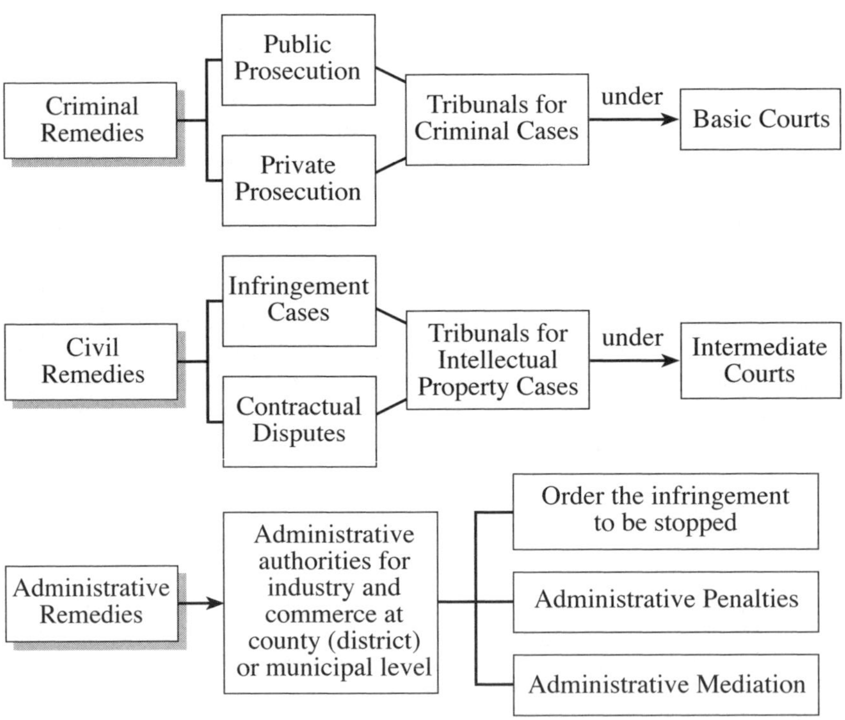


*Figure 8.5 The Chinese system of legal remedies for trade secrets*

Article 18 of the Chinese *Civil Procedure Law* provides that the basic people's courts[15] shall have jurisdiction as courts of first instance over civil cases. Article 19 further provides that the intermediate people's courts shall have jurisdiction as courts of first instance over 'major cases involving foreign interests, cases that have major impact on the area under their jurisdiction; and cases under the jurisdiction of the intermediate people's courts as determined by the Supreme People's Court'. 'Major cases involving foreign interests' refers to cases with foreign elements that involve large sums of money, complicated circumstances and a large number of parties living abroad. In 1998, the Supreme People's Court promulgated the *Memorandum of Certain National Courts' Working Conference on the Trial of Intellectual Property Cases* (hereinafter the '*Memorandum*') which, taking into account the characteristics of civil disputes over intellectual property and the real situation of judicial personnel, has provided guidance for issues regarding the judicial procedure and application of law in intellectual property cases such as the scope of admission, jurisdiction and so on. The '*Memorandum*' provides that disputes in respect of the ownership of, infringement of and contracts involving a trade secret are all within the scope of civil disputes over intellectual property. In respect of civil disputes over intellectual property, except for a few basic courts which have established specialized intellectual property tribunals and which may have jurisdiction as the court of first instance, the intermediate court, if so determined by the high court, taking into consideration the circumstances of the case, shall be the court of first instance for this type of case. Therefore, since 1998, the majority of civil disputes involving trade secrets have been tried by the intermediate courts of the provincial capital as the court of first instance.

However, the adjustment to the current policy shall bear in mind the integrity of the whole system. Inconsistency in the legal framework for the protection of trade secrets has arisen from the fact that, at present, the hierarchical jurisdiction of civil cases involving trade secrets and that of criminal ones have not been synchronized. Our Criminal Procedure Law provides that the intermediate people's courts shall have jurisdiction as courts of first instance over criminal cases punishable by life imprisonment or the death penalty and criminal cases with foreign elements (article 20). Cases involving trade secrets infringement fall within the jurisdiction of basic people's courts as the court of first instance.

---

15 The term 'basic people's court' refers to Chinese judiciaries at the lowest level which are also referred as 'primary people's court'. Therefore there are two English translations for the same Chinese term ('Ji Ceng Fa Yuan') which appeared in officially translated laws. Compare Article 8 of Civil Procedure Law and article 19 of Criminal Procedure Law on www.chinacourt.org, which is sponsored by the Supreme People's Court. (Note by the translator.)

Thus the following inconsistency regarding the trial of trade secrets cases appears: while simple (civil) cases have to be tried by intermediate courts, more complicated (criminal) cases might be tried by basic courts. Compared to the civil remedy, the criminal remedy is more serious as it involves not only economic punishment such as fines, but also deprivation and restriction of personal liberties of the defendant, and not only penalties against the entity which has committed the infringement, but also against its key managing personnel. Therefore, the criminal remedy for the purpose of punishing crimes, in terms of the sum of money involved, the degree of complexity, the seriousness of the circumstances and so on, is much more important than the civil remedy for the purpose of compensating the right holder. Furthermore, since difficult issues such as the definition of trade secrets, the acquisition of evidence and procedural guarantees and the rest are involved, trade secret civil cases are all tried by collegial panels in the intermediate courts.[16] In contrast, judges in the basic courts often lack experience. Therefore, this inconsistency in respect of misplaced hierarchical jurisdiction has a direct negative impact on the quality of the trial of criminal cases involving trade secrets and also makes it easier for certain parties to bring malicious law suits.

### The Function and Status of Criminal Penalties in the Protection of Trade Secrets shall be Clarified

At present, the protection of trade secrets under criminal law is one of the key issues attracting the attention of legal scholars in China. Although the number of criminal cases involving the infringement of trade secrets is still relatively small, it has been rising continuously in recent years. According to the statistics, from 1998 to 2002, cases involving trade secrets infringement investigated by the police at various levels have exceeded 500 in number, which accounts for 9 per cent of all criminal cases involving intellectual property infringement, and 600 million yuan is the sum of money involved, which accounts for 32 per cent of all the money involved in criminal cases involving intellectual property infringement.[17] From 2000 to 2003, national courts at various levels have adjudicated 1369 criminal cases of intellectual property infringement involving 722 people, among which 8.6 per cent are trade secrets infringement crimes. These are therefore second only to trademark infringement crimes (75 per

[16] Collegial panels are the basic units in each court. They are not permanent bodies but organized to adjudicate individual cases. A collegial panel is composed of three to seven judges, the number of which must be odd. Simple civil cases, economic cases, minor criminal cases and cases that are otherwise provided for in law can be tried by a single judge. (Note by the translator.)

[17] The source: see http://www.chinaiprlaw.cn/file/200412213887.html.

cent).[18] Cases involving the infringement of know-how account for the majority of all criminal cases of trade secrets infringement.

It is necessary to protect trade secrets with the criminal law. However, Chinese criminal cases involving trade secrets have revealed many incidents of abuse of the criminal law or of arbitrary criminalization. The judiciaries of certain places, acting as the 'hit man' of one party to the competition, have been using the instrument to battle against crimes to promote local protectionism. In order to protect local business, they have been interfering in economic disputes under the name of criminal law through trade secrets infringement charges with insufficient evidence. The criminal procedure is an important instrument to protect the society and to maintain the market order and fair competition, which, if abused, might become an instrument facilitating unfair competition and which has a negative impact on the healthy development of the socialist market economy.

Two factors that have caused this phenomenon have been identified by scholars: (i) the traditional trend of the wide application of the criminal procedure has led to the presumption that the criminal law is the cure for all sorts of problems and can be used without hesitation; (ii) the lack of independence of the judiciary from local governments has led to the abuse of criminal procedure to attack competitors or to prevent the normal transfer of personnel in order to protect local economic interests.[19]

In addition, deficiencies of the Chinese legislation, especially the related provisions of the Criminal Law, are also the cause of the abovementioned phenomenon. These deficiencies include the following.

## The Ambiguity Regarding the Definition of 'Serious Loss'

Under the Chinese law, the demarcation line between general infringing activities and the crime of trade secrets infringement is drawn according to the degree or amount of losses suffered by the right holder. The crime of trade secrets infringement in the current Criminal Law refers to acts that have broken the state legislation on the protection of trade secrets, infringed others' trade secrets and caused serious losses to the right holder. Since a breach of the Anti-Unfair Competition Law is the prerequisite for an act to be a crime of trade secrets infringement, such act has certain common characteristics with a civil act infringing trade secrets.

---

18 The Third Civil Chamber of the Supreme People's Court, *Guidance and Reference for Intellectual Property Trials* (Vol. 8), Law Press, Beijing, 2004, at p. 3.

19 Professor You Wei, *Speech at the Conference on Application of Law on Crimes of Trade Secrets Infringement* (see http://www.sfyj.org/list.asp?unid=722).

Firstly, the perpetrators of both acts have the same characteristics: natural persons above age 16 and having legal capacity, legal persons or non-legal personality organizations having legal capacity. The natural persons mentioned above include all external and internal employees of the right holder and experts who have acquired the trade secrets through their working relationship with the right holder.

Secondly, the infringing activities conducted by the infringer are similar. They both include (i) obtaining a trade secret from the right holder through theft, enticement, coercion, or other illegitimate means; (ii) disclosing, using or allowing others to use such trade secret obtained through the illegitimate means identified above; (iii) disclosing, using or allowing others to use the trade secret in his possession in breach of a contractual obligation of confidence or an obligation of confidence imposed by the right holder of such trade secret (iv) for the third party, who knows or should know the illegal activities mentioned in the previous sections obtaining, using or disclosing another's trade secret.[20] The first three activities are a direct infringement of another's trade secrets involving the acquisition of trade secrets from the right holder by the infringer by legitimate or illegitimate means. The last activity refers to the act of a third party indirectly infringing trade secrets.

Thirdly, both the wilful infringement and the infringement due to the negligence of the third party constitute a crime. Article 219 of the Criminal Law provides that whoever engages in the abovementioned activities infringing trade secrets and causes serious losses to the right holder of such trade secrets, shall be sentenced, in cases where the loss suffered by the right holder is serious, to fixed-term imprisonment of not more than three years or criminal detention in conjunction with, or independently of, a statutory fine. In cases where the loss suffered by the right holder is extremely serious, such a person shall be sentenced to fixed-term imprisonment of not less than three years but not more than seven years, in conjunction with a statutory fine. Article 12(6) of the *Interpretation on Several Issues Concerning the Application of Law in Trials of Theft Cases* adopted by the Supreme Court in 1998 clearly provides that the theft of trade secrets such as technical achievements and so on shall be punished in accordance with article 219 of the Criminal Law. Article 65 of the *Regulation on the Threshold of Prosecuting Economic Crimes* adopted by the Supreme People's Procuratorate and the Ministry of Public Security on 18 April 2001 provides that the infringement of trade secrets shall be prosecuted if one of the following conditions is satisfied: (i) the economic loss suffered by the right holder is estimated at more than half a million yuan; (ii) the right holder has been forced into bankruptcy or other serious consequences.

20 Article 219 of Criminal Law and article 10 of Anti-Unfair Competition Law.

However, since this regulation is neither a legislative nor a judicial interpretation, the guidance provided by it is not binding for the courts.

Therefore, in 2004, the Supreme People's Court and the Supreme People's Procuratorate jointly enacted the *Interpretation on Several Issues Concerning the Application of Law in Handling Criminal Cases Involving Intellectual Property* in order to provide guidance for the procuratorates and courts to prosecute and adjudicate crimes of trade secrets infringement in accordance with the Criminal Law. This interpretation has provided detailed explanations for related provisions of the Criminal Law. Its Article 7 explains circumstances under which infringement of trade secrets will cause the right holder 'serious losses' and 'extremely serious consequences' as provided for in the Criminal Law. If the infringement that is prohibited by the law has caused the right holder to suffer a loss exceeding the sum of 500 000 yuan, a 'serious loss' of the right holder shall be established. If the infringement has caused the right holder to suffer a loss exceeding the sum of 2.5 million yuan, 'extremely serious consequences' shall be identified. Obviously, the interpretation has adopted the threshold in the abovementioned regulation and drawn a line between crimes and those infringements that have not yet constituted crimes. However, it remains unclear in the interpretation whether the 500 000 yuan loss refers to the value of the trade secret and the media bearing such secret or the actual loss of interest suffered by the right holder. Therefore, the question of how to count the loss is still haunting the judicial practice.

## The Way to Count the 'Serious Loss' is Lacking Rationality

Because of the special nature of the trade secret, it is hard for some right holders to count the losses they suffered. Therefore, article 20 of the Anti-Unfair Competition Law provides that, if the loss of the right holder is difficult to establish, the amount of the compensation shall be equal to the profit gained by the infringer during the period of the infringement. Therefore, in the trial of criminal cases of trade secrets infringement, some procuratorates and courts have, when the right holder can not provide the sum of its actual loss, been using 'the profit gained by the infringer' as the reference to count the loss of the right holder and to decide whether the infringement constitutes a crime. It is argued that this approach has mixed up the distinction between criminal and civil principles. The loss of the right holder and the gain of the infringer are two completely different concepts and their scopes are not identical. Equating the loss of the right holder to the gain of the infringer is inconsistent with the basic principle of the criminal law: *Nulla poena sine lege*. The direct consequence of this equation is that the scope of the application of the Criminal Law has been widened.

Traditionally, Chinese criminal law has been mainly concentrating on those acts that cause serious harm to society, citizens and properties. Therefore, in the Criminal Law, many crimes are crimes of consequences: only when the defendant has conducted acts prohibited by the law and caused serious losses to the society or others will the act of the defendant be punished by the Criminal Law. However, it is worth considering whether this doctrine of the criminal law is sufficient for the protection of intellectual property. The classification of the crime of trade secrets infringement as a crime of consequences and the ambiguity surrounding the assessment of such consequences have caused not only undesirable flexibility regarding the key issue of differentiating crimes from general infringements, but also difficulties in finding crimes and in criminal adjudication.

## The Legal Nature of the Employee's Obligation of Confidence in Respect of Trade Secrets shall be Clarified

The question whether the employee's obligation to maintain the confidentiality of its employer's trade secrets during the period of employment is statutory or contractual in nature has been troubling China's judicial circles and has directly influenced the fair trial of this type of case. Can the employee, in breach of the professional code of conduct, disclose, use or allow others to use trade secrets of the employer in his possession if no clear reference has been made in the employment contract to the obligation of confidence?

For historical reasons, China's employment regime has, for a long time, been subject to a regime of highly centralized state administration under which the labour force has been allocated according to central plans and all employees were naturally also the 'master' of the enterprise that they were working for. However, together with the reform of the economic regime and the establishment of the labour market, the employment relationship has changed dramatically. This change manifests itself not only in the allocation of the labour force by the market, but also in the employment now being based upon hiring by enterprises and the regime of collective labour contracts established in 1999.[21]

However, current Chinese legislation including the Labour Law dedicated to the regulation of the employment relationship has not provided a clear legal definition of the nature of the current labour/employment relationship. Therefore, the employee's obligation of confidence lacks a logical legal base. Furthermore, the wording of some related provisions in certain regulations is ambiguous. For example, article 3 of *Several Regulations on Prohibiting*

---

21 Baohua Dong, *Theory of Labour Law*, World Books Press, Beijing, 1999, at p. 63.

*Activities Infringing Trade Secrets* adopted by the State Administration for Industry and Commerce provides that activities infringing trade secrets, which shall be prohibited, include, inter alia, '(iv) disclosing, using or allowing others to use trade secrets of the right holder by its employee in breach of the contractual agreement entered with or the requirement of confidentiality imposed by the right holder'. It is not clear whether 'the requirement of confidentiality imposed by the right holder' mentioned above is statutory in nature. Another example is article 22 of the Labour Law, which provides: 'The parties to a labour contract may agree, in the labour contract, upon issues such as the duty to maintain trade secrets of the employer. The employee who has failed to fulfil such duty and caused economic loss to the employer shall be liable to pay compensation.' Article 1 of the *Letter on Infringement of Trade Secrets Involved in Labour Disputes* enacted by the Secretariat of the Ministry of Labour and Social Security further provides that, 'if terms regarding maintaining confidentiality of trade secrets have been incorporated into a labour contract and subsequently a labour dispute has arisen because the employee has failed to fulfil such obligation of confidence and caused infringement of the employer's trade secrets, the Arbitration Committee for Labour Disputes shall accept the application for arbitration in respect of such dispute and give an award in accordance with relevant regulations and the agreement of confidentiality contained in the labour contract'. It is not clear whether these provisions of the Labour Law are suggesting that the effect of the employee's obligation of confidence is based solely upon contractual agreement. If such obligation is statutory, even in the absence of a contractual agreement, the employee shall observe the duty of confidentiality and be liable to pay compensation for any breach of such duty, but if such obligation is only contractual, then, in the absence of any or explicit references in the labour contract, there is no legal basis for the employer to impose an obligation of confidence upon its employees.

Owing to the ambiguity of Chinese law, many employers have tried to protect their trade secrets by signing a confidentiality agreement with their employees. However, the employers worry that the clauses of such an agreement will not be able to cover all their trade secrets.

## Legislation on the Non-competition Agreement/Promise shall be Improved

Since the function of trade secrets has become more and more important in current economic life and the awareness of the society has improved dramatically, more and more Chinese enterprises have paid special attention to including a confidentiality agreement within their employment contracts, and they often try to include a non-competition clause to prevent employees from working for competitors in order to prevent the leaking of trade secrets through the transfer of employees. However, it is a difficult issue and a challenge for the Chinese legislator and judiciary to draw a fair balance between the commercial interest of enterprises and the labour right of employees, when considering the scope, reasonable compensation and duration of the non-competition agreement.

The main difficulty met by the courts in the trial of disputes involving non-competition agreements is that the scope of application of the national legislation is limited to senior administrative personnel of the enterprise. While certain ministerial/departmental rules and local regulations have extended the scope to cover normal employees, these regulations are not universally applicable.

Article 61 of the Company Law provides that any board director or manager shall refrain from engaging, independently or together with others, in any business similar to that of the current company for which he is working or any activity detrimental to that company. Any gains obtained from such illegal businesses or activities shall belong to the employing company. The chairman, deputy chairman of the board of directors, any director or manager of a wholly state-owned company, unless otherwise authorized by the state investing authority or other authorities, cannot take office as a member of the managerial staff of other companies including limited companies, public listed limited companies or other business organizations.

The Partnership Law provides that partners shall refrain from engaging, independently or together with others, in any business competing with the partnership. Any partner who has engaged in businesses competing with the partnership or made deals with the partnership in breach of article 30 and has caused losses to the partnership or to other partners, shall be liable to pay compensation in accordance with the law.

The Sole Proprietorship Law provides that the person entrusted or hired by the investor to run the business of the sole proprietorship shall not engage in any business competing with the sole proprietorship without the consent of the investor.

The *Notice on Several Issues Concerning the Transfer of Employees of Enterprises* enacted by the Ministry of Labour provides that the employer may require the employee knowing the trade secret, for a certain period (no more than three years) after the termination of the employment contract, not to work for competing entities producing similar products or engaging in similar business, not to compete by himself with the employer through producing similar products or by engaging in similar businesses, provided that the employee receives a certain amount in economic compensation from the employer.

Article 7 of the *Several Opinions on Strengthening Administration of Know-how during the Transfer of Scientific and Technological Personnel* adopted by the State Science and Technology Commission provides that the entity may conclude non-competition agreements with administrative staff, scientific and technological staff and other related personnel. If such non-competition agreements have been reached, the entity shall pay a certain amount in compensation to those members of staff. The non-competition agreement shall be automatically terminated if the obligator has sufficient evidence proving (i) that national policies on scientific and technological staff have not been followed by the entity; or (ii) obvious unfair treatment; or (iii) the non-payment or the delay of payment without justification in breach of the non-competition agreement. The duration of the non-competition agreement shall not exceed three years.

Article 5 of the *Notice on the Protection of the Intellectual Property Achieved from Key National Scientific and Technological Research Projects* adopted by the Department of Science and Technology of the State Administration of Building Materials provides that main research fellows in charge of a certain specific project can not be transferred to another entity during the process of research. The person who retires, who is on unpaid leave, quits or applies for transfer, may not engage in any technical work related to the research work of the project within one year after leaving the original unit.

In respect of adopting local regulations on the protection of trade secrets, Shenzhen Special Economic Zone and Zhuhai Municipality are in a leading position, promulgating the *Regulation on the Protection of Enterprises' Know-how* which includes regulations on non-competition agreements. Article 16 of the *Shanghai Regulation on Labour Contracts* enacted by Shanghai People's Congress in 2001 provides that parties to the labour contract may incorporate a non-competition clause in the labour contract or confidentiality agreement in respect of employees who have a duty to maintain the trade secrets of the employer, and that they may agree upon the compensation to be paid to the employee after the termination of the labour contract. The scope of the non-competition agreement is limited to stipulating that the employee may not engage, by himself or for others, in any business competing with the former employer for a certain length of time after leaving the employment. The duration of the non-competition agreement is subject to the parties of the labour contract but shall not exceed three years unless otherwise provided in laws and administrative regulations.

Among the abovementioned laws, regulations and regulatory documents, the regulations in respect of non-competition contained in the Company Law, Partnership Law and Sole Proprietorship Law mainly concern senior managerial staff during the term of employment and remain silent about the non-competition obligation of normal employees, especially that of technical staff. The *Notice on Several Issues Concerning the Transfer of Employees of Enterprises*, the *Several Opinions on Strengthening Administration of Know-how during the*

*Transfer of Scientific and Technological Personnel*, and the *Notice on the Protection of the Intellectual Property Achieved from Key National Scientific and Technological Research Projects* are general internal rules of certain ministries or departments and have no authority. The regulations adopted by Shenzhen, Zhuhai and Shanghai are local regulations that do not have general applicability.

## CONCLUSION

Protection of trade secrets in China has been through a process of improving from no protection to protection, from a piecemeal approach to consolidated protection, from protection that was narrow in scope to wide protection, from domestic law protection to protection under bilateral agreements, international treaties and global conventions. However, as with the protection of other intellectual properties, China still has a huge task in establishing a coherent regime of trade secrets protection. This task is particularly difficult because, for historical reasons, the enactment of Chinese laws, including those regarding trade secrets, has been subject to external pressures and a lack of basic infrastructure, which has influenced, to a certain extent, the fairness and effective implementation of the legislation. Therefore, the improvement of the Chinese legal framework on the protection of trade secrets will be based upon experiences of other jurisdictions, taking into consideration, as the starting point, the reality of the country and the need for further development. It will aim at establishing a trade secrets protection regime with special characteristics and in accordance with international standards, in order to facilitate the advance in technology and investment and to protect the public interest.

# 9. Protection of traditional knowledge: protecting poor countries' intellectual property?

**Zhu Lanye***

## INTRODUCTION

Ever since the Uruguay Round took intellectual property as one of the negotiation topics and the Agreement on Trade-Related Aspects of Intellectual Property Rights (TRIPS) was concluded, intellectual property has become a hot topic to which all countries in the world pay much attention. During the first few years of operation of the World Trade Organization (WTO), several disputes regarding intellectual property had been brought to the Dispute Settlement Body (DSB) each year, many of which were disputes between developed country members. However, when we entered the twenty-first century, it seems that intellectual property disputes fell silent; they even seem to have disappeared.[1] If one observes things carefully, one may find that the issue of intellectual property did not disappear from the WTO. In the first five years after the establishment of the WTO, the disputes mainly concerned the traditional categories of intellectual property, such as patent, copyright and trademark. In 2003, Australia filed a complaint regarding geographical indications to the WTO, which brought back to the agenda a similar case filed by the United States five years earlier. Out of this came the first panel regarding geographical indications since the WTO was

* Professor, East China University of Politics and Law.

1 According to the statistics, 22 cases relating to intellectual property rights had been brought to the Dispute Settlement Body (DSB) of the WTO from 1 January 1995 to the end of 2000. Of these cases 15 were between developed country members; the other seven cases were brought by developed country members against developing country members. From 1 January 2001 to the end of 2005, only two cases relating to intellectual property rights were brought, one between the developed country members, one brought by a developing country member against a developed country member (WT/DS/OV/25, www.wto.org).

established.[2] Besides, during the Doha Development Agenda negotiations, quite a few members, including the United States, raised the issue of the establishment of a multilateral system of notification and registration of geographical indications for wines and spirits.[3] This means that the intellectual property rights protection in a non-traditional area[4] has been brought to the public's attention.

## THE RISE OF TRADITIONAL KNOWLEDGE PROTECTION AT INTERNATIONAL LEVEL

In recent years, a new issue, the protection of traditional knowledge, has become the focus of discussions between developing and developed countries. In the thousand years of historical development, different nations in different

---

[2] Complaints by the United States (WT/DS174) and Australia (WT/DS290). The US and Australia separately requested consultations with the EC in respect of the alleged lack of protection of trademarks and geographical indications for agricultural products and foodstuffs in the EC. The US and Australia contended that EC Regulation 2081/92, as amended, does not provide national treatment with respect to geographical indications and does not provide sufficient protection to pre-existing trademarks that are similar or identical to a geographical indication. The US considered this situation to be inconsistent with the EC's obligations under the agreement, including but not necessarily limited to articles 3, 16, 24, 63 and 65 of the agreement. The dispute was resolved by a panel. The panel agreed with the United States and Australia that the EC's geographical indication regulation does not provide national treatment to other WTO Members' right holders and products, because (i) registration of a geographical indication from a country outside the European Union is contingent upon the government of that country adopting a system of geographical indication protection equivalent to the EC's system and offering reciprocal protection to EC geographical indications; and (ii) the Regulation's procedures require applications and objections from other WTO Members to be examined and transmitted by the governments of those Members, and require those governments to operate systems of product inspection like EC Member States. Therefore, foreign nationals do not have guaranteed access to the EC's system for their geographical indications, unlike EC nationals; otherwise, there is no finding that the substance of the EC system of geographical indication protection, which requires product inspection, is inconsistent with WTO obligations; and the panel agreed with the EC that, although its geographical indication regulation allows it to register geographical indications even when they conflict with a prior trademark, the regulation, as written, is sufficiently constrained to qualify as a 'limited exception' to trademark rights. However, the panel agreed with the United States and Australia, that the TRIPS Agreement does not allow unqualified coexistence of geographical indications with prior trademarks. The DSB adopted the Panel report on 20 April 2005.

[3] TN/IP/10, TN/IP/8 (www.wto.org).

[4] This author regards the patent, trademark and copyright as traditional areas of intellectual property.

parts of the world formed an abundant cultural tradition and also accumulated 'technical knowledge',[5] widely known to the public in a particular region. This group of knowledge with its rich content and uncertain external boundary is hard to define. There are many questions relating to traditional knowledge. Is it possible to protect such a group of knowledge with a certain system? Ought this kind of knowledge to be protected at all? The World Intellectual Property Organization (WIPO) has organized a series of research seminars and established the Intergovernmental Committee on Intellectual Property and Genetic Resources, Traditional Knowledge and Folklore to coordinate further research between WIPO and other international organizations, such as UNESCO, the Convention on Biological Diversity (CBD) and the Food and Agriculture Organization of the United Nations (FAO) on the basis of the work.

The further away a region is located from modern civilization, the more one sees the possibility that there exists some knowledge and unique culture accumulated thanks to the primitive status of the residents. The knowledge has been handed over from generation to generation in that group of people through oral means. This might be what we call 'traditional knowledge'. Let us look at two examples first. *Curcuma longa* is a kind of plant with its rootstock the colour of yellow ginger. Indian people use it as a spice in their cooking and the plant is also used as a medicine to cure wounds and rashes. Suman K. Das and Hari Har P. Cohly, two Indian citizens working with a medical centre in Mississippi, were granted a US patent for 'the application of *Curcuma longa* in curing wounds' (US patent No. 5,401,504). The Indian Commission of Science and Industry Research (CSIR) requested that the US Patent and Trademark Office (USPTO) cancel the patent. CSIR pointed out that *Curcuma longa* has been used in India to cure wounds and rash for several thousand years; therefore its medical use is not new. CSIR submitted evidence, including ancient Sanskrit text and 1953 publications of the Indian Medical Association, to support its request. The USPTO in the end supported CSIR's objection and cancelled the patent.

For generations, the local witch doctors in the Amazon catchments use the bark of *ayahuasca* to make a drink. The local people call it the 'water of death cane', because the witch doctors claim that they can use the drink at religious ceremonies to diagnose and cure diseases, to meet the soul of the ancestors and to predict the future. Loren Miller, an American, obtained the plant when visiting the area and claimed that he had found a new variety of B.caapi. Miller called the plant Da Vine, and obtained plant patent No. 5751 in 1986. In 1999,

---

5 For instance, most Chinese rural people know that a slight headache or fever can be cured by scraping a certain part of the neck, chest or back of the sick person ('Gua Sha').

the Coordinating Body of Indigenous Organizations of the Amazon Basin (COICA), the Center for International Environmental Law (CIEL) and the Amazon Alliance for Indigenous and Traditional Peoples of the Amazon Basin filed application to the USPTO to cancel the patent. These organizations objected to the granting of the patent, claiming that, according to their research on prior art, the Da Vine plant was neither novel nor non-obvious. They also pointed out that, because of the unique status of the plant in the Amazon catchments, granting a patent to the plant was against the social and moral principle of the patent law. The USPTO pointed out in 1999 that Da Vine was not substantially different from the sample provided by CIEL and decided that the patent should not have been be granted. However, the response from the patentee persuaded the USPTO to change its position. The USPTO decided that the flower and the leaves of the applicant were different than those grown in nature and announced in 2001 that the patent was valid.[6]

The movie *Lion King*, with Elton John and Hans Zimmer composing the music, conquered the audience with its story, its scenario and its music, which was full of the lingering charm of Africa. The movie was a hit in 1994. The song 'The Lion Sleeps Tonight' was captivating, but no one knew that the song was actually adapted from a Zulu folk song by M. Lebo, a singer in Africa, who not only rewrote the music but also finished the writing of the lyrics, the matching music and the recording. In 1994, the song was used in the *Lion King*. It is estimated by Disney Company that the royalties from the use of this song reached US$20 million, but Lebo only got a nominal one pound.[7]

The above examples are only a few among many. Because traditional knowledge mainly exists in areas where there is little influence of modern civilization, the ones who are familiar with the traditional knowledge are people in developing countries. On the one hand the developed countries call for protection of intellectual property and use every possible means, from concluding international treaties to taking unilateral measures, to strengthen the protection. On the other hand, the knowledge accumulated in the developing countries over thousands of years are not protected, being used free of charge, or even becoming others' property. Since the developing countries are playing an increasingly important role in the arena of the international economy, the issue of traditional knowledge has been put on the agenda.

---

6 Source of the two cases: 'Integrating Intellectual Property and Development Policies, Chapter 4: Traditional Knowledge and Geographical Indications' (http://www.blogchina.com/new/display/12651.html), accessed 31 October 2004.

7 Tang Congrong, 'Focusing on Big Events in the Development of International Intellectual Property Protection System', *China Intellectual Property*, 20 October 2004, p. 3

## THE ISSUES SURROUNDING INTERNATIONAL PROTECTION FOR TRADITIONAL KNOWLEDGE

The issues being studied by international organizations such as the World Intellectual Property Organization (WIPO) at the early stage include the following. What is traditional knowledge? Does it need protection? If protection is necessary, what form should it take? When the study went on, further questions were raised. What makes traditional knowledge different from ordinary knowledge? How can the value of tradition knowledge be recognized and protected by people outside the place where traditional knowledge is held and how at the same time can the way it is protected be accepted by and be favourable to the nation or tribe who created or inherited the traditional knowledge? Is it enough to provide protection for the knowledge itself? When discussing protection, there is another issue we should consider. Traditional knowledge is usually accumulated and developed in a certain area, a nationality or a tribe, over a long period of time. When providing protection, it should not be taken away from the surroundings where it is formed and developed. This is because the form of traditional knowledge not only has its cultural background, but also has its spiritual, legal and even scientific backgrounds. It can even be said that some traditional knowledge itself is the combination of customary law, taking into it the social life, the belief of people and a unique way of protection of its own.

No matter whether it is for cultural, scientific research or commercial purposes, or whether it is out of ignorance or recognition, modern society is showing increasing curiosity towards the aboriginal and traditional culture and traditional knowledge, which is so different from modern civilization. Traditional knowledge and traditional culture are utilized to produce new products, from toys to fashion and pharmaceuticals. Artists have for a long time been taking materials and inspiration from aboriginal culture and have created unique cultural products. The aboriginal culture has direct tourist value, which has been recognized by the market. The issues are the following. How can the development of the market be of benefit to the people who created the culture, or who are part of the culture? When making use of the commercial value of the traditional knowledge, how can we keep the tradition and not divorce it from the land on which it is grown?

Traditional knowledge is a very complicated issue. Not only does it relate to the history, culture and tradition of different nations, but also it is not fixed or free of change. Traditional knowledge itself is growing and changing. WIPO also recognizes that it is facing a series of challenges. This is a new area of international cooperation, where the object of research and protection has profound historical roots. This is an international issue where global cooperation is necessary; but what it relates to is the culture or tradition in a specific area. Coordination in the international law field usually relates to countries, but the ultimate goal of the research is to set up a legal framework for the regulation of certain knowledge, which relates to cross-border tribes, villages and people. For reasons related to the above mentioned complexity, the Intergovernmental Committee has not made any breakthrough since it was established in 2001.

In 2003, the WIPO Assembly requested that the Intergovernmental Committee speed up its work and put its emphasis on the international level. Not long ago, the Intergovernmental Committee held its first meeting since WIPO assigned this new task to it in 2003. It was decided that specific measures would be taken to shift the focus of the work to intellectual property and genetic resources, traditional knowledge and folklore, and to do some basic work for the protection of traditional knowledge and folklore.

At its first meeting, the Intergovernmental Committee first discussed the necessity of aboriginal groups taking part in the work of the Committee. The Committee admitted 10 NGOs, nine of them representing aboriginal groups or associations. This brought the number of NGOs participating in the Intergovernmental Committee with special approval as observers to more than 90. The Committee discussed measures to encourage representatives of traditional knowledge holders to participate in the work. The Committee also opened a new website to let people know the viewpoint of the traditional knowledge holders and the issues they are interested in (http://www.wipo.int/tk/en/igc/ngo/index.html).

The Committee also compiled two sets of key materials about traditional knowledge and folklore. Each set includes a survey of the ultimate goal of protection and key principles. It also includes the analysis of different plans of policy selection and legal framework. These materials are the international framework for the further development of the international protection of traditional knowledge and folklore.

Specific topics discussed by the Committee include strengthening preventive protection of traditional knowledge and genetic resources to prevent the illegal obtaining of patents. The Committee made efforts to raise the understanding of the countries in the area of the protection of traditional knowledge and the application of the patent examination system regarding traditional knowledge. It also drafted the guidelines for maintaining traditional knowledge and guiding the negotiations regarding interests related to traditional knowledge and intellectual property systems. It is now inviting suggestions and comments to improve the guidelines.

The basis of the work of the Committee is the agenda, including dialogue with traditional knowledge holders, sharing country experience and international policy debate inside WIPO. The agenda continued in 1998 and 1999, where discussions were held with about 3000 representatives from 60 different places, who represented the aboriginal groups and other stake holders. The demand and expectation expressed by these representatives and the policy raised by WIPO members set the direction for the work of the Intergovernmental Committee. The preparatory work combines the practice, legal materials and policy, which laid a foundation for further international work, which is more coordinated and focused. WIPO should make continuous efforts in a mutually supportive way with other international organizations to resolve issues that the aboriginal people are interested in.[8]

## THE EXISTING INTELLECTUAL PROPERTY RIGHTS

Although there has not been any definite answer to the issue of traditional knowledge protection, in practice, there are also examples where traditional knowledge holders protect their rights through the existing intellectual property system.

The San are a group of people living in the Kalahari desert. They eat Hoodia cacti for both food and drink when they travel and hunt for a long time. This had been a long tradition until it was discovered in 1937 by some Dutch anthropologists who were studying San people. Scientists of the South African Committee of Industry and Science Research (CSIR) found the report of the anthropologists several decades later and started doing research on this plant. They were granted a patent in 1995 for the element of Hoodia (P57) which can restrain appetite. In 1997, CSIR granted a licence to Phytopharm, a UK biotechnology company; and Pfizer Inc. of the US spent US$320 million to get permission to develop and sell P57. Pfizer Inc. plans to develop a medicine for weight control and adiposis. It is estimated that the market value of the medicine could exceed £6 billion. When this became known to the San people, they threatened to file a law suit against bio-pirating. The San people claimed that their traditional knowledge was stolen and the CSIR did not follow the regulations of the CB (Commision on Biodiversity) that require informed consent by all owners of traditional knowledge, including both the discoverers and the users. Phytopharm alleged that it carried out an extensive search but could not find any 'owners of the knowledge' and that the remaining San people stayed in tents 1500 miles away from their original tribes. The CSIR alleged that they were prepared to notify the San people about the research and were ready to share the interests, but hope that this could be done after the medicine had

8 Zhang Ying, 'China bio-diversity intellectual property information', (http://www.biodiv-ip.gov.cn/xgdt/gjdt/t20040427_28601.htm), accessed 31 October 2004.

been determined to be effective. In March 2002, the CSIR reached an understanding with the San people. The San people, as the custodians of the traditional knowledge relating to Hoodia, would share the future patent royalties. Although what the San people get is probably a small portion of the final turnover, the huge potential market means it may still be a large amount.[9]

In Australia, the folk artists created artistic works, including some designs based on legend. Their works were welcomed by local citizens and were full of primitive simplicity. The artists found that a company imported rugs with the designs they created on the products. With the help of the Australia National Folk Art Promotion Association, three artists brought a case against the importer, Indofurn Pty. Ltd. One of the plaintiffs was Bunduk Marika, a famous artist, who pointed out that they had the right to create fine art works according to the legends because they were owners of the piece of land. She was worried that, when the tribe people learned that the designs had been used on ordinary products, they would take away her right to use the stories. The claims of the artist were supported by the court and the court ordered the defendant to stop selling rugs bearing the design of the plaintiffs, transfer the unsold rugs to the artists and pay 18 640 Australian dollars in damages.[10]

## A CHINESE PERSPECTIVE

China is a country with 5000 years of history and 55 minorities. In this long history, people of all nationalities created abundant culture and traditional knowledge. Therefore the protection of traditional knowledge is also very important to China.

With the assistance of international organizations, the Chinese Government makes efforts to catalogue and protect traditional knowledge. For instance, the China Agriculture Science Academy cooperates with the International Research Institute of Plant Genetic Resource to study the genetic diversity, growing, storage, processing and usage of taro in Yunnan province. It was found that local farmers could effectively preserve and manage the diversity of the plant. With the support of the Ford Foundation, the Kunming Flora Research Institute of the China Science Academy did research on the traditional production method of '*dao geng huo zhong*' (slash-and-burn cultivation)[11] by Hani and Jinuo minorities in the Xishuangbanna area. It was found

---

9 See *supra*, note 6.

10 *Milpurrurru and Ors* v. *Indofurn Pty Ltd and Ors*, 30 IPR 209.

11 This is a primitive farming method of burning the grass and bushes on the land and using the ashes as fertilizer, digging holes in the ground and sowing the seeds.

that many traditional methods pay attention to the preservation of the forest. On the land cultivated by slash-and-burn cultivation, many varieties of plants having special economic and ecological value, such as banyan and wild mango, have been saved. This shows the traditional farming method plays an irreplaceable role in preserving the biodiversity of the place.

The Chinese Government also did some legislative work. For instance, the Regulations on Protection of Traditional Craft and Fine Arts published in May 1997 and the Regulations on Yunnan Province Protection of Traditional Folk Culture implemented on 1 September 2000 are examples of legislative work.

## CONCLUSION

However, compared with the huge amount of traditional knowledge existing today, all work done cannot meet the requirement of protection, not to say adequate and effective protection. As mentioned in the first part of this chapter, before the answers to many questions are found, this topic will be a long-term important task of WIPO. The existing intellectual property system is obviously not suitable to be used directly on traditional knowledge protection. The developing countries should cooperate and find a better means to protect traditional knowledge.

# 10. Legal issues regarding contracts of technology import: a Chinese lawyer's perspective

**Zou Weining***

## INTRODUCTION

After China's accession to the WTO, in order to honour the commitments undertaken upon accession, the Chinese government has amended a series of laws and regulations according to WTO rules and international customs. This chapter will discuss some issues regarding contracts of technology import from a Chinese lawyer's perspective, based on experiences the author gained from providing legal services in relation to such contracts.

## I THE EVOLUTION OF CHINESE LEGISLATION ON TECHNOLOGY IMPORT AND THE CURRENT LEGAL ENVIRONMENT

Until 1 January 2002, there had been an approval system for contracts of technology import that entered into effect in accordance with the *Regulation on the Administration of Contracts of Technology Import* enacted by the State Council in 1985.[1] The approving authority, the Ministry of Foreign Trade and

* Partner, Jun He Law Office (Beijing).

1 Article 4 of the *Regulation on the Administration of Contracts of Technology Import* provides that: 'The recipient and the supplier shall conclude in written form a technology import contract (hereinafter referred to as "the contract"). An application for approval of the contract shall be submitted by the recipient, within thirty days from the date of conclusion, to the Ministry of Foreign Trade and Economic Cooperation of the People's Republic of China or any other agency authorized by the Ministry (hereinafter referred to as "the approving authority"). The approving authority shall approve or reject the contract within sixty days from the date of receipt. Contracts approved shall come into effect on the date of approval. Contracts on which the approving authority does not make a decision within the specified period of time shall be regarded as approved and shall come into effect automatically.'

Economic Cooperation (hereinafter MOFTEC) and its affiliated agencies, had been conducting a thorough review of all aspects of the contracts of technology import submitted for approval in accordance with the *Regulation on the Administration of Contracts of Technology Import* and its implementing measures.

The 1985 *Regulation on the Administration of Contracts of Technology Import* has been revoked by the *Regulation of the People's Republic of China on Administration of Import and Export of Technologies* (hereinafter the *Regulation on Technology Import and Export*) which entered into force on 1 January 2002. The old approval system has been replaced by a new system which divides technologies for import into three categories: technologies that are prohibited from importation, technologies that are restricted in terms of importation and that are subject to a licensing requirement, and technologies that can be imported freely but that are subject to a registration requirement.

At present, China's legal environment regulating contracts of technology import mainly consists of laws, administrative regulations and ministerial rules, and judicial interpretation.

### A Laws

(i) the Foreign Trade Law, as amended on 6 April 2004;
(ii) the Contract Law, which entered into force on 10 October 1999;
(iii) the Patents Law, that was amended for a second time on 25 August 2000.

### B Administrative Regulations and Ministerial Rules

These mainly include the *Regulation on Technology Import and Export* that was enacted by the State Council and that entered into force on 1 January 2002, and a series of ministerial rules adopted by the Ministry of Commerce (the former MOFTEC) regarding the implementation of the *Regulation on Technology Import and Export*, for example *Measures for the Administration of Registration of Technology Import and Export Contracts of the People's Republic of China* and *Catalogue of Technologies Prohibited from or Restricted to Import.*

### C Judicial Interpretation

This refers to the *Interpretation of the Supreme People's Court on Several Issues Concerning the Application of Laws in the Trial of Cases of Civil Disputes Arising from Technology Contract*, which entered into force in January 2005.

# II LEGAL ISSUES INVOLVING TECHNOLOGY IMPORT CONTRACTS

## A China's Administration of Technology Import Contracts

According to the *Regulation on Technology Import and Export*, the administration of import of technologies is based on the categorization of the technology in question into three categories: technologies that are prohibited from importation, technologies that are restricted in terms of importation, and technologies that can be imported freely. It provides that technologies that are prohibited from being imported shall not be imported (article 9) and technologies that are subject to restricted importation can be imported only with licences (article 10).

For technologies that are subject to restricted importation, the procedure is as follows (articles 11–16):

1. The importer shall submit an application for technology import to the foreign trade authority under the State Council (Ministry of Commerce and its agencies) together with supporting documents such as approval documents from the relevant authorities when necessary.
2. If the application is approved, the importer will be issued a Preliminary Licence for the importation of the technology, upon which the importer may enter into contracts of technology importation only once he has received such a licence.
3. Upon signing the contract, the importer shall submit a copy of the contract, together with other supportive documents, to a foreign trade authority under the State Council (Ministry of Commerce and its agencies) in order to apply for a Licence of Import of Technologies.
4. The foreign trade authority under the State Council (Ministry of Commerce and its agencies) shall, upon reviewing the authenticity of the contract, decide to grant or not to grant the Licence of Import of Technologies.
5. If it decides to grant the licence, the foreign trade authority under the State Council shall issue the Licence of Import of Technologies. The contract of import of technologies shall enter into force on the date on which the licence is issued.
6. The applicant shall present the licence in order to go through the formalities at the authorities of foreign exchange, banking, taxation and customs.

Technologies that can be imported freely may be imported only by registering the importation contracts. The contracts of importation of technologies that can be imported freely shall become effective in accordance with the law and shall not be subject to the registration of the contracts (article 17). The procedure is as follows (articles 18–20):

1. The importer shall submit to the foreign trade authority under the State Council, for the purpose of registration, an application letter, copies of the contracts of importation of technologies and documents proving the legal status of the parties to the contract.
2. The foreign trade authority under the State Council shall register the contract and issue a registration certificate within three days of receiving the application documents.
3. The applicant shall present the certificate in order to go through the formalities at the authorities of foreign exchange, banking, taxation and customs.

It is clear from the procedure mentioned above that, although the registration of the technology import contract (for those that can be imported freely) is not a prerequisite for the contract to become effective, the importer can only pay the contract price through the bank after the registration of the contract. Without registration, the exporter will not be paid in foreign currency.[2]

## B Applicable Law and Approval, Registration and Entry into Force

Article 126(1) of the Contract Law provides that 'Parties to the contract with foreign elements may choose the law applicable to any future contractual dispute except if otherwise provided in laws. If parties to the contract with foreign elements have not made a choice, the law of the nation which is most closely connected to the contract shall apply.' Since there is no specific provision regarding the applicable law in cases of technology import contracts,[3]

---

2 The *Regulation on Technology Import and Export* and *Measures for the Administration of Registration of Technology Import and Export Contracts of the People's Republic of China* have not made it clear who is responsible for the registration of contracts regarding technology imported freely. However, since the exporter is located in foreign countries, it is normally the importer that shall make the registration. Projects participated in by the author normally required that the importer should make the registration. It is possible that, if the importer has failed to make the registration, the bank cannot pay out in foreign currency. In practice, the foreign exporter may demand that the importer make the registration and acquire the registration certificate. The bank can also make the payment in accordance with effective ruling of a court of law or an arbitration body.

3 Article 126(2) of the Contract Law provides, in particular, that in cases of sino-foreign joint venture contracts, cooperation contract and joint exploration of natural resources contracts, Chinese law shall apply.

parties to technology import contracts may choose the law of another nation as the applicable law of the contract.

However, if a foreign law is chosen to be the applicable law of a technology import contract, it is questionable whether, during the review (in cases of restricted technology) or registration process, the authority shall conduct the review or registration in accordance with Chinese law or the foreign law chosen in the contract.

Obviously, in cases of restricted technologies, Chinese authorities can only review the contents of the contract and decide whether or not to grant the licence according to Chinese law. For technologies that can be imported freely, although the *Regulation on Technology Import and Export* provides that the foreign trade authority *shall* register the technology import contracts, in practice, the Ministry of Commerce has refused to register those contracts that are in breach of any compulsory requirement of Chinese law. Therefore, even if the parties agree that a foreign law shall apply to the technology importation contract, the contract cannot contain any content that is contradictory to any compulsory requirement of Chinese law. Otherwise, the contract will not be approved or registered, and the contract will not be able to become effective (in cases of restricted technology), or even after the contract becomes effective, the contract price cannot be paid to the exporter through the bank.

## C The Guarantee of the Licensor

Article 24 of the *Regulation on Technology Import and Export* provides that: 'The licensor in a contract of technology import shall guarantee that it is the lawful proprietor of the said technology and therefore has the right to license the technology. If the licensee is charged for infringement by a third party because of its use of the technology pursuant to the contract terms, the licensee shall promptly notify the licensor who shall, once notified, assist the licensee in removing the obstruction. If others' legitimate rights are infringed because of the licensee's use of the technology pursuant to the contract terms, the licensor shall take the liability.'

In some technology importation contracts, foreign licensors require to be exempted from liabilities in infringement resulting from the use of the technology by the licensee. The Ministry of Commerce has rejected this contractual clause which is obviously against Chinese law. It states that 'the obligation of guarantee by the licensor is compulsory and cannot be given up. If the contract does not contain a term of guarantee or the content of such term exempts the licensor from its obligation of guarantee, the authority may require that contract to be amended or reject the application for a license or for registration'.

Article 353 of the Contract Law provides that, 'unless otherwise agreed between the parties, the licensor shall accept liability in case another's legitimate rights are infringed by the licensee while implementing the patent or using the technical know-how pursuant to the contract'. Read in conjunction with article 24 of the *Regulation on Technology Import and Export*, the phrase 'unless otherwise agreed between the parties' shall not be understood as meaning that the parties to the contract may agree to exempt the licensor from liability in case of infringement of a third party's rights by the licensee because of the use of the technology. This phrase can only mean that, under the precondition that the licensor is taking the liability, the licensor and the licensee may agree upon a limitation of such liability such as in terms of the amount of damages to be paid. This type of reasonable limit on the licensor's liability will normally be accepted by the Chinese Ministry of Commerce.

## D The Ownership of Technical Improvements

Article 354 of the Contract Law provides that: 'The parties may stipulate in a technology transfer contract the method of sharing technological achievements obtained from the follow-up improvements made in the exploitation of a patent or the use of know-how in the light of the principle of mutual benefit. Where there is no such agreement in the contract or such agreement is unclear and nor can it be determined according to the provisions of Article 61 of this Law, the other parties shall have no right to share the technological achievements made by one party in the follow-up improvement.' In principle, the know-how gained in the follow-up improvement shall be owned by the party which initiated such improvement, but the parties may agree upfront a way to share such achievements based on the principle of mutual benefit. The provision on 'sharing' explicitly eliminates the possibility that the licensor would enjoy a monopoly over all fruits of follow-up improvements by any party.

Article 27 of the *Regulation on Technology Import and Export*, provides that: 'During the term of validity of a contract of import of technologies, the right over any improvement of the technology shall be vested with the party which has made the improvement.'

Some foreign licensors want to incorporate in the contract a clause stating that any improvement made by the licensee in the process of using the technology shall belong to the licensor. This is clearly against article 27 of the *Regulation on Technology Import and Export*. The Ministry of Commerce has made it clear that such arrangement cannot be made through an agreement between the parties.

Now the common contract clause regarding the ownership of the improvement of the technology is that the improvement of the technology shall belong to the party which made the improvement, but that party commits itself to allowing the other party to the contract to use such improvement upon the payment of a reasonable fee. That clause has been accepted by the Ministry of Commerce.

## E Limitation on Sales and Parallel Import

Article 29(7) of the *Regulation on Technology Import and Export* provides that the contract of technology import shall not 'unreasonably restrict the export channel of the product produced by the licensee using the imported technology'.

The difference between economies leads to the fact that the same product is manufactured at different costs in different countries. It is possible that the product manufactured more cheaply in one country may be exported to the country where the product is produced at a higher cost. There is still much debate among Chinese legal scholars regarding such issues of parallel import.

Regarding the issue of parallel import, article 46 of the Provisions of the Supreme People's Court *on Several Issues in the Trial of Cases of Disputes over Patents Infringement (draft version, dated November 2003)* provides that 'in the cases where the patented product domestically manufactured or obtained through patented process by the patentee or with its authorization is exported but subsequently imported back into the country, or the patented product manufactured or obtained through patented process abroad by the patentee or with its authorization is imported into the country, the people's court shall deal with the issue according to Article 63(1) of the *Patent Law*,[4] except where there have been explicit limits on the geographical scope of the sale of the patented product incorporated in the sales contract or the licensing contract. The sole proprietorship or exclusive exploitation rights regarding such patent which have been properly declared according to the law shall not be influenced'.

This provision is still under discussion as a draft and has not yet been adopted by the Supreme Court. However, it is clear from the above provision that, in order to protect the interest of Chinese licensees, the licensee may, in the licensing contract, limit the parallel import into China of the patented products manufactured abroad. In correspondence, it is only fair for foreign exporters of technology to be allowed to confer certain sales limits upon Chinese importers. These reasonable limits are not only

4 Article 63(1) provides that the use, sale or offer to sell a patented product, after the sale of the product that was made or imported by the patentee or with the authorization of the patentee, or that was directly obtained by using the patented process, shall not be deemed as the infringement of the patent.

accepted by Chinese laws and regulations, but they are also recognized by the judiciary.

## CONCLUSION

The new system for technology importation contracts represents a vast improvement over the old system and it reflects China's WTO commitments. Parallel importation however remains, as in many other countries, a difficult issue.

# PART IV

# The development agenda, TRIPS and China

# 11. The WTO–TRIPs patent regime after Doha: promises and realities

**Sigrid Sterckx***

## 1. A BRIEF HISTORY OF THE CONFLICT OVER IPRS BETWEEN INDUSTRIALIZED AND DEVELOPING COUNTRIES

In a brilliant book by a science journalist which was published six years ago, it was noted:

> The emerging battles over knowledge assets are increasingly vital to each of us. . . . their effects are pervasive, influencing our jobs, our schools, and our relations with colleagues and neighbors. The results of these battles shape the type of medical care we receive and the availability of the food in our refrigerators. Battles over ownership of the rights to the world's storehouses of knowledge already have largely determined who is rich and who is poor in our society. On a global scale, these battles have begun to foster international conflicts, a trend that is sure to grow in coming years.[1]

Indeed, in the meantime the international conflicts over access to information and to products embodying information have clearly intensified.

These conflicts originated as early as the 1970s, when the developing countries took the lead in an attempt to have the international treaties on intellectual property revised. In the early 1980s, both the industrialized countries and the developing countries advocated a revision of the Paris Convention (1883), an important multilateral treaty on patents. Yet, as a result of conflicting views on the patent system, none of the revision attempts yielded concrete results. The two sides had opposite intentions.

The industrialized countries wanted higher and well-maintained protection standards for intellectual property. In the US, various industrial lobbies reported enormous losses that were attributed to infringements of the intellectual property

* Professor, Department of Philosophy and Moral Science, University of Ghent.

1 Shulman, Seth (1999), *Owning the Future*, New York: Houghton Mifflin, Preface, p. xiv.

rights of American companies. These infringements were primarily linked to the legal protection, perceived as poor, in the developing countries.

The developing countries maintained (1) that the evolution of the regimes of intellectual property protection in industrialized countries has always been determined by what these countries consider as their national interest; and (2) that developing countries need lower protection standards in view of their economic development needs.

The following quotation on the TRIPs negotiations, from a WTO official, illustrates the conflict between industrialized countries and developing countries:

> Developed countries, and particularly the most industrialized among them, saw intellectual property . . . as the legitimate basis . . . to earn trading advantage. . . . They also argued that, in the absence of such protection, and the promise of later reward, research and development which led to inventions . . . would simply not take place. . . . Developing countries . . . did not see reason to give support to international standards of protection that would require them to pay large sums to use technology they needed or which might even deny them access to that technology.[2]

The US, later followed by other industrialized countries, were of the opinion that intellectual property formed a suitable GATT theme considering its growing significance as a component of national prosperity and as an object of international trade. Furthermore, a number of industrialized countries felt that the developing countries had too much influence (in number) in the traditional forum for intellectual property negotiations, the World Intellectual Property Organization (WIPO). The introduction of the intellectual property theme on the GATT agenda was not without a struggle, but in the end the US prevailed.

Seven years after the start of the so-called ‘Uruguay Round’ of the GATT negotiations (1986–93) there came about the TRIPs agreement (Agreement on Trade-Related Aspects of Intellectual Property Rights) (Annex 1C of the Agreement Establishing the World Trade Organization, signed on 15 April 1994).

Champions of a worldwide upgrading of the intellectual property protection standards often refer to economic arguments. Gadbaw and Richards, for example, mention the following arguments (which are adopted uncritically by many commentators) in the introduction of their extensively quoted book, *Intellectual Property Rights – Global Consensus, Global Conflict?*

---

2 Croome, John (1995), *Reshaping the World Trading System. A History of the Uruguay Round*, Geneva: World Trade Organization [hereafter Croome, 1995], pp. 131–2.

> There are significant benefits which any nation can obtain by putting into place an effective regime of intellectual property protection. Specifically, intellectual property protection provides an incentive to businesses to conduct domestic R&D activity, encourages the transfer of state-of-the-art technology into the economy and its diffusion within the economy, and creates an incentive for foreign direct investment.[3]

They immediately continue, however, by recognizing that these arguments alone are not sufficient to convince the developing countries that they need to reform their regimes of intellectual property (in the sense of a better protection for the holders of intellectual property rights). Apparently, these theoretical arguments have to be used in combination with the application of 'other forms of persuasion':[4]

> Only when the potential loss of other economic benefits is introduced into the equation have governments of (developing nations( concluded that it is in their interest to reform their intellectual property regimes.[5]

The US have heavily influenced this 'equation'. Their threats of lifting preferential duty-free treatment under the Generalized System of Preferences, on the one hand, and import restrictions under Section 301 of the American trade law, on the other, have been very effective in persuading the governments of a number of developing countries and newly industrialized countries.

## 2. THE OUTCOME: A MAXIMALIST RIGHTS CULTURE

In the last 30 years the concept of patentability has been significantly expanded: more and more domains previously excluded from patent protection have been encapsulated in the patent system, the remaining exclusions are being interpreted more narrowly, the concept of 'patent infringement' is being interpreted in favour of patent proprietors and the arsenal of strategies for the maintenance of patent rights has increased.

Indeed, as observed recently by Professor James Boyle from Duke Law School:

> The assumption seems to be that to promote intellectual property is automatically to promote innovation and, in that process, the more rights the better. But both assumptions are categorically false. Even where intellectual property rights *are* the

---

[3] Gadbaw, R. Michael and Richards, Timothy J. (1988), 'Introduction', in Gadbaw and Richards (eds), *Intellectual Property Rights – Global Consensus, Global Conflict?*, Boulder: Westview Press, p. 20.

[4] Ibid.

[5] Ibid., p. 21.

> best way to promote innovation, and there are many areas where they are not, it is only by having rules that set the correct *balance* between the public domain and the realm of private property that we will get the innovation we desire. Yet trade treaties require very high 'floors' of international intellectual property protection while rarely imposing 'ceilings', even though too *much* intellectual property protection is just as harmful, and as distorting of trade flows, as too *little*.[6]

The maximalist rights culture tends to cause a selective blindness in the decision makers in some policy making fora. The World Intellectual Property Organization (WIPO), for example, seems to be increasingly obsessed with the promotion of intellectual property rights. Part of WIPO's mission within the UN system is 'promoting creative intellectual activity', and indeed the promotion of IPRs may be one way to go about achieving that goal. But unfortunately, at the same time, WIPO is forgetting or ignoring the other aspect of its mission: 'facilitating the transfer of technology related to industrial property to the developing countries in order to accelerate economic, social and cultural development'. Even for the industrialized countries, the maximalist rights approach is bad policy. It reflects the interests of a very narrow range of interests, and it does so with remarkably little public scrutiny. This is problematic, because the implications of intellectual property policy are so far-reaching that they demand a much more participatory procedure. The participation of civil society groups, for example, must be increased.

Admittedly, some flexibility has been built into the WTO–TRIPs Agreement, but this will not solve the problems of imbalance, for various reasons. Most developing countries lack the technical and legal expertise to understand the scope of those flexibilities and to take full advantage of them. They should receive technical assistance from organizations like WIPO to help them in this regard, but instead they are being persuaded, mainly in the context of bilateral negotiations on Free Trade Agreements, to adopt 'TRIPs-plus' levels of IPR protection.

## 3. THE WTO MINISTERIAL DECLARATION ADOPTED AT DOHA; THE DOHA DECLARATION ON THE TRIPS AGREEMENT AND PUBLIC HEALTH

The 4th Session of the WTO Ministerial Conference, held at Doha, Quatar, 9–14 November 2001, resulted in the so-called 'Doha Declaration'.[7] In the

---

6 Boyle, James (2004), 'A manifesto on WIPO and the future of intellectual property', *Duke Law & Technology Review*, **9**, 1–12, at 2–3.

7 WTO document WT/MIN(01)/DEC/1, 20 November 2001.

context of the topics that concern us here, the most important part of that Declaration is the second paragraph, according to which:

> International trade can play a major role in the promotion of economic development and the alleviation of poverty. We recognize the need for all our peoples to benefit from the increased opportunities and welfare gains that the multilateral trading system generates. The majority of WTO Members are developing countries. We seek to place their needs and interests at the heart of the Work Programme adopted in this Declaration. . . . We shall continue to make positive efforts designed to ensure that developing countries, and especially the least-developed among them, secure a share in the growth of world trade commensurate with the needs of their economic development. In this context . . . balanced rules . . . have important roles to play.

On the subject of '*The TRIPs Agreement and Public Health*', a separate Declaration came out of the WTO Ministerial Conference at Doha.[8] Civil society groups in both developing and industrialized countries have, particularly in recent years, intensified their efforts to force the problem of the lack of access to healthcare in general, and drugs in particular, onto the political agenda. Indeed, more than a third of the world's population has no access to essential drugs. Most of these people live in developing countries. Obviously, access to drugs in developing countries is determined by several factors. Hardly any drugs to combat tropical diseases are being developed, but even *existing* drugs are often not available to the patients who need them. One of the important determinants of access to drugs is the working of the patent system. This has been recognized by several prominent academic experts, as well as in fora such as the UN Commission on the Promotion and Protection of Human Rights, which adopted a resolution in August 2000 declaring that there are apparent conflicts between the TRIPs regime, on the one hand, and human rights (including the right to health), on the other.

In many respects, the TRIPs Agreement represents a fundamentally new situation for developing countries. The industrial sector in which this is most clearly the case is, without any doubt, the pharmaceutical sector. Many developing countries want to use the patent system to boost local industries, also in the field of pharmaceuticals. They have therefore traditionally excluded pharmaceutical products from patent protection; only processes for the production of pharmaceuticals could be patented. In the pharmaceutical sector a product patent refers to the chemical structure of a drug, regardless of how it was manufactured and of the purpose it serves. Process patents offer protection for the way in which the final product is made and for the way in which the product is used to reach certain goals (in the case of drugs: the treatment of specific

8 WTO document WT/MIN(01)/DEC/2, 20 November 2001.

diseases). A process patent offers a 'strong' form of protection only if there is no other (financially sound) way of producing the product in question, other than through the process covered by the process patent. In the pharmaceutical sector, this is rarely the case, so product patents are most wanted.

Apart from the ban on pharmaceutical product patents, most developing countries have traditionally quasi automatically imposed a regime of compulsory licences on patented inventions in the pharmaceutical domain. The objective is the same: to guarantee that the local industry is given the opportunity to play a significant role in the manufacturing of pharmaceuticals.

As a result of the implementation of the TRIPs Agreement in the developing countries it becomes increasingly difficult for them – and probably even impossible – to pursue a 'selective' patent granting policy, certainly as far as pharmaceuticals are concerned. Drugs cannot be excluded from patentability under TRIPs, with far-reaching potential consequences for access to drugs for millions of people who desperately need them. Hence a number of developing countries pushed for the adoption of the *Doha Declaration on the TRIPs Agreement and Public Health.*

The essence of the Declaration is to be found in paragraph 4:

> We agree that the TRIPS Agreement does not and should not prevent Members from taking measures to protect public health. Accordingly . . . we affirm that the Agreement can and should be interpreted and implemented in a manner supportive of WTO Members' right to protect public health and, in particular, to promote access to medicines for all.
>
> In this connection, we reaffirm the right of WTO Members to use, to the full, the provisions in the TRIPS Agreement, which provide flexibility for this purpose.

This is somewhat fleshed out in the fifth paragraph:

> Accordingly . . . we recognize that these flexibilities include:
>
> . . .
>
> (b) Each Member has the right to grant compulsory licenses and the freedom to determine the grounds upon which such licenses are granted.
>
> (c) Each Member has the right to determine what constitutes a national emergency or other circumstances of extreme urgency, it being understood that public health crises, including those relating to HIV/AIDS, tuberculosis, malaria and other epidemics, can represent a national emergency or other circumstances of extreme urgency.
>
> (d) The effect of the provisions in the TRIPS Agreement that are relevant to the exhaustion of intellectual property rights is to leave each Member free to establish its own regime for such exhaustion without challenge, subject to the MFN [Most Favoured Nation] and national treatment provisions of Articles 3 and 4.

Subparagraph (b) is important because developing countries that are planning to grant compulsory licences are sometimes put under great pressure (for example via threats to withdraw investments), primarily by the US, not to do so. However, the system of compulsory licences enables a country to factor national interests into its patent system and allows it to achieve a better balance between the rights and the obligations of patent holders. Therefore it should be used to the full, especially in 'vital' sectors such as drugs.

Subparagraph (c) is important in that it stresses that every member state has the sovereign power of decision to proclaim a (national) state of emergency. Subparagraph (d) recognizes the right of every state to allow parallel import of medicines. This is a welcome signal, since the US has repeatedly proclaimed that such parallel import is not allowed by virtue of article 28 TRIPs (which gives a description of the rights conferred by patents; import is one of the things listed in that article).

The sixth paragraph of the Declaration runs as follows:

> We recognize that WTO Members with insufficient or no manufacturing capacities in the pharmaceutical sector could face difficulties in making effective use of compulsory licensing under the TRIPs Agreement. We instruct the Council for TRIPs to find an expeditious solution to this problem and to report to the General Council before the end of 2002.

Pursuant to art. 31(f) TRIPs, compulsory licences must be used predominantly for the supply of the domestic market of the member state that issued the compulsory licence and can, therefore, only be used to a limited extent for export. If a country has insufficient or no manufacturing capacities and the drugs offered by foreign manufacturers are too expensive, the country should be allowed to look elsewhere for a suitable supplier. Until recently, this did not really pose a serious problem because a number of developing countries – with India as the most prominent example, had a good production capacity and were able to export their drugs, even when these were patented in other countries.

The *least developed* countries have been granted a postponement until 2016 to conform their drug-related patent provisions to the WTO–TRIPs Agreement, but in view of the fact that the *developing* countries that can export drugs to them (such as India) must acknowledge drug patents since 1 January 2005, the less developed countries will encounter even more serious problems. In this context, compulsory licences are essential and will become increasingly critical.

As foreseen, paragraph 6 of the Doha Declaration led to negotiations in the TRIPs Council. The discussions in the Council concerning export strategies went off the rails during a debate about the question for which diseases the export of drugs under compulsory licence should be allowed. When the president of the TRIPs Council proposed a draft in December 2002 stating that the Doha Declaration was *not* limited to HIV/AIDS, malaria and tuberculosis, the

US (as the only country among the then 145 WTO members) refused to accept this draft and negotiations were broken off. Numerous countries were opposed to a limitation of diseases for which medicines can be exported under compulsory licences and felt that this could not be the subject of negotiations. They rightly observed that the Doha Declaration states that the TRIPs Agreement has to be implemented in such a way as to give *everyone* access to medicines.

In a letter addressed to the trade ministers of all WTO members the US Trade Representative, Robert Zoellick stated:

> It became clear to us that some WTO members and advocacy organizations sought to expand the scope of disease beyond that intended at Doha to allow countries to override drug patents to treat a wide range of public health concerns, including obesity, asthma, cancer, diabetes, among others – even including the use of Viagra. We were seriously concerned that this approach would undermine the WTO rules on patents that provide incentives for the development of new pharmaceutical products.[9]

Given the fact that North America, Europe and Japan together represent 80 per cent of the global pharmaceutical market, and that of the remaining 20 per cent, Africa represents only 1 per cent, Zoellick's concern about an 'undermining' of incentives for drug development was without foundation. The continuation of pharmaceutical R&D is not dependent on the markets of developing countries. Moreover, his mentioning Viagra was grotesque; as if Viagra is the true reason behind the wish of developing countries to gain access to essential medicines.

A third objection the US has repeatedly referred to involves the risk of cheap medicines intended for the South being diverted to the North. However, this objection is unjustified:

> There are billions of generic pills being produced each year around the globe that have not been diverted into the U.S. and Europe. Not only do U.S. and Europe outlaw such diversion, but they guard their borders with remarkable efficiency. As a matter of law and of practicality, the U.S. and Europe are in total control of the diversion risk. Rich consumers in London, Paris, and New York are not going to buy black market, smuggled heart medicines out of the trunk of a Chevy.[10]

Moreover, if the colour, shape and packaging of the drugs intended for poor countries are modified, the risk of diversion to the US and Europe should not be an issue.

On 30 August 2003, an agreement on the implementation of paragraph 6 of

---

9 InsideHealthPolicy.com, Daily Updates, 17 January 2003.
10 Ip-health mailing list, 23 December 2002.

the Doha Declaration was adopted by the WTO General Council.[11] This agreement was based on a compromise worked out by the Chair of the TRIPs Council and a 'Statement by the Chair' requested by the US as a condition to accept this compromise. The agreement involved a temporary waiver from the obligation, set out in article 31(f) TRIPs, to use compulsory licences predominantly for the supply of the domestic market. Meanwhile, this agreement has been made permanent, as explained below.

The waiver allowed countries producing patented pharmaceutical products under compulsory licence to *export* those products to eligible importing countries, provided that several conditions are met. Unfortunately, in view of the fact that those conditions are particularly burdensome, the agreement can hardly be called an 'expeditious solution' (as called for in paragraph 6 of the Doha Declaration).

Moreover, virtually no countries have implanted the waiver in their national laws. Only Norway, Canada and India have done so, while the EU and the Republic of Korea have adopted laws that are about to come into force. China is reported[12] to have implemented a limited version of the waiver. An order to that effect was issued on 29 November 2005 and came into force on 1 January 2006. However, the Chinese order only applies to 'infectious diseases', while the WTO Agreement includes all diseases.

Without going into all the details, some of the conditions that are being imposed are the following:

a. an entity in the importing country (a country with insufficient or no drug manufacturing capacities) must seek a voluntary licence from the patent holder;
b. if efforts to obtain a voluntary licence fail, a compulsory licence must be applied for and the compulsory licence must be obtained in the importing country;
c. the importing country, unless it is a Least Developed Country, must demonstrate that it has insufficient capacity to produce the drug locally;
d. the importing country must notify the TRIPs Council if it decides to use paragraph 6 of the Doha Declaration;
e. the interested importing country or entity must identify a potential exporter;
f. that potential exporter must first try to obtain a voluntary licence on commercially reasonable terms for a commercially reasonable period of time;

11 See document IP/C/W/405.

12 See the IP-related website of the World Health Organization (www.ip-watch.org), under the section 'Public Health'.

g. if such a voluntary licence is refused by the patent holder, the potential exporter must seek a compulsory licence from its own government;
h. if a compulsory licence is granted, the exporter must then formulate the drug and investigate the shape, colouring, labelling and packaging of the patent holder's product in the importing country, in order to differentiate the product for export;
i. the exporting country must notify the TRIPs Council of the grant of the licence and its conditions;
j. the exporter has to seek product registration and prove bio-equivalence, when required by national law in the importing country;
k. if in the importing country data exclusivity[13] is granted, the exporter will have to obtain authorization from the owner of the data to use them, or he will have to develop his own toxicity and efficacy studies (unless the use of the data is included in the compulsory licence);
l. before shipment of the drug starts, the holder of the compulsory licence for exportation must post information on a website about the quantities that will be supplied and the distinguishing features of the product (colour and so on).

This series of steps must be repeated over and over again, as each time a country registers as an eligible importer, new voluntary licences must be sought and, if refused, new compulsory licences for export need to be obtained.

Clearly, these conditions are not economically viable. The mechanism is so burdensome for potential suppliers that it will hardly encourage them to use it. Moreover, such a complex mechanism does not pose a risk to the position of owners of drug patents; it will provide little or no incentive to lower drug prices or to negotiate voluntary licences.

The temporary waiver approved in August 2003 was made permanent on 6 December 2006, when the decision was taken to amend the TRIPs Agreement. The amendment will become part of TRIPs once it is ratified by two-thirds of WTO member states. The deadline is 1 December 2007.

The amendment consists of three parts. First, an Article 31*bis* has been added to the TRIPs Agreement itself. Second, an Annex has been added to the TRIPs Agreement, which provides a number of definitions and explains the

---

[13] Data exclusivity implies that, for a specified period of time, drug regulatory authorities prevent the use of registration data – test data and other data relating to the safety and efficacy of the drug provided by an originator of a pharmaceutical product – in the process of registration of a generic version of the same product. Data exclusivity is separate from patents, although it can have the effect of artificially extending the period of monopoly protection of a drug or of creating a monopoly in a country where the drug is not even patented.

terms for using the system. An 'eligible importing Member', for instance, is defined as 'any least-developed country Member, and any other Member that has made a notification to the Council for TRIPS of its intention to use the system [. . .]' (Annex, para. 1). An 'exporting Member' is defined as 'a Member using the system to produce pharmaceutical products for, and export them to, an eligible importing Member' (ibid.).

The terms for using the mechanism are set out in paragraph 2 of the Annex:

> (a) the eligible importing Member(s) has made a notification to the Council for TRIPS, that:
> (i) specifies the names and expected quantities of the product(s) needed;
> (ii) confirms that the eligible importing Member in question, other than a least-developed country Member, has established that it has insufficient or no manufacturing capacities in the pharmaceutical sector for the product(s) in question [. . .]; and
> (iii) confirms that, where a pharmaceutical product is patented in its territory, it has granted or intends to grant a compulsory licence in accordance with Article 31 and 31*bis* of this Agreement and the provisions of this Annex;
> (b) the compulsory licence issued by the exporting Member under the system shall contain the following conditions:
> (i) only the amount necessary to meet the needs of the eligible importing Member(s) may be manufactured under the licence and the entirety of this production shall be exported to the Member(s) which has notified its needs to the Council for TRIPS;
> (ii) products produced under the licence shall be clearly identified as being produced under the system through specific labelling or marking. Suppliers should distinguish such products through special packaging and/or special colouring/shaping of the products themselves, provided that such distinction is feasible and does not have a significant impact on price; and
> (iii) before shipment begins, the licensee shall post on a website the following information:
> – the quantities being supplied to each destination as referred to in indent (i) above; and
> – the distinguishing features of the product(s) referred to in indent (ii) above;
> (c) the exporting Member shall notify the Council for TRIPS of the grant of the licence, including the conditions attached to it. The information provided shall include the name and address of the licensee, the product(s) for which the licence has been granted, the quantity(ies) for which it has been granted, the country(ies) to which the product(s) is (are) to be supplied and the duration of the licence. The notification shall also indicate the address of the website referred to [. . .] above.

Further, the Annex provides that importing countries must take reasonable measures to prevent re-exportation of the products, and encourages both importing countries and exporting countries to use the system in a way which promotes technology transfer and capacity building in the pharmaceutical sector. The Council for TRIPs is responsible for an annual review of the functioning of the system.

Finally, an Appendix to the abovementioned Annex is included, which deals with the assessment of the lack of manufacturing capacity in the importing countries. This Appendix is identical to an annex to the August 2003 decision.

Non-governmental organizations have heavily criticized the amendment, arguing that it makes a flawed agreement permanent. As Doctors Without Borders (MSF) put it in their briefing note for the WTO Hong Kong Ministerial Meeting:

> To date there is no experience using the mechanism – not one patient has benefited from its use – despite the fact that newer medicines, such as second-line AIDS drugs, are priced out of reach of poor patients. Delaying the amendment would have been a far better option, as it would have ensured the possibility of testing and improving the mechanism in practice. The amendment has made permanent a burdensome drug-by-drug, country-by-country decision-making process, which does not take into account the fact that economies of scale are needed to attract interest from manufacturers of medicines.

According to Ellen 't Hoen, Director of Policy Advocacy for the MSF Access to Essential Medicines Campaign: 'There is a glaring lack of evidence that the measures proposed by the WTO would actually resolve the difficulties we are facing [. . .] Since 2003, we have tried to place drug orders under the 'August 30' decision. But these attempts have not yet been successful.'

Several NGOs have stated that the amendment was rushed through for political reasons, so that the WTO would have something to show at the Hong Kong Ministerial Meeting, as no progress had been achieved in other areas. According to German Velasquez, Associate Director of the Department of Technical Cooperation for Essential Drugs and Traditional Medicine at the WHO, the African countries were pressurized by the US, the EU and the WTO's Director General to come to an agreement. Velasquez observed that an entire week of informal meetings on the topic was held at which major potential exporting countries such as Argentina, Brazil and India were not even consulted.[14]

The pharmaceutical industry has welcomed the amendment.

[14] See the World Health Organization's IP-Watch, www.ip-watch.org, posting of 14 December 2005.

## 4. THE NEED TO RETHINK THE WTO–TRIPS PATENT REGIME

While tariffs and other barriers to trade in traditional manufactured goods have been lowered, and tariffs on agricultural products may also go down, attempts are being made to *re-regulate* the global market in ways that will hamper innovation – particularly so-called 'follow-on' innovation, but also innovation in highly industrialized countries. By this re-regulation, I mean the constant strengthening of intellectual property rights. Just when some developing countries were starting to climb the ladder of economic development, they may have found that this re-regulation of the world economy removes the ladder from under their feet.

The great majority of inventions come about in OECD countries, where most of the R&D is conducted and where most patent applications are filed. Developing countries are often labelled 'follower' countries. They are, to a great extent, dependent on imported technologies. Technological change in these countries is largely driven by adaptation of such technologies, so it is important for them to get access to those technologies.

As noted earlier, some commentators argue that the strengthening of IPRs is actually a good thing for developing countries, as it will enable them to attract more Foreign Direct Investment (FDI), more technology transfer and more local R&D. There may well be some truth in this story,[15] but it also involves problems which go beyond the lack of infrastructure which prevents the technological development of so many developing countries. To mention but a few potential problems:[16] the Foreign Direct Investments necessary for local innovation may not respond in any significant way to levels of intellectual property rights protection; technology transfer, in the form of licensing, may continue to lag because the owners of the technologies fear competition from developing countries; the products that actually reach developing countries may be too expensive or too obsolete to improve their position in terms of competitiveness. Moreover, the strengthening of IPRs may prevent access to the products and processes which developing countries need most.

As I remarked in the second section of this chapter, this re-regulation of the world economy is certainly not driven by the developing countries. They have not defined or influenced the norms embedded in the TRIPs Agreement. This has

---

15 For a discussion of empirical economic research on these questions, see Keith E. Maskus (2000), *Intellectual Property Rights in the Global Economy*, Washington, DC: Institute for International Economics.

16 See Jerome H. Reichman (2003), 'Managing the challenge of a globalized intellectual property regime', paper prepared for the ICTSD–UNCTAD Dialogue, 2nd Bellagio Series on Development and Intellectual Property, 18–21 September 2003 [hereinafter Reichman (2003)], p. 2.

been the work of a very narrow range of business interests. In spite of the rhetoric, the resulting norms are not intended to enhance the development prospects of developing countries. On the contrary, these norms make it more difficult for so-called 'second-comers' or 'follow-on' innovators, anywhere in the world, to get access to and be able to use products and processes which, before, were in the public domain and could potentially be used to adapt them to local needs.

The TRIPs Agreement does refer to the importance of technology transfer. Article 7 provides:

> The protection and enforcement of intellectual property rights should contribute to the promotion of technological innovation and to the transfer and dissemination of technology, to the mutual advantage of producers and users of technological knowledge and in a manner conducive to social and economic welfare, and to a balance of rights and obligations.

Article 66(2) specifically deals with technology transfer:

> Developed country Members shall provide incentives to enterprises and institutions in their territories for the purpose of promoting and encouraging technology transfer to least-developed country Members in order to enable them to create a sound and viable technological base.

However, this remains a very vague commitment, which is much less easily enforceable than many other aspects of TRIPs. Until now, no concrete examples of such incentives have been reported.

In theory, stronger IPRs can encourage technology transfer, but they also enable technology owners to choose not to transfer the technologies, or to transfer them only to markets of other industrialized countries. As to the *actual* effect of IPRs on technology transfer (or, put differently, as to the question whether a strengthening of patent rights in a particular country increases the transfer of technology to that country) there is not much empirical evidence yet. This is in part due to the fact that, until recently, hardly any empirical research on this issue was available. Moreover, the issue is a very complex one.

Recent research seems to indicate that, particularly in patent-sensitive industries, international trade flows respond positively to a strengthening of patent rights among middle-income and large developing countries, but *not* among poor countries.[17] The same would seem to hold for inward FDI.[18]

---

[17] See Pamela J. Smith (2001), 'How do foreign patent rights affect U.S. exports, affiliate sales, and licenses?', *Journal of International Economics*, **55**, 411–40.

[18] Ibid. See also OECD (2003), *The Impact of Trade-Related Intellectual Property Rights on Trade and Foreign Direct Investment in Developing Countries*, Doc. TD/TC/WP(2002)42/FINAL.

Developing countries should be careful to avoid two extremes:[19] free riding and a further privatization of the public domain. Free riding practices which allow 'second comers' to appropriate the innovations of 'first comers' almost immediately, without contributing their fair share to the costs, should be prohibited everywhere, that is, also in developing countries. For such practices undermine incentives to invest in new technologies. In the past, some developing countries have been unwilling to accept this principle – this is one of the reasons why the forum for international negotiations on intellectual property shifted from WIPO to GATT.

The other extreme that should be avoided is a further privatization of scientific and technological information. The more the balance between private and public interests tilts in favour of private interests, the more the public domain shrinks, the more it becomes expensive or impossible to get access to information and hence innovation is delayed or made impossible.

If we can agree that patents are not ends in themselves, then we can also agree that patent policy should be used as a tool to promote technological development in developing countries, to improve their economic competitiveness. This implies that the stage of development of a country should be taken into account in intellectual property policies. They should not be put under pressure to implement inappropriately high (even 'TRIPs plus') standards of protection. Countries which are now among the group of industrialized countries have regularly adapted the 'architecture' of their patent regime to their level of economic development, and also in function of what they considered to be their 'national interest' at a given moment in history.

Indeed, empirical economic research shows that it depends on the concrete economic circumstances whether or not a 'strengthening' of the patent system will be advantageous to a particular country. We can distinguish between three stages. The level of economic development of countries situated in the *first stage* is very low. These countries dispose of hardly any technological infrastructure and produce very few or no patentable inventions at all. Such countries get no benefits out of a patent system since their problem is not a lack of inventions but the limited possibilities to use the available technology (that is, 'older' inventions which, because of the expiration of their patents, belong to the public domain).

Countries that have entered the *second stage* are capable of using more sophisticated technologies and can become technology copiers, or 'duplicative imitators'. The economy of these countries generally grows very rapidly, not least thanks to such imitation. At this stage, it is in the interest of the country

---

19 Reichman (2003), p. 4.

to have weak patent protection, so as to enable imitation and adaptation. Later in this stage, 'duplicative imitation' can be replaced by 'creative imitation', which involves a greater extent of adaptation of imported technologies. In the course of this process, domestic R&D will increase. Japan, Korea, Brazil, Mexico, Malaysia and the export-intensive regions of China can be seen as examples of countries which moved from the stage of 'duplicative imitation' to the stage of 'creative imitation'. Many middle-income developing countries are still at the 'duplicative imitation' stage, and the least-developed countries are not even there yet.

In the *third stage*, countries are capable of producing top-level inventions. From this point on, it can become beneficial for a country to introduce strong patent protection.

## 5. CONCLUSION

Economic research shows that the nature of technology transfer and the utility of intellectual property rights follow a kind of 'technology ladder'. However, in the continuous process of the 'strengthening' of patents, little or no attention is paid to the economic circumstances in poor countries. The fact that the patent system has very diverse effects in different *industries* – and this is also true in industrialized countries – is also ignored. A strongest-possible and long-lasting patent protection is pursued in all countries and all fields of industry: a 'one size fits all' (viz. extra large) approach.

I would not go as far as Jagdish Bhagwati, one of the most prominent economists of our time, who has claimed in the *Financial Times*:

> [Intellectual Property Protection] is not a 'trade' issue; the WTO ought to be about lowering trade barriers and tackling market access problems. The inclusion of IPP has turned the organization into a royalty collection agency.[20]

Intellectual property rights do have trade related aspects, but this is precisely why scientists, consumers and patients in both industrialized and developing countries should be so worried about the maximalist rights approach that is currently taken in the field of intellectual property. The urgent challenge we are facing today has been summarized in simple words, but very much to the point, in the recent report of the UK Commission on Intellectual Property Rights:

---

20 Jagdish Bhagwati (2002), 'Patents and the Poor', *The Financial Times*, 16 September.

> Developed countries should pay more attention to reconciling their commercial self-interest with the need to reduce poverty in developing countries, which is in everyone's interest. Higher IP standards should not be pressed on developing countries without a serious and objective assessment of their impact on development and poor people. We need to ensure that the global IP system evolves so that the needs of developing countries are incorporated and, most importantly, so that it contributes to the reduction of poverty in developing countries by stimulating innovation and technology transfer relevant to them, while also making available the products of technology at the most competitive prices possible.

Intellectual property protection is not per se hostile to the interests of developing countries, but the system should be adapted to reflect *their* innovation and investment needs. To the extent that this is difficult or impossible, alternative models should be developed that promote the needs of developing countries at much lower social costs than the models that are currently in place.

# 12. Intellectual property rights and WTO compliance: Chinese and European perspectives

**Fientje Moerman***

## INTRODUCTION

We are all greatly impressed by the changes that China has undergone; your country has undeniably become a high-tech economy within the shortest imaginable time. Yet some Chinese sectors and areas have developed more slowly or to a lesser extent, and others still exhibit certain social and economic needs. You undoubtedly expect more wealth creation and hope that this, combined with current improvements in the technology domain, will ultimately boost the well-being and comfort of your numerous citizens even further. Right now, the strength that China has already acquired and the future promise it holds in many areas of industry and commerce make it a great import–export partner.

China's volume of trade in its own finished hi-tech products is constantly growing. All these elements make your country a formidable competitor, and the development of your country's trade imbalances with other trading blocs means that you are – and will continue to be – viewed with admiration, as well as with suspicion by some countries.

## INTELLECTUAL PROPERTY IN BELGIAN–CHINESE TRADE RELATIONS

As the minister in charge of economic affairs and innovation in Flanders, the northern part of Belgium, it is my job to conduct a policy that further enhances

* Deputy Minister-President and Flemish Minister for Economics, Business, Science, Innovation and Foreign Trade, Flemish Regional Government, Flanders, Belgium. This is the text of the speech delivered in Shanghai on 24 November 2004 at the Shanghai Conference on Intellectual Property Rights (IPR) and WTO Compliance – Chinese and European Perspectives.

Flanders' position. I am determined to protect what we have won through hard work and as a result of our fortunate geographical location at a place that serves as a major crossroads for people, goods and ideas. Our western part of Europe is right next door to France and serves as a sea-gate to Germany and the heart of Europe. Flanders lies to the south of the Netherlands and is just a few miles away from Great Britain. We have strong historical traditions and great intellectual wealth. Unlike the USA we do not have a major film or music industry, nor are we a world player in owning copyright on printed works, and our language is not a world language. But we do have some interesting musicians and singers, and some famous cartoonists. We also have some valuable trademarks, though we do not own major global brands. Technologically we are a very advanced society, and we are proud of our innovation in areas such as the chemical sector, in microelectronics, engineering, information technology, pharmaceuticals and biotech industries, as well as in breeding rights.

It is in this context that I wish to join you in focusing on the topic of your conference, on the current challenges facing us with regard to protecting intellectual property rights, and on the strengths and weaknesses of Flanders and Belgium in this connection.

In 1990, in the *Journal of Economic Literature*, the American economist Zvi Griliches clearly described the aim of the patenting process. The patents system is designed to protect inventors. A temporary monopoly for inventors guarantees them sufficient reward for their efforts at innovation. The aim here is to ensure that the incentives to innovate are sufficiently high and that as a result sufficient efforts are made to innovate, enabling companies, regions and countries to benefit from the headway made. Furthermore, thanks to the patents system, the associated, clearly defined proprietary rights lower the transaction costs associated with licensing agreements and facilitate trade in technological know-how.

From a socio-economic viewpoint there is also an additional advantage, for the information contained in the patent enters the public domain and therefore prompts wider dissemination of technological innovations. In fact, the patent system plays an important role in facilitating the flow of information, because it helps to prevent the needless duplication of R&D and can thus trigger swifter technological progress.

In recent years there has been a clearly rising trend in patents awarded to Flanders and Belgium, a development that has been noticeable within the systems presided over by both the EPO (European Patent Office) and USPTO (United States Patent and Trade Office). In fact we belong to one of the most dynamic regions in Europe in this respect (here I would refer you to the Flemish 2003 book of indicators and to the as yet unpublished 2005 version).

However, companies continue to dominate the field, accounting for more than 80 per cent of all patent applications and even 90 per cent or thereabouts of awarded patents. This concentration applies both to Belgium as a whole and also to Flanders, and is along similar lines to developments in other 'small' countries, like the Netherlands. The role played by universities and public research establishments remains limited, though here too the trend is towards ever greater involvement.

The top companies in Belgium and Flanders are Agfa-Gevaert (Flanders-'Fl'), Janssen Pharmaceutica (Fl), Solvay (Belgium-'B'), Alcatel-Bell (Fl), Picanol (Fl), Bekaert (Fl), New Holland (Fl), Raychem, now Tyco (Fl,), TotalFina (B), Innogenetics (Fl), GlaxoSmithKline (BE), UCB (B), Procter and Gamble (Fl), Xeikon (Fl), Barco (Fl), Atlas Copco (Fl), GB Boucherie (B), Plant Genetic Systems & Aventis CropScience (Fl), Michel Van de Wiele (Fl) and Heraeus Electronite (Fl).

An analysis of these top companies reveals the strong foreign presence of a majority of patent applicants, yet such studies also highlight the fact that the top patent applicants from Flanders and Belgium are amongst the top players in Europe in their respective domains. In other words, there is a high level of concentration, though the actors involved have established a strong position for themselves on the international market.

The main areas of technology in which Flemish and Belgian companies hold patents include optics, organic fine chemistry, packaging and printing, textiles and paper, pharmaceutics and cosmetics. If we look at the categories of technology involved, the strong areas include agriculture, food processing, raw materials processing and biotechnology.

## REFORM OF THE INTERNATIONAL INTELLECTUAL PROPERTY SYSTEM

My country has traditionally contributed a great deal to the market economy system. Nevertheless – even as a liberal politician – I freely accept that in this debate social policy and health policy must also play their role if intellectual property rights are to function optimally.

Clearly, patents are crucial for stimulating research into a given technology and its development into applications, and they also play a key role in stimulating economic development driven by such technology. But there is a fundamental difference between the raw materials of this economy and its products. Let me explain. The present trend towards patenting genetic material (genes, series of genes, gene fragments, recombinant proteins, transgenic plants, and so on) is coming up against serious difficulties of both an ethical and an economic kind (concentration of the control of materials). Scientists feel in a dilemma here, and questions are being asked about the patenting of the human genome (or indeed other genomes). The applications based thereon could equally be marketed by patenting specific applications. For instance, just think of the debate about the patented BRCA (breast cancer) genes: a single company owns exclusive rights to all applications based on these genes, although it really developed a specific tracing method that makes use of the BRCA sequences in question. A thorough international debate on all these issues is an important and extremely urgent priority.

Furthermore, steps need to be taken to prevent technology and intellectual property rights from being concentrated among too limited a number of players. After all, a situation like that would place them in too powerful a position, making consumers, farmers, scientists and developing countries overly dependent on them.

Specifically, where the pharmaceutical sector is concerned, national and international governments and institutions should be forced to draw up suitable rules and regulations that will encourage pharmaceutical companies to develop products that meet society's real needs, and thus be induced to invest more in the development of drugs designed to combat diseases which occur primarily in the South. What is more, regulation must guarantee that the barriers for new entrants are sufficiently low to enable smaller companies and research establishments to gain a secure foothold in terms of proprietary rights.

One highly critical consideration is that free, unattached scientific research in this sector must not be hindered by excessively extensive patents. Today, what is known in the business as the lack of 'freedom to operate' is already hindering the development of potentially interesting applications. I should like to point out in this connection that Belgium may be considered moderate or well-balanced in terms of its economic gains from the value of intellectual rights and its use of rights owned by others.

Just like China, we too are respectful of the basic notions involved, being firm believers in the protection of private rights. At the same time, I think the system needs to be altered. Scientific and technological progress must be made in the 'general interest', including – indeed, especially so – in developing countries. Some technologies (and here again I am thinking of gene technology) can complement other possibilities and have the potential to make a positive contribution, for example by yielding high-quality food, better drugs, and so on. However, if this is to happen, researchers will need to be pointed in the right direction, and we will have to work together with agricultural organizations and processors in the respective developing countries themselves. Moreover, technology will have to be made available under decent conditions.

I would suggest that a review of some of the policy considerations behind the patents system may lead us to distinguish better between patents, shortening the duration of some. That same exercise might also prompt us to diversify the type of protection provided, depending on the type of knowledge or of field of technology in question. Information technology does not seem to justify or even require patent protection lasting 20 years.

The complexity of the international situation can hopefully be reduced in a conventional manner, namely by further improving international treaties on patent cooperation and harmonizing the relevant procedures. The ever-growing backlog in patent examinations also needs to be addressed, and here too an attempt should be made to engage in international cooperation under a more 'international' or transnational patent system.

The patents system has been expanding into new sectors of technology and even into business techniques; meanwhile new types of intellectual property are emerging. The manner in which claims are formulated and protected – pending possible future disputes heard by national courts – has also been criticized. Patent examiners are increasingly finding themselves faced with clusters of patents and walls of claims that are artificially constructed by companies and applicants seeking to assure themselves some form of strategic protection. They try and use them as bargaining chips when negotiating the adoption of industry-wide standards and when entertaining the notion of swapping patents. Practices such as these will inevitably leave out the less sophisticated inventors, the smaller entities like universities, and the less wealthy applicants, maybe including those from less well developed countries.

Already some commentators and students of this phenomenon have expressed fears that innovation may end up being stifled by the practices characterizing the present system and by the awarding of excessively long-lasting patents and by too great a degree of uncertainty regarding multiple and overlapping patent claims.

## CONCLUSION

These are some of my concerns. As a business lawyer I could see myself working within the system. As a politician, I must say that we should make sure the system continues to evolve sensibly.

I certainly look forward to hearing more about the role that China will play in this matter . . . and I trust this role will be substantial and will benefit the developing world. China proved to be a rule-abiding, moderate WTO member when it came to debating the rights of the least developed countries at the Cancún Conference. I also trust that your country has an impeccable sense of timing, and that any Chinese intervention in this debate will take place at the most effective juncture and in the most suitable forum.

# PART V

# Postscript

# 13. The agenda for the future

**Paul Torremans***

One of the major points to emerge from the essays in this book is that TRIPs is not perfect and nor is it the final stage in the development of the international intellectual property framework. China has now entered the international intellectual property scene and one can hope and expect that it will play a major constructive role in its future developments. On too many occasions in the past China has been threatened with trade sanctions for not doing enough to protect intellectual property, while China itself has then reacted by looking inward and doing enough to thwart these threats by increasing protection for intellectual property. This strategy is counterproductive. The Chinese economy needs an efficient intellectual property system, including its enforcement arm, if it is to develop further. There will be ever more Chinese, as well as foreign, intellectual property to protect. Various authors have demonstrated in this book that this message has now been taken on board by the Chinese authorities and that they are developing an intellectual property system along these lines. China is ready to move on and to play a proactive role in the international intellectual property arena. Its main trading partners are therefore also well advised to move on from their strategy to spur on China by threatening trade sanctions to a more constructive attitude that encourages the formation of a strategic partnership to further develop the international protection of intellectual property. Those of us who attended the conference in Shanghai in November 2004, which is so intimately linked to the research that led to this book, were particularly encouraged to hear the delegates from the European Commission at that conference endorse this idea of a constructive strategic partnership.[1]

In spite of the obvious importance of these issues at intergovernmental level, the main emphasis of the debate in practice and in this book is placed on

* Professor, School of Law, University of Nottingham, UK and Faculty of Law, University of Ghent, Belgium.

1 The concept of a constructive strategic partnership has been defended ardently by academics such as Professor Peter Yu for a number of years, see Yu (2001), 'From pirates to partners: protecting intellectual property in China in the twenty-first century', **50**, *American University Law Review*, 131.

intellectual property rights for individual right holders and their enforcement. Several authors explain the significant changes that have taken place on this point in China over the last few years. Their conclusion that a comprehensive and modern system of intellectual property rights that can cope with the demands of the modern global and networked economy has emerged is not to be doubted. At the same time, there is still work to be done. Intellectual property and the economy it supports are constantly changing and there are still areas here where work remains to be done. The protection of trade secrets in the workplace and the protection of traditional knowledge were singled out in this respect.

This brings us to the core issue of enforcement. Major problems existed in relation to enforcement of intellectual property rights in China, in part because the rights issue was addressed first, only to reveal that the enforcement mechanisms could not follow. There are several essays in this book that analyse the colossal efforts that have been undertaken by the Chinese authorities to address these issues and to provide an efficient enforcement system that is fully TRIPs-compliant. It is fair to say, though, that enforcement remains a problematic issue. This is explained very well from a practising lawyer's perspective in another essay in the book by Jingzhou Tao. From that perspective several foreign multinational companies that operate in China feel they are losing the battle to protect their intellectual property. They feel that the enforcement system is still letting them down. The broader overall picture may, however, be a bit more complex.[2] The problems these companies face may to a large extent be due to their unduly heavy reliance on legal tactics as the sole instrument to safeguard and enforce their intellectual property rights. Their operations in China are seen as a low cost, especially when it comes to labour costs, consisting of a production facility only, and consquently they fail to factor intellectual property properly into their strategic and operational decisions, as they would do in their home country. Strategic and operational decisions tend to be taken outside China anyhow in those cases. Executives, even in intellectual property-sensitive industries, tend to think only of keeping production costs down and of the flexibility with which their Chinese production facilities need to be able to respond to global changes in demand. The protection of intellectual property is seen as a legal problem only and one they mostly only pay attention to when it has been stolen and when, in other words, the problem is already there. This reactive rather than proactive attitude is not helpful. Indeed, the most successful companies take strategic and operational action to protect their intellectual property before it is stolen and before it

---

2 See M. Dietz, L.S. Shao-Tin, and Y. Lei (2005), 'Protecting intellectual property in China: litigation is no substitute for strategy', *The McKinsey Quarterly*, issue 3.

becomes a problem. This in turn significantly lowers their litigation costs and it improves the chances that their intellectual property will remain safe.

As part of such a proactive approach, companies should of course register their trademarks and patents with local authorities and they should prosecute infringers rigorously, but also with prudence. Prudence is essential as one does not want to acquire a reputation for making groundless threats or of going into battle without being properly prepared. Rigour is essential because one needs to be seen to be taking intellectual property protection and enforcement very seriously. The new stronger Chinese intellectual property legislation will in this respect significantly assist right holders, but nevertheless litigation is no substitute for strategy, irrespective of the country concerned. China is no different on this point. The best right holders reduce the chance that competitors will steal their intellectual property by carefully selecting which products and technologies to sell and manufacture in China. One could, for example, avoid manufacturing everything in one plant and instead import a key piece, such as a chip or the software, from abroad. This strategy is even applied in Europe as a precaution, so why not apply it in China too? By separating functions and keeping technological details secret in this way, a right holder can significantly reduce the possibility of an intellectual property leak.

Operational action is also a critical component of such a proactive approach. The vast majority of companies implement essential security measures, such as the use of surveillance equipment or firewalls, to prevent large file transfers. The best players go significantly further, though. It is indeed good practice to cultivate an awareness of intellectual property and the need to protect it amongst staff. Rather than focus solely on cheap and readily available labour, one should screen all job candidates for high ethical standards and, once they become employees, they should be given proper training to cultivate these standards and this awareness. Attracting staff with international experience of gaining a degree from a foreign country where there is a long-established intellectual property culture for key positions may also assist. Such staff can also help train the others. Employment contracts should also reflect the importance of intellectual property and its enforcement. Know-how secrecy clauses and non-competition clauses to deal with issues when staff leave their employment are essential, but still too often neglected, tools in this respect. Professor Hailing Shan makes this abundantly clear in Chapter 8.

Strong protection for intellectual property also means that right holders need to monitor the activities of their Chinese business partners on a continuing basis. One needs to audit the compliance of one's partners frequently or rigorously to prevent intellectual property leaks, for example through unauthorized resale of parts.

Legal means alone are not enough to protect intellectual property. A company that is exploiting its intellectual property in China (or elsewhere) should assign specific responsibility for its intellectual property to senior managers who are familiar with all aspects of the business and who can implement the proactive strategy set out above. Achieving the right mix of legal, operational and strategic considerations is a difficult balancing act and companies will not always be able to get it right.

A final point that is to be taken account of is that foreign companies often expect to find in China the same enforcement system which they work with at home. This then often leads to complaints if the different Chinese system does not produce the results that are expected if one tries to use it in the same way as one uses the system at home. This is not a sensible strategy. Instead right holders should use all the aspects and specificities of the Chinese enforcement arsenal. The specific role of administrative enforcement of intellectual property rights is a prime example of such a specificity.

Overall, China has made tremendous progress in the area of intellectual property rights and enforcement. However, in order to address the challenges of the future, a somewhat different approach will be needed. China and its main trading partners will need to work together in the future in a constructive strategic partnership at the international level. Right holders will need to mirror that by working in partnership with the enforcement authorities by adopting a proactive approach that does not only rely on legal means and that takes account of the specificities of the Chinese economic, social and legal context.

# Bibliography


Alford, W.P. (1995), *To Steal a Book Is an Elegant Offense: Intellectual Property Law in Chinese Civilization*, Stanford: Stanford University Press.

Attaran, A. and L. Gillespie-White (2001), 'Do patents for antiretroviral drugs constrain access to AIDS treatment in Africa?', **286**, *Journal of the American Medical Association*, 1886.

Baohua, D. (1999), *Theory of Labour Law*, Beijing: World Books Press.

Barry, R. (1996), 'The effect of GATT and TRIPS on U.K. patent law', **81**, *Patent World*, 13.

Bhagwati, J. (2002), 'Patents and the poor', *The Financial Times*, 16 September.

Birks, P. (1985), *Introduction to the Law of Restitution*, Oxford: Oxford University Press.

Blakeney M. (1994), 'Well-known marks', *European Intellectual Property Review*, 481.

Boyle, J. (2004), 'A manifesto on WIPO and the future of intellectual property', *Duke Law & Technology Review*, **9**, 1–12.

Browning T. and C. Wang (2004) 'Ten years of enforcement in China', *Managing Intellectual Property*, February, China Intellectual Property Focus, p. 38.

Chakravarthi, Raghavan (2000), 'ASEAN for protecting indigenous/traditional knowledge', *Third World Network*, 5 May.

Cheetham, S.P. (1999), 'Protection of intellectual property rights in luxury goods', in Mark A. Cohen, A. Elizabeth Bang and Stephanie J. Mitchell (eds), *Chinese Intellectual Property Law and Practice*, London: Kluwer Law International, p. 386.

Chen Zhaokuan, C. (1998–99), 'Administrative management and enforcement of copyright in China', *Duke Journal of Comparative & International Law*, **9**, 249.

Chow, D.C.K. (2000), 'Counterfeiting in the People's Republic of China', *Washington University Law Quarterly*, **78**(1), Spring, 22.

Chow, D.C.K. (2002), *A Primer on Foreign Investment Enterprises and Protection of Intellectual Property in China*, The Hague: Kluwer Law International, p. 228.

Clarke, D.C. (1999), 'Private enforcement of intellectual property rights in China', *National Bureau of Asian Research*, p. 35.

Coleman, A. (1992), *The Legal Protection of Trade Secrets*, London: Sweet & Maxwell.

Crespi, S. (1992), 'Patents and plant variety rights: is there an interface problem?', *International Review of Industrial Property and Copyright*, 168.

Croome, J. (1998), *Reshaping the World Trading System. A History of the Uruguay Round*, Geneva: WTO and Deventer: Kluwer Law International.

Davis, M.H. (2003), 'Some realism about indigenism', **11** *Cardozo Journal of International and Comparative Law* 815.

Dietz, M., S. Shao-Tin and Y. Lei (2005), 'Protecting intellectual property in China: litigation is no substitute for strategy', *The McKinsey Quarterly*, issue 3.

Dinwoodie, G.B. and Rochelle C. Dreyfuss (2004), 'TRIPS and the dynamics of intellectual property lawmaking', **36** *Case Western Journal of International Law*, 95.

Drahos, P. (2001), 'BITs and BIPs: bilateralism in intellectual property', **4** *Journal of World Intellectual Property*, 791

Dreyfuss, R.C. (2004), 'TRIPS-Round II: should users strike back?', **71** *University of Chicago Law Review*, 21.

Endeshaw, A. (1996), *Intellectual Property in China: The Roots of the Problem of Enforcement*, Singapore: Acumen Publishing, p. 114.

Feder, G.S. (1996), 'Enforcement of intellectual property rights in China: you can lead a horse to water but you can't make it drink', *Virginia Journal of International Law*, **37**(1), 253.

Ficsor, M. (2002), 'How much of what? The "three-step test" and its application in two recent WTO dispute settlement cases', **192** *Revue Internationale du Droit d'Auteur*, 111.

Fink, C. (2001), 'Patent protection, transnational corporations, and market structure: a simulation study of the Indian pharmaceutical industry', **10** *Journal of Industrial Competition and Trade*.

Ford, S. (2000), 'Compulsory licensing provisions under the TRIPS Agreement: balancing pills and patents', **14** *American University International Law Review*, 941.

Gaster, J. (1999), *Der Rechtsschutz von Datenbanken. Kommentar zur Richtlinie*, 96/9/EG, Köln: Carl Heymanns Verlag.

Gaster, J. (2000) 'The EC sui generis right revisited after two years: a review of the practice of database protection in the EU Member States', **5** *Communications Law*, 87.

Gervais, D. (2002), '"Feist goes global": a comparative analysis of the notion of originality in copyright law', **49** *Journal of the Copyright Society of the USA*, 949.

Gervais, D. (2002), 'The internationalization of intellectual property: new challenges from the very old and the very new', **12** *Fordham Intellectual Property Media and Entertainment Law Journal*, 929.

Gervais, D. (2003), 'Spiritual but not intellectual? The protection of sacred intangible traditional knowledge', **11** *Cardozo Journal of International and Comparative Law*, 467.

Gervais, D. (2003) *The TRIPs Agreement: Drafting History and Analysis*, 2nd edn, London: Sweet & Maxwell.

Gervais, D.J. (2005), 'Towards a new core international copyright norm: the reverse three-step test', **9** *Marquette Intellectual Property Law Review*, 1

Ginarte, Juan C. and Walter G. Park (1997), 'Determinants of patent rights: a cross-national study', **26** *Research Policy*, 283.

Ginsburg, S. (2002), 'Towards supranational copyright law? The WTO panel decision and the "Three-Step Test for Copyright Exceptions" ', **187** *Revue Internationale du Droit d'Auteur*, 3.

Gomez, B. and Peggy B. Hu, 'Intellectual property enforcement high on US–China agenda', published by Usinfo.State.Gov. (available online, US Government website).

Gopakumar, K.M. (2004), 'The WTO deal on cheap drugs: a critique', **7** *Journal of World International Property*, 99.

Gregory, A. (2003), 'Chinese trademark law and the TRIPS Agreement – Confucius meets the WTO', in Deborah Cass (ed.), *China and the World Trading System: Entering the New Millennium*, Cambridge: Cambridge University Press, p. 321.

Guangliang, Zh (2003), *Civil Remedies for Intellectual Property*, Beijing: Law Press, p. 62.

Guo, Shoukang (eds) (2002), *Intellectual Property Law*, Beijing: Law Press.

Heald, P.J. (2003), 'Misreading a canonical work: an analysis of Mansfield's 1994 study', **10** *Journal of Intellectual Property Law*, 309–18

Heald, P.J. (2003), 'Mowing the playing field: addressing information distortion and asymmetry in the TRIPS game', **88** *Minnesota Law Review*, 249

Holder, S. (2002), 'Preliminary injunctions for intellectual property infringements in the PRC', *International Newsletter*, Rouse & Co., 13 March.

Homere, J.R. (2004), 'Intellectual property rights can help stimulate the economic development of least developed countries', **27** *Columbia Journal of Law and the Arts*, 277.

Johnson, J.M. (2002), 'Solving China's counterfeiting problem', *Managing Intellectual Property*, Issue 155, December 2001/January 2002, p. 4.

Kitch, E.W. (1994), 'The patent policy of developing countries', **13** *University of California in Los Angeles Pacific Basin Law Journal*, 166, 169–78.

Kunimi, M. (2001), 'TRIPS Agreement, is it really successful achievement in the WTO? The difficulty of balancing between public and private interests', **3** *Oregan Review of International Law*, 46.

Kur, A. (1996), 'The right to use one's own trade mark: a self-evident issue or a new concept in German, European and international trade mark law?', *European Intellectual Property Review*, 198.

Kuruk, P. (2004), 'Bridging the gap between traditional knowledge and intellectual property rights: is reciprocity an answer?', **7** *Journal of World Intellectual Property*, 42.

Lagerqvist, Th. and M.L. Riley (1997), 'How to protect intellectual property rights in China', in Mary L. Riley et al. (eds), *Protecting Intellectual Property Rights in China*, Hong Kong: Sweet & Maxwell Asia, p. 31.

Landes, W.M. and R.A. Posner (2004), 'The Political Economy of Intellectual Property Law, Washington, AEI – Brookings Joint Center for Regulatory Studies.

Magarinos, C.A., L. Yongtu and F. Sercovich (eds) (2003), *China in the WTO: The Birth of a New Catching-Up Strategy*, New York: Palgrave Macmillan, p. 165.

Maskus, K.E. (1998), 'The role of intellectual property rights in encouraging foreign direct investment and technology transfer', **9** *Duke Journal of Comparative and International Law*, 109.

Maskus, E. (2000), 'Intellectual property rights and economic development', **32** *Case Western Reserve Journal of International Law*, 471.

Maskus, K.E. and J.H. Reichman (2004), 'The globalization of private knowledge goods and the privatization of global public goods', **7** *Journal of International Economic Law*, 279.

Maskus, K. (2000), *Intellectual Property Rights in the Global Economy*, Institute for International Economics, pp. 199–205.

Massouye, C. (1978), 'WIPO guide to the Berne Convention', Geneva: WIPO.

Massouye, C. (1981), 'Guide to the Rome Convention and to the Phonograms Convention', Geneva: WIPO.

McGrath, M. (1996), 'The patent provisions in TRIPS: protecting reasonable remuneration for services rendered – or the latest development in Western colonialism?', *European Intellectual Property Review*, 398.

Mendes da Costa, P. (1992), 'Patent harmonization through GATT: TRIP or trap?', **45** *Patent World*, 23, at 25.

Mercurio, B.C. (2004), 'TRIPS, patents, and access to life-saving drugs in the developing world', **8** *Marquette Intellectual Property Law Review*, 211.

Miller, T. (1998), 'Inventions made in USA: foreign "equality" under applicable international treaties', **5** *International Review of Industrial Property and Copyright*, 587.

Mugabe, J. (1998), 'Intellectual property protection and traditional knowledge: an exploration in international policy discourse', November, available at wipo.int.

Murphy, M. (2003), 'Supreme people's court widens litigation options', *Managing Intellectual Property*, November, p. 1.

Okediji, R.L. (2003), 'The international relations of intellectual property: narratives of developing country participation in the global intellectual property system', *Singapore Yearbook of International Law*, Singapore: National University of Singapore, **7** at 315 (vol 7).

Okediji, R.L. (2004), 'Back to bilateralism? Pendulum swings in international intellectual property protection', **1** *University of Ottowa Law and Technology Journal*, 125.

Pitman, B. Potter and Michel Oksenberg (1999), 'A patchwork of IPR protections', *China Business Review*, **26**(1), January/February, 9.

Pollock, F. and F.W. Maitland (1968), *History of English Law*, vol. I, Cambridge: Cambridge University Press, p. 221.

Primo Braga, C.A. and C. Fink (1998), 'The relationship between intellectual property rights and foreign direct investment', **9** *Duke Journal of Comparative and International Law*, 163.

Rangel-Ortiz, H. (1995), 'Trademarks, NAFTA and TRIPS – an update', *Trademark World*, 29, at 31.

Reichman, J.H. (1995), 'The know-how gap in the TRIPS Agreement: why software fared badly, and what are the solutions', **17** *Hastings Communication and Entertainment Law Journal*, 763.

Reichman, J.H. (2000), 'The TRIPS Agreement comes of age: conflicts or cooperation with the developing countries?', **32** *Case Western Reserve Journal of International Law*, 441.

Reinbothe, J. and A. Howard (1991), 'The state of play in the negotiations on TRIPS', *European Intellectual Property Review*, 158.

Report of the Working Party on the Accession of China (2001), WT/ACC/CHN/49 (WTO document available online), Geneva: WTO, 1 October.

Ricketson, S. and J. Ginsburg (2006), *International Copyright and Neighboring Rights: The Berne Convention and Beyond*, Oxford: Oxford University Press.

Riley, M.L. (2002), 'Enforcement of intellectual property rights in China (and the trouble you face if you don't)', Issue 12, *International Company and Commercial Law Review*, 458.

Ruichun, D. (1998–99), 'China's intellectual property rights protection towards the 21st century', **9** *Duke Journal of Comparative & International Law*, 215.

Ryan, M.P. (2002), 'Knowledge-economy elites, the international law of intellectual property and trade, and economic development', **10** *Cardozo Journal of International and Comparative Law*, 271.

Schiappacasse, M. (2004), 'Intellectual property rights in China: technology transfers and economic development', **2** *Buffalo Intellectual Property Law Journal*, 164.

Scotchmer, S. (2004), *Innovation and Incentives*, Cambridge, Mass: MIT Press, p. 329.

Scotchmer, S. (2004), 'The political economy of intellectual property treaties', **20** *Journal of Law, Economics and Organization*, 415, 435–6.

Shulman, Seth (1999), *Owning the Future*, New York: Houghton Mifflin.

Shunde, L. (2002), 'TRIPS and the Intellectual Property Law of our country I', **58** *Survey of Scientific and Technological Achievement*.

Simone, J.T. (1999), 'China's IPR enforcement mechanisms', **26**(1) *China Business Review*, January/February, 14.

Smith, P.J. (2001), 'How do foreign patent rights affect U.S. exports, affiliate sales, and licenses?', **55** *Journal of International Economics*, 411–40.

Sprigman, Ch. (2004), 'Reform(aliz)ing copyright', **57** *Stanford Law Review*, 485.

Srividhya, Ragavan (2004), 'The Jekyll and Hyde story of international trade: the Supreme Court in *PhRMA* v. *Walsh* and the TRIPS Agreement', **38** *University of Richmond Law Review*, 777.

Stanley, C.L. (2003), 'A dangerous step toward the over protection of intellectual property: rethinking *Eldred* v. *Ashcroft*, **26** *Hamline Law Review*, 679.

Stewart, G.R., M.J. Tawfik and M. Irish (1995), *International Trade and Intellectual Property: The Search for a Balanced System*, Boulder: Westview Press.

Su, E. (2000), 'The winners and the losers: the agreement on the trade-related aspects of intellectual property rights and its effects on developing countries', **23** *Houston Journal of International Law*, 169.

Sun, A.Y. (2001), 'Reforming the protection of intellectual property: the case of China and Taiwan in light of WTO accession', Maryland Series in Contemporary Asian Studies, no. 4, p. 25.

Taubman, A.S. (2003), 'TRIPS goes east: Chinese interests and international trade in intellectual property', in Deborah Cass (ed.), *China and the World Trading System: Entering the New Millennium*, Cambridge: Cambridge University Press, p. 347.

Torremans, P. (2005), *Holyoak and Torremans Intellectual Property Law*, 4th edn, Oxford: Oxford University Press.

Tully, L.D. (2003), 'Note, Prospects for Progress: The TRIPS Agreement and Developing Countries After the DOHA Conference', **26** *Boston College International and Comparative Law Review*, 129.

United States – Section 110(5) of the Copyright Act, Panel Report WT/DS160/R, (2000) (WTO document available online).

Vandevelde, K.J. (1998), 'The political economy of a bilateral investment treaty', **92** *American Journal of International Law*, 621.

Vivas-Eugui, D. (2003), 'Regional and bilateral agreements and a TRIPS-plus world: the free trade area of the Americas' (FTAA).

Wager, H. (1996), 'Substantive Copyright Law in TRIPS', in H. Cohen Jehoram et al. (eds), *Trade Related Aspects of Copyright*, Deventer: Kluwer, p. 34.

Wang, Xuezheng (2004), 'WTO accession and trademark protection in China', *Frontline Issues of Protection of Intellectual Property Right in China and TRIPs*, Beijing: Law Press China.

Weeks, A.M. (2000), 'IPR protection and enforcement: a guide' **27**(6) *China Business Review*, November/December, p. 29.

Wenwei, Z. (2006), 'Hot Interpretation of the Industry Circle on Measures for the Protection of Intellectual Property Rights during Exhibitions', *China Trade Daily*, 21 March.

Wheare, H.J.H. (1998), 'Enforcement', in *IP Protection in China: Practical Strategies*, 2nd edn, Hong Kong: Asia Law & Practice, p. 36.

Xu, Chao (2004), 'Legal regime of copyright and the amendment of copyright law', *Frontline Issues of Protection of Intellectual Property Right in China and TRIPs*, Beijing: Law Press China.

Yahong, Li (2002), 'Pushing for greater protection: the trend toward greater protection of intellectual property in the Chinese software industry and the implications for rule of law in China, **23** *University of Pennsylvania Journal of International Economic Law*, 637.

Yang, D. (2003), 'The development of intellectual property in China', **25**(2), *World Patent Information*, p. 139.

Yang, D. and P. Clarke (2004), 'Review of the current intellectual property system in China', **3**(1), *International Journal of Technology Transfer and Commercialisation*, p. 19.

Yu, P.K. (2002), 'The second coming of intellectual property rights in China', Occasional Papers in Intellectual Property from Benjamin N. Cardozo School of Law, Yeshiva University, no. 11, Benjamin N. Cardozo School of Law, Yeshiva University, pp. 17–18.

Yu, P.K. (2003), 'China and the WTO: progress, perils, and prospects', **17** *Columbia Journal of Asian Law*, 1.

Yu P.K. (2004), 'Currents and crosscurrents in the international intellectual property regime', **38** *Loyola of Los Angeles Law Review*, 323.

Zheng, Chengsi (1997), *Copyright Law*, 2nd edn, Beijing: Renmin University Press.

# Index